MICHAEL J. SCHELL

W9-CAA-836

BASEBALL'S ALL-TIME BEST HITTERS

How Statistics Can Level the Playing Field

PRINCETON UNIVERSITY PRESS   PRINCETON, NEW JERSEY

Published by Princeton University Press, 41 William Street, Princeton,
New Jersey 08540
In the United Kingdom: Princeton University Press, Chichester, West Sussex

Library of Congress Cataloging-in-Publication Data

Schell, Michael J., 1957–
Baseball's all-time best hitters : how statistics can level the
playing field / Michael J. Schell
p.   cm.
Includes bibliographical references (p.   ) and index.
ISBN 0-691-00455-2 (alk. paper)
1. Batting (Baseball) — United States — Statistics.   2. Baseball players — Rating
of — United States.   3. Baseball players — United States — Statistics.   I. Title.
GV869.S34   1999
796.357'0973 — dc21   98-33356
                                                            CIP

Photos from National Baseball Hall of Fame Library, Cooperstown, N.Y., unless
otherwise credited
Photos of Tony Gwynn and Wade Boggs from Photo File Inc.
Photo on p. 13 from CORBIS/Bettmann
Photo on p. 133 from CORBIS/Farrell Grehan

This book has been composed in Electra.

The paper used in this publication meets the minimum requirements of
ANSI/NISO Z39.48-1992(R1997) (*Permanence of Paper*)

http://pup.princeton.edu

Printed in the United States of America

1   3   5   7   9   10   8   6   4   2

1   3   5   7   9   10   8   6   4   2
(Pbk.)

BASEBALL'S ALL-TIME BEST HITTERS

To My Parents, Joseph and Irene Schell

CONTENTS

CONTENTS

LIST OF FIGURES

LIST OF TABLES

TECHNICAL NOTES

Who are the greatest all-time hitters in baseball? That was a question that fascinated me as a twelve-year-old in 1969 when I first discovered baseball and it still fascinates me today. I remember poring over the list of the year-by-year batting champions from an almanac. The consistency of Ty Cobb's name certainly left an impression. I also loved numbers. Today I am a professional statistician. What better combination of interests could there be than baseball and numbers?

That my "life" in baseball began in 1969 is probably not accidental to my decision to write this book. *Street and Smith's Baseball* preview in 1969 included an article on the recent decline in batting averages. The overall batting average in the American League had slipped to an all-time low of .230.

To longtime baseball fans, 1968 is known as "the year of the pitcher." Carl Yastrzemski of the Boston Red Sox was the only American Leaguer to top .300 that year, winning the batting title with a .301 average. The situation was not much better in the National League, whose .243 league batting average was the lowest in sixty years and third lowest ever. Bob Gibson, a fireballer for the St. Louis Cardinals, had a 1.12 ERA for the year and pitched 13 shutouts. Taking nothing away from Gibson, major league baseball wanted more hitting.

The powers-that-be voted to lower the pitcher's mound from 15 inches above home plate to 10 inches above the level of home plate. I remember reading one pitcher lament in spring training in 1969, "I don't like it. It's like pitching out of a foxhole." They also shrank the strike zone. The result was that, in 1969, batting averages went up 7 points in the National League and 16 points in the American League.

The *Street and Smith's Baseball* article described eras in baseball which featured strong differences in batting average. The 1969 season provided direct evidence about how rule changes can affect batting averages from one year to the next. Thus, it seemed possible to me that batting averages decades apart could also differ for reasons other than absolute player ability. Since no rule changes have been made since 1969 with the express intent of raising the individual hitter's batting average, the recent fan is probably less aware of this. (The designated hitter rule in the American League raised the *league* batting average, not an *individual's* batting average.)

Batting averages were relatively stable for an unprecedented quarter of a century, from 1969 to 1993. Now we are again experiencing rising batting averages and an onslaught of home runs. Because these changes were not planned, baseball pundits are confused. Commentators have come up with numerous explanations, such as: the ball is juiced, the players are stronger, the new ballparks are "friendlier" to the hitter, the pitchers are worse.

I believe that all of the explanations except the last one have some merit. Pitching doesn't suddenly go bad in one or two years. Recent changes in the game are shifting the balance toward the hitter. I recently heard a baseball commentator suggest that the mound be *raised* next year! Does this mean that today's pitchers are worse and need help? If so, does that imply that Mays, McCovey, Aaron, Bench, Carew, Killebrew, and Yastrzemski weren't good in the 1960s and needed help when the mound was *lowered*?

The aim of this book is to identify the 100 all-time best hitters, where "best hitters" means the best hitters for average. Adjustments will be made for both major and subtle changes that have occurred throughout the game's history in order to better determine who these players are. There will be some important changes from the traditional list. In particular, the recent and current hitters are much better than the traditional list reveals.

I wish to acknowledge those who have made many fine suggestions and comments during the writing of this book. Special thanks go to Sean O'Brien, Michael O'Malley, Joseph Schell, David Stephan, Michael Symons, and Bill Whitaker, who looked at several drafts of the book and whose insights are sprinkled throughout. I also thank Joe Black, Isaac Kim, Basia Korycka, Inchull Lee, Yuhua Lin, Noreen Martinez, Pete Palmer, Tom Ruane, Eddie Schell, Neil Traven, and Craig Turnbull, who read and critiqued parts of the book. I thank Bea Shube for her support and editorial insights. Pete Palmer also provided home and away ballpark data from 1993 to 1997 that were extremely useful.

I thank my many friends from the department of Biostatistics and the Lineberger Comprehensive Cancer Center at the University of North Carolina at Chapel Hill, who gave me tremendous personal support while I wrote this book.

I further thank my editor, Trevor Lipscombe, whose enthusiasm for the book was evident from his first reply letter. He, copy editor Bill Laznovsky, and the staff of Princeton University Press provided great encouragement to me by their interest during my months of writing.

BASEBALL'S ALL-TIME BEST HITTERS

INTRODUCTION In the Dugout

Never did I expect that writing this book would lead me into the San Diego Padres dugout. On July 28, 1997, however, two hours before that evening's game against the Philadelphia Phillies, there I was! Tony Gwynn had just returned his Louisville Slugger to the bat rack after batting practice.

"Tony!—I'm Michael Schell," I called out. Tony Gwynn, the 7-time batting champion from the San Diego Padres, turned toward me and replied, "Soooo—you're the guy!"

A month earlier I had sent a press release to the media relations people at the Padres saying that Gwynn was on the verge of clinching his standing as the best pure hitter in baseball history. A week earlier I had sent him a congratulatory note after he got the clinching hit. Two days before, sportswriter Wayne Lockwood presented my findings in the *San Diego Union-Tribune*.

"I'll talk with you in a minute," Gwynn added as he headed to chat with some early-bird fans that he knew.

I waited expectantly and a little nervously. Shaun O'Neill, a sports reporter for the *North County Times* told me that Gwynn was a very unassuming ballplayer who would downplay what I was going to say but would listen intently.

"You're putting pressure on me!" Gwynn moaned jokingly as he approached.

He was hitting .391 and the media had been hounding him for weeks about the possibility of becoming the first player in 56 years to hit .400 for the season. That week, in fact, Gwynn was on the cover of both *Sports Illustrated* and *The Sporting News*.

"You've got no pressure from me," I countered, "you've already done it!"

He sat down beside me and said, "Show me what you found."

That's what I plan to do in this book—show the reader what I've

3

found by developing a method to compare players across baseball history, from the first pitch in 1876 to the present day.

The Tyranny of Traditional Top Hitters Lists

Most baseball encyclopedias and many almanacs have lists of top lifetime hitters or single season batting champions. Young fans memorize the names — Ty Cobb, Rogers Hornsby, Ted Williams, Babe Ruth — and often their lifetime batting averages as well (.366, .358, .344, .342, respectively). These players have become mythological heroes of the game.

There is some sadness, though, among fans today since our favorite active players — Tony Gwynn, Mike Piazza, Ken Griffey Jr. are — hopelessly out of the top positions. Gwynn would rank 16th, Piazza 21st and Griffey fails to make the top 100. Moreover, Hall of Famers Hank Aaron and Willie Mays and all-time hits leader Pete Rose are off the list, while a host of relatively unknown players like Bibb Falk, Cecil Travis, Rip Radcliff, and Elmer Smith are on it. How can this be?

Knowing how extraordinary these current and recent players are, we become mystified by those on the list. How did they do it? Why were they so much better? The punch line, which is the subject of this book, is that they are *not* so much better. We fans have been misled by the averages. It is the unfortunate fact of life that fair appraisals of anything rarely come without effort.

Grandparents may tell you about how they bought a house for $15,000. Did they also tell you, however, that they only earned $6,000 per year then, too? Simply defined statistics, like *batting average* (which equals hits divided by at bats), may be fine to make comparisons between ballplayers playing in the same year in the same ballparks against the same pitchers. But why should these averages be used at all to compare a player who played at night in a domed stadium with astroturf with another player who played only day games in the open air on natural grass?

The question of who the greatest hitters are is a subject of considerable interest to baseball fans. It is a source of argument between father and son, between Dodger and Yankee fan, between the pure hitter fan and the slugger fan. The good news is that we can reasonably answer this question, when it is clearly posed. This is the legacy provided by baseball, which has a wealth of statistical data over a hundred-year period. The bad news is that the answer is not easily found in the baseball encyclopedias and almanacs. It is the aim of this book to identify the 100 greatest hitters, by applying four adjustments to the standard batting average.

"Best Hitter" Defined

What does the phrase "best hitter" mean? Hitting is composed of many things. For example, Tony Gwynn is excellent at getting hits but relatively few of his hits are home runs. On the other hand, Mark McGwire is only average in getting hits but they go a country mile when he does connect! So which one is the "better" hitter?

There are many different baseball statistics. Batting average and slugging average both combine singles, doubles, triples, home runs, and outs into single measures. Batting average is computed by totaling the different kinds of hits and dividing by the number of at bats, while slugging average totals the number of bases that you reach on the hits before being divided by the total number of at bats. However, both of them ignore factors like the walk average, number of RBIs and less well-measured things like hit-and-run or clutch hitting ability. There are other ballplayer abilities as well, such as run scoring, base stealing, and fielding. Bill James, with his *Runs Created* formulae, and John Thorn and Pete Palmer, with their *Total Player Rating*, have combined batting, fielding, and stealing data into a single rating. Both composite statistics are useful and interesting.

The statistics of Bill James and Thorn and Palmer seem to be searching for the best *players*. Statistics that combine various hitting events, which may include weighting of the values of singles, doubles, triples, and home runs (and possibly walks, strikeouts, or other batting events) are searching for the best *batters*. The search in this book is for the best *hitters*, that is, the players with the best chance to get a hit in a given at bat. Thus, we will use the preeminent baseball statistic, the *batting average*. However, we will adjust this average for each year in baseball history based on the ease with which hits could be attained and the player's home ballpark. This leads to batting averages that are *relative* to the league batting averages. Consequently, the talent pool of the league must also be considered. Also, at bats late in the careers of the longest playing stars will not be included, since batting ability clearly wanes then. Because these adjustments are needed to *level the playing field*, standard batting average lists do not properly order the top hitters.

Minimum Requirements of Qualifying Players

In order to determine the 100 greatest hitters of all time there must be a minimum playing time. I have chosen 4000 at bats as the minimum. One could choose 4000 plate appearances, which includes both at bats and walks and a few other minor events, so as not to penalize individuals who walked frequently. However, since the focus here is on the ability to hit, not the ability to get on base, a minimum of at bats is used. A player who plays full-time will get 400–600 at bats per year, so 4000 at bats represents 7 to 10 years of full-time play.

This minimum — 4000 at bats — is close to those used by the three major contemporary baseball encyclopedias. *The Baseball Encyclopedia* uses the same definition. *The Sports Encyclopedia: Baseball* also requires a 10-year career. *Total Baseball* requires appearances in 1000 games. Thus, *Total Baseball's* top 100 list includes 5 players who have fewer than 4000 at bats, including Bob Fothergill, who had a mere 3265. The others are John McGraw, Mike Donlin, Dale Mitchell, and Taffy Wright.

It is particularly regrettable that John McGraw is left out. This outstanding, turn-of-the-century third baseman is in the Hall of Fame as the manager who skippered many successful New York Giant teams. He was a very good hitter and one of the best players of his day at drawing a walk. Had he not been so good at walking, he would easily have gotten the extra 76 at bats to qualify. He will be included when on base average is considered later in the book.

I also require that the player be retired or have at least 8000 at bats, if he is still active. (This additional requirement will be explained further in the chapter on late career declines.) Thus 10 active players (as of spring 1998) are included: Harold Baines, Wade Boggs, Joe Carter, Chili Davis, Gary Gaetti, Tony Gwynn, Rickey Henderson, Paul Molitor, Tim Raines, and Cal Ripken Jr.

Through 1995, 8259 players have played major league baseball, excluding the Negro Leagues. However, only 836 players — who will be called *qualifying players* — qualify for consideration, by having had at least 4000 at bats and being retired or having had at least 8000 at bats, if still active. Thus, the top 100 hitters are members of an elite group — comprising only 1.2% of all major league batters and 12% of qualifying players.

Unfortunately, records from the Negro Leagues are incomplete although they are now being compiled and included in baseball encyclopedias. As a result, they are not ranked in this book.

Batting Average Data Sources

There is no universally accepted list of top hitters. Besides the minimum eligibility criteria, reference books differ on how many hits and at bats each player actually had. Fortunately, this problem is largely limited to players from the 19th and early part of the 20th century. For example, Cap Anson, who played from 1876 to 1897 batted .329 = (3000 / 9108) according to *The Baseball Encyclopedia, Tenth Edition,* 1996, .329 = (2995 / 9101) according to *Total Baseball, Fifth Edition,* 1997, and .333 = (3022 / 9067) according to *The Sports Encyclopedia: Baseball, Seventeenth Edition,* 1997.

Total Baseball received much of its information from sabermatricians (members of the Society for American Baseball Research — SABR), who carefully researched box scores for many of these discrepancies. Thorn and Palmer described some of the corrections that they made to "official" major league records in the "Errors and Controversies" section of the introduction of the Player Register for *Total Baseball,* 1989. Since I believe that it provides the most accurate numbers available, *Total Baseball* will be the principal data source for hits and at bats for players in this book.

The Traditional Top 100 Hitters List

Table I gives the traditional list of top 100 hitters. This is *not* my list of top 100 hitters. However, this list is useful as a starting point. A look at the traditional list shows that 48 hitters were in their prime during the 1920s and 1930s! On the other hand, only 8 players on the list were in their prime on or after 1960.

Table I   The Traditional List of Top 100 Hitters

Rank	Player	Average	Mid Yr	Top 5
1	Ty Cobb	.366	1917	16
2	Rogers Hornsby	.358	1926	12
3	Joe Jackson	.356	1914	7
4	Ed Delahanty	.346	1896	9
5	Ted Williams	.344	1950	12
6	Billy Hamilton	.344	1895	7
7	Tris Speaker	.344	1918	13
8	Dan Brouthers	.342	1892	11
9	Babe Ruth	.342	1925	8
10	Harry Heilmann	.342	1923	8
11	Pete Browning	.341	1888	8
12	Willie Keeler	.341	1901	10
13	Bill Terry	.341	1930	7
14	George Sisler	.340	1923	7
15	Lou Gehrig	.340	1931	9
16	Tony Gwynn	.340		13
17	Jesse Burkett	.338	1898	7
18	Nap Lajoie	.338	1906	7
19	Riggs Stephenson	.336	1928	2
20	Al Simmons	.334	1934	7
21	Paul Waner	.333	1935	8
22	Eddie Collins	.333	1918	11
23	Wade Boggs	.331		11
24	Stan Musial	.331	1952	16
25	Sam Thompson	.331	1896	5
26	Heinie Manush	.330	1931	6
27	Cap Anson	.329	1887	10
28	Rod Carew	.328	1976	12
29	Honus Wagner	.327	1907	13
30	Tip O'Neill	.326	1888	5
31	Jimmie Foxx	.325	1935	7
32	Earle Combs	.325	1930	1
33	Joe DiMaggio	.325	1944	6
34	Babe Herman	.324	1936	2
35	Hugh Duffy	.324	1897	3

(continued)

Table I   The Traditional List of Top 100 Hitters *(continued)*

Rank	Player	Average	Mid Yr	Top 5
36	Joe Medwick	.324	1940	6
37	Edd Roush	.323	1922	7
38	Sam Rice	.322	1925	0
39	Ross Youngs	.322	1922	3
40	Kiki Cuyler	.321	1930	3
41	Charlie Gehringer	.320	1933	5̲
42	Chuck Klein	.320	1936	4̲
43	Pie Traynor	.320	1929	1
44	Mickey Cochrane	.320	1931	2
45	Ken Williams	.319	1922	2
46	Kirby Puckett	.318	1989	5̲
47	Earl Averill	.318	1935	1
48	Arky Vaughan	.318	1940	4̲
49	Roberto Clemente	.317	1964	10
50	Chick Hafey	.317	1931	1̲
51	Joe Kelley	.317	1900	1
52	Zach Wheat	.317	1918	6
53	Roger Connor	.317	1889	6̲
54	Lloyd Waner	.316	1936	1
55	Frankie Frisch	.316	1928	2
56	Goose Goslin	.316	1930	2̲
57	George Van Haltren	.316	1895	1
58	Bibb Falk	.314	1926	1
59	Cecil Travis	.314	1940	3
60	Hank Greenberg	.313	1939	2
61	Jack Fournier	.313	1920	4
62	Elmer Flick	.313	1904	5̲
63	Bill Dickey	.313	1937	0
64	Johnny Mize	.312	1945	6̲
65	Joe Sewell	.312	1927	0
66	Fred Clarke	.312	1905	2
67	Barney McCosky	.312	1946	2
68	Bing Miller	.312	1929	2
69	Hugh Jennings	.311	1905	1
70	Fred Lindstrom	.311	1930	2

(continued)

Table I   The Traditional List of Top 100 Hitters *(continued)*

Rank	Player	Average	Mid Yr	Top 5
71	Jackie Robinson	.311	1952	<u>4</u>
72	Baby Doll Jacobson	.311	1921	0
73	Rip Radcliff	.311	1939	1
74	Ginger Beaumont	.311	1905	<u>3</u>
75	Mike Tiernan	.311	1893	3
76	Denny Lyons	.310	1891	2
77	Luke Appling	.310	1940	**3**
78	Irish Meusel	.310	1921	1
79	Elmer Smith	.310	1894	1
80	Bobby Veach	.310	1919	2
81	Jim O'Rourke	.310	1890	5
82	John Stone	.310	1933	0
83	Jim Bottomley	.310	1930	2
84	Sam Crawford	.309	1908	8
85	Bob Meusel	.309	1925	0
86	Jack Tobin	.309	1921	1
87	Spud Davis	.308	1937	0
88	Richie Ashburn	.308	1955	**4**
89	King Kelly	.308	1884	**6**
90	Jake Beckley	.308	1898	3
91	Paul Molitor	.308		6
92	Stuffy McInnis	.308	1918	0
93	Don Mattingly	.307	1989	<u>4</u>
94	Joe Vosmik	.307	1937	<u>1</u>
95	Frank Baker	.307	1915	3
96	George Burns	.307	1922	3
97	Matty Alou	.307	1967	<u>4</u>
98	Hack Wilson	.307	1929	0
99	Johnny Pesky	.307	1948	3
100	George Kell	.306	1950	<u>7</u>

Notes:

Mid Yr = year that the player attained half of his career at bats (blank for active players).

Top 5 = number of years among the league's top 5 hitters.

Underline = one batting title; bold = two or more titles.

As the book develops, I will drop and add players to the list, changing it after each adjustment. The ranking of players who remain on the list will also change, sometimes rather dramatically. After all adjustments have been made, only 18 of the 50 hitters from 1920–39 will remain. On the other hand, the number of players whose prime was 1960 or later will jump from 8 to 39.

A Note About Statistical Methods

This book makes use of statistical methods. They are presented as simply as possible and it is my intention that readers with no prior statistical knowledge will still enjoy this book and understand the basic ideas.

The use of statistics is the way that science often judges whether or not an idea that somebody dreams up is supported by the data. When the evidence from data is overwhelming, no statistics are needed. It is only in close cases that statistical analysis is needed. Just as a microscope enhances the seeing power of the eye, so statistics allows us to obtain convincing evidence about some question with less data than is required to have *overwhelming* evidence.

I am a professional statistician in a cancer research center. The center seeks knowledge on how to prevent and best treat cancer. Since it is important to make discoveries in cancer as soon as possible, statisticians are part of the team. Why shouldn't we use the same tools scientists do so that we can make additional discoveries about baseball?

Statistical methods or concepts used in this book have been placed in boxes labeled *Technical Notes*. These may be skipped without interrupting the flow of the book. Use of the statistical method or concept will usually immediately follow the box. Readers who are not interested in these details can look at the interpretation that I provide. Once a statistical method is introduced, it may be used several times in the book. A list of the Technical Notes is given at the beginning of the book for easy reference.

Organization of the Book

The book is divided into two parts: Methods and Findings. Chapters 1–5 comprise the Methods section. In chapter 1, the basic characteristics of the players eligible for consideration in the top 100 are described. In chapters 2–5 the four adjustments to batting averages will be introduced and applied. Chapters 6–12 comprise the Findings section. In chapter 6 the fully adjusted top 100 hitters are identified. Later chapters deal with top hitters by position, top single-season batting averages, the best batting teams of all-time, ballpark effects for the 20th-century stadiums, top players for on base percentage, who should really be in the Hall of Fame, where today's hitters would place among the top 100 hitters, and a wrap-up. Readers who can't wait for the top 100 list can jump to chapter 6.

PART I   The Method

Tony Gwynn

On Deck with the Qualifying Players

1

We're in the on deck circle, getting ready to bat. Before we undertake the four adjustments needed to identify the top 100 hitters in baseball history, we need to warm up a little. We'll do this by looking at the players from which the top 100 hitters will emerge. In the introduction, we identified these players. They are called the *qualifying players* — 836 players who, through the 1997 season, have had at least 4000 at bats and have retired from baseball or who have had at least 8000 at bats, regardless of their retirement status.

Who are these players? We know at least that their managers rated their abilities highly. After all, they couldn't have had 4000 at bats unless their manager penciled their name onto the lineup card day after day. Did the game change over the years, leading managers to favor different types of players in different eras? Let's find out.

Batting Average

Managers clearly want players who can hit for average. Figure 1.1 shows the percentage of qualifying players in 10-point groups. For example, 18% of the players batted between .260 and .269. The averages range from .218 for George McBride to .366 for Ty Cobb. The average of the batting averages of all qualifying players is .279, with three-quarters of the players hitting between .250 and .299.

George McBride was the regular shortstop for the Washington Senators from 1908 to 1916. McBride earned his keep by being an excellent fielder. The shortstop position is the place where managers are most willing to give up batting points for good fielding.

Figure 1.1 Batting Average Profile of Qualifying Players

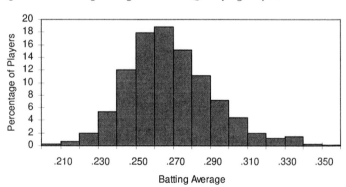

THE METHOD

Cobb was . . . well, if you don't know yet, it's high time you learned! Ty Cobb was the aggressive, spike sharpening centerfielder for the Detroit Tigers. According to baseball reference books, he is credited with having the highest lifetime average of all time. He won 10 to 12 batting titles (more about this later) in a 13-year stretch from 1907–19. He was also a great base stealer, resulting from a potent combination of speed and spike. In recent years, several books have been written about him and one was made into a movie entitled simply *Cobb*.

Picture Cobb and McBride as contrasting bookends in the fortunes of baseball. They faced each other on the field 22 times a year for 9 years. Cobb's shortstop teammate was Donie Bush, a lifetime .250 hitter who walked a lot. Cobb also had shared the outfield with fellow Hall of Famer Sam Crawford, a .309 hitter with the highest lifetime number of triples. McBride's teammate in centerfield was Clyde Milan, a .285 hitter. Chick Gandil, who averaged .293 for the Senators from 1912 to 1915, was the only other "decent" hitter on McBride's team. From 1908–11, Detroit won two league titles and averaged 91 wins in 154-game seasons. Washington averaged 60 wins, finishing 7th or 8th each year in an 8-team league. Just as you might expect. From 1912–16, however, Detroit slipped to 80 wins a year, in spite of adding .310-hitting Bobby Veach in 1914 — and Washington passed by them, averaging 85 wins.

How was this possible? Two explanations come to mind. First, Detroit had the best hitter's park in the American League at that time, while Washington had the worst. So perhaps the batting average differences weren't so great as they seem (more about this later). Second, Washington had Walter "Big Train" Johnson on the mound for them, who didn't need a lot of runs to eke out wins for his team. Johnson is considered by many to have been the greatest pitcher ever. Interesting — Johnson was able to take a team with the weakest "qualifying" hitter and still outwin Detroit, a team with the game's best hitter. Clark Griffith, the owner of the Washington Senators, tried to hire Cobb away from the Tigers. Baseball history would surely have been changed greatly if Cobb and Johnson had played on the same team!

At Bats

When baseball players are listed by decreasing number of at bats, the best players seem to be at the top. Why is this? The primary reason seems to be that better hitters are likely to stay in the lineup and hence

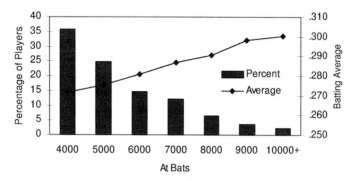

Figure 1.2   Batting Average by At Bats

have longer careers with more at bats. Figure 1.2 shows the percentage
of players with a given range of at bats and their average batting average. The number of players drops dramatically as the number of at bats
increases. Their batting averages go up 2 to 7 points for each additional
1000 at bats.

Table 1.1 shows representative retired players in the different at
bat groups who primarily played after 1972. For the first column of
names, one player was chosen for each at bat group starting alphabet-
ically with the A's. For the second column of names, the selections
started with the M's. While this is a very small sample of players, it
illustrates the point that better hitters tend to have more at bats.

Batting Handedness

Although most batters are right-handed, 34% are left-handers. This is
much higher than the percentage of those who write left-handed in the
U.S. population, which is about 10% according to the World Book En-

Table 1.1   Recently Retired Players in Different At Bat Groups

AB	Name	BA	Name	BA
10000+	George Brett	.305	Pete Rose	.303
9000–9999	Bill Buckner	.289	Joe Morgan	.271
8000–8999	Don Baylor	.260	Graig Nettles	.248
7000–7999	Dusty Baker	.278	Gary Matthews	.281
6000–6999	George Bell	.278	Garry Maddox	.285
5000–5999	Tony Armas	.252	Rick Manning	.257
4000–4999	Alan Ashby	.245	Candy Maldonado	.254

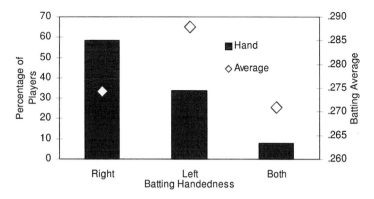

Figure 1.3   Batting Average by Batting Handedness

cyclopedia. Left-handers bat 14 points higher than right-handers who, in turn, bat 3 points higher than switch-hitters (Fig. 1.3).

Position

Pete Rose started his career at second base, moved to the outfield, then to third base, and finally to first base. So what position should be given for Rose? *The Baseball Encyclopedia* and *Total Baseball* both require a player to play at least 1000 games at a position in order to qualify for it, and we will do the same. If a player does not qualify at a position, he qualifies as a utility player if he plays at least 500 games in his non-primary position. Otherwise, he qualifies at no position. Let's take a look at some examples.

Pete Rose played 1327 games in the outfield, 939 at first base, 634 at third, and 628 at second. He qualifies as an outfielder.

Jackie Robinson played 751 games at second base, 256 games at third base, 197 games at first base, 152 games in the outfield, and 1 game at shortstop. Since Robinson did not qualify at his primary position — second base — and played 606 games in non-primary positions, he qualifies as a utility player.

Frank Chance, the first baseman in the famed Chicago Cub double play combo "Tinker to Evers to Chance," played 997 games at first base, 186 games as a catcher, and 72 games in the outfield. He fell three games short of qualifying at first base and qualifies at *no position*. Most of the players who qualify at "no position" had fewer than 5000 career at bats (Chance had 4299 AB).

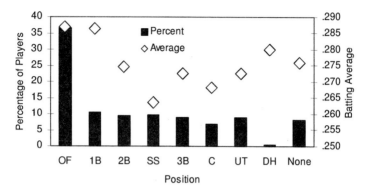

Figure 1.4 Batting Average by Position

Only three players qualify at two different positions. Stan Musial played 1896 games in the outfield and 1016 games at first base. We will consider Musial to be an outfielder. Ernie Banks played 1259 games at first base and 1125 games at shortstop. Even though he played more games at first, we will consider Banks to be a shortstop, since he is usually placed with the shortstop lists. Harold Baines qualifies both as an outfielder and a designated hitter (DH), but has played more games as a DH and will be counted there.

The designated hitter was only established in 1973 and is used only by the American League. As a result, a scant 3 players qualify to date — Harold Baines, Don Baylor, and Hal McRae. (Paul Molitor also has had over 1000 games as a designated hitter. However, he has been "qualified" as a utility player since he played extensively at third, second, and first base, which certainly showed his "utility" to the team in the field.)

Figure 1.4 shows the percentage of qualifying players and overall player batting averages at each position. Outfielders and first basemen bat more than 10 points higher than the other positions (excluding the DHs). Shortstops and catchers, at the two most demanding defensive positions, have the lowest batting averages.

Decade of Mid-Career

Baseball is often divided into eras depending on the dominant features of play. *Sports Encyclopedia: Baseball* divides baseball history into 6 eras (although some of the era names are mine): the 19th century era (1876–1900); "dead ball" era (1901–19); "lively ball" era (1920–45);

post–World War II era (1946–60); expansion era (1961–72); and designated hitter era (1973–present).

A player's performance is usually better understood in the light of when he played. Ty Cobb played from 1905–28 — in both the "dead ball" and "lively ball" eras. The *mid-career year* gives a snapshot summary of when a player played. The *mid-career year* is the year when the player attained half of his total career at bats. Cobb had 11,434 career at bats, so his mid-career year, 1916, occurred when he attained his 5717th at bat.

Batting averages vary greatly by the decade of mid-career of ballplayers, with the overall averages among the players ranging from the upper .260s in the 1960–80s to .295 in the 1920–30s, as Figure 1.5 shows. This variation of nearly 30 points is quite substantial. The big rise in the 1920s partly explains why the era from 1920–45 is often called the "lively" ball period. Many baseball writers claim that a livelier ball was introduced in 1920, although other writers dispute the claim. I will discuss the variation in batting averages over time in greater detail in chapter 3.

The drop in the number of players whose mid-careers were in the 1940s was due to the military service of players during World War II. An average of 27 players per team (including pitchers) missed at least one full season, serving tours of duty sometime between 1942 and 1945. These 427 players missed an average of 2.4 full seasons. These players had shortened careers and some never returned to baseball.

Figure 1.5   Batting Average by Decade of Mid-Career

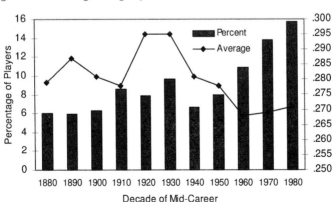

Looking at Pairs of Player Characteristics

We have seen how hitters' batting averages differ by four hitter characteristics — how many at-bats they had, what handedness they had, what
position they played, and when they played. Sometimes new insights
arise when looking at pairs of characteristics. Four pairs will now be
presented.

Batting Handedness and Position

We saw earlier that 34% of the players are left-handed. This percentage, however, varies considerably by position. Figure 1.6 shows that
while the *majority* of outfielders and first basemen are left-handed, very
few shortstops are. In fact, there are only 4 left-handed shortstops, and
the last, Arky Vaughan, was in mid-career in 1938! Also, note that the
middle infield (2B and SS) have higher percentages of switch-hitters
than the other positions.

We saw earlier that left-handed batters hit 14 points better than
right-handed batters. However, Figure 1.7 shows that the difference
ranges from 3–8 points for most positions and the exceptions — shortstops, second basemen, and third basemen — do not have many left-
handed hitters. How can this be? This paradox is largely due to the fact
that the positions with the best hitters overall — the outfield and first
base — have the highest percentage of left-handed hitters.

Figure 1.6 **Batting Handedness by Position**

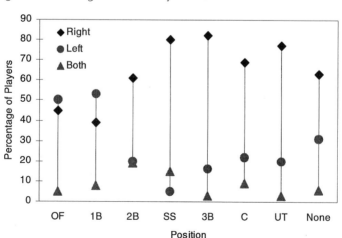

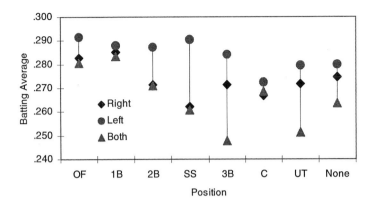

Figure 1.7   Batting Average by Batting Handedness and Position

Position by position, right-handers bat several points better than switch-hitters. Thus, apparently players become switch-hitters to become competitive with more gifted single-handed players.

Batting Handedness and Decade of Mid-Career

Figure 1.8 shows the major shifts in batting handedness over baseball history. In 1880–89, the first full decade of major league baseball, only 24% of the players were left-handed and none were switch-hitters. By the 1890s, 36% of the players were left-handed and 6% were switch-hitters. Those percentages remained relatively constant until 1970, when the percentage of switch-hitters climbed from 6% to 13%, with a corresponding decrease in left-handed hitters.

Figure 1.8   Batting Handedness of Players by Era

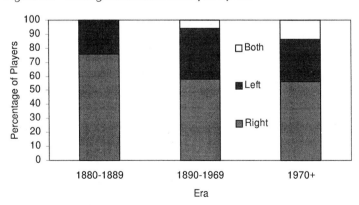

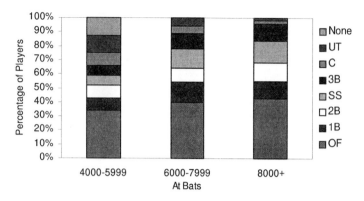

Figure 1.9   Percentage of Players by Position and Number of At Bats

Position and At Bats

Figure 1.9 shows the job "insecurity" of catchers. Catchers represent 9% of the players with careers of between 4000 and 5999 at bats. The percentage drops to 5% for the 6000–7999 at bat group and a scant 2% of players with 8000 or more at bats. The most "secure" infield position is shortstop.

Why do catchers and shortstops have such different prospects? After all, both are highly skilled positions defensively and shortstops hit even less than catchers. Clearly, the strain of catching takes a severe toll.

Utility players and players who don't qualify at a position ("None") tend to have fewer at bats. This is built into the very definitions of the categories since, given enough at bats, a player will qualify somewhere (Fig. 1.9).

Position and Decade of Mid-Career

From 1890 to the present, the percentages of qualifying players at different positions have been relatively constant. However, the percentages were quite different in 1880–89. None of the early players qualified as a catcher and only one — Jack Glassock — qualified as a shortstop. On the other hand, 28% did not qualify at a position ("None") and 20% qualified as utility players. Two reasons for the high percentages at these two "positions" is that players in the 1880s played fewer games and changed positions much more often. It is surprising how quickly the position profile settled down to a constant pattern (Fig. 1.10).

THE METHOD

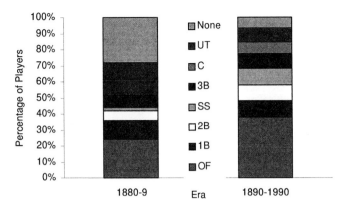

Figure 1.10   Players by Position before and after 1890

An Analysis of the Traditional Top 100 Hitters List

Of the players in the traditional top 100 hitters list presented in the introduction (Table I), 59 are outfielders and 15 are first basemen, while at most 6 players play at any of the other positions. There are 59 left-handers, quite a bit higher than the overall rate of 34%. The most striking feature, however, is the decade when these hitters were in mid-career.

The mid-career year for each of the top hitters is given in Table I. The top 100 hitters are concentrated in a couple of decades, quite different from the percentage of qualifying players overall by decade of mid-career, as Figure 1.11 shows.

Figure 1.11   Percent of Players from Decade in the
Traditional Top 100 List

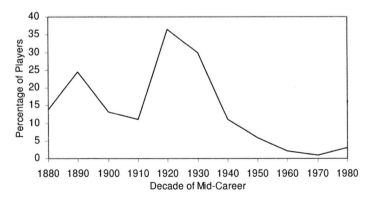

Almost half of the traditional top 100 hitters were in mid-career between 1920–39, although only 17% of the qualifying players played then. Moreover, only 8 top hitting players were in mid-career after 1960, although 41% of all batters played then. Visually, these percentages look quite different. We might raise the question whether these differences are due to chance alone or whether there is some identifiable "association" between the decade of mid-career and being a top 100 hitter. This can be answered using a chi-square test.

The chi-square p-value to test for the association of the decade of mid-career and being a top 100 hitter is less than .0001. Thus, the evidence is quite strong that the percentage of players by decade of mid-career of traditional top 100 hitters does not closely match the percentage of qualifying hitters overall.

Stepping Up to the Plate

Four adjustments—for late career batting declines, hitting feasts and famines, the talent pool, and ballpark effects—are needed to *level the playing field* for batting averages. A basic assumption behind these adjustments is that there is an equal proportion of hitters who are "great" across baseball history. Consequently, one would reasonably expect the percentages of qualifying players that are "true" top 100 hitters to be fairly constant across the decades. We have just seen that this is *not* the case for the traditional top hitter list. We will see progressive improvement in the "constancy" over the four adjustments to batting averages (both graphically and by having a *p*-value above .05 for the chi-square test for the association between the decade of mid-career and being a top 100 hitter).

The traditional top 100 hitters account for 451 single-year top 5 finishes, including 125 batting championships. These numbers are impressive at first blush. However, nine of the players never finished in the top 5 in hitting in any year and 30 others had only 1 or 2 top 5 finishes. We will see improvements in these totals after the proposed adjustments.

In the next four chapters we will examine each of the four adjustments in turn, see why it is needed, learn how to make it, and discover what its effects are. Just like a ballplayer—we'll reach home only after touching each of the bases.

Ty Cobb

First Base —— Adjusting for Late Career Declines

2

Avid baseball fans know that players with long careers perform below their peak ability during their last several seasons. Indeed, many fans hope that their favorite players retire before their skills wane so that they will only be able to remember the peak performance or so that their averages don't drop. Let's look at two players — Hank Aaron and George Van Haltren.

Hank Aaron, a Hall of Famer who played for the Milwaukee Braves, Atlanta Braves, and Milwaukee Brewers from 1954–76, is baseball's all-time home run hitter with 755 home runs. Aaron also won two batting titles, in 1956 and 1959, and finished among the top 5 hitters in 9 other years. Over the course of his 23-year career, Hank Aaron batted .305. In his autobiography, *I Had a Hammer* (p. 202), Aaron, early in his career, viewed himself primarily as a good hitter for average, not as a home run hitter:

> I took home my second batting title in 1959 with an average of .355. . . . I still led the league with 223 hits, and at age twenty-five, I was the second youngest player to reach 1,000, after Ty Cobb. Pete Rose did it when he was twenty-seven. Although it was still way off in the future, my career goal at the time was to get 3,000 hits. I was still putting more emphasis on base hits than home runs, and I think my 1959 season answered anybody who thought I was swinging for the fences.

George Van Haltren, an outfielder who played from 1887 to 1903, principally for the New York Giants, is relatively unknown. In his 17-year career, Van Haltren placed among the top 5 hitters only once — a 5th place finish in the American Association in 1891. Van Haltren's lifetime batting average was .316.

The figure below compares Aaron and Van Haltren at 1000 at bat intervals (which I called *milestone-at-bats*) over the course of their careers. At every milestone-at-bat, Aaron's average was higher than Van Haltren's. At 8000 at bats, Aaron, with a .3164 average, held a slight advantage over Van Haltren's .3158 average. However, after only 21 more at bats, Van Haltren retired with a .3157 average, placing him 57th on the all-time batting average list. On the other hand, Aaron had over 4000 more at bats, finishing second on the all-time at bat list with 12,364. However, his average dropped 11 points to .305, one point below the 100th best player on the traditional batting average list (Fig. 2.1).

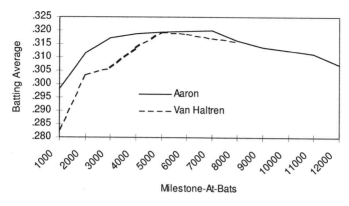

Figure 2.1   Aaron vs. Van Haltren at Milestone-At-Bats

Although Aaron had a superior batting average to Van Haltren at each milestone-at-bat, Van Haltren ranks among the top hitters, while Aaron does not. A great case could be made that Aaron was at least as good a hitter as Van Haltren. We are looking for batting performance here, not the wisdom of early versus late retirement!

Batting Average Trends over a Player's Career

Let's look at the batting averages of *longtime* players — those who reached 8000 at bats. Reaching 8000 at bats for a career is a real accomplishment. Of over 8300 hitters in major league history, only 105 have attained 8000 at bats including 9 active players. This elite group of hitters is packed with Hall of Famers and at least one future Hall of Famer — Tony Gwynn — who singled on his 8000th at bat in San Diego on July 28, 1997. The significance of the moment was noted since the ball was thrown back to the Padre dugout to be saved.

It does not matter when in the order of adjustments the one for late career declines is applied, since the adjustment only involves deciding which at bats should be considered. To understand the 8000 at-bat cutoff choice, it is best to look at it *after* the other adjustments have been made. Applying it *first*, however, quickly moves the best players up the ranks. Thus, the other three adjustments developed in this book (including the ballpark played in) have been applied to the batting averages shown in this chapter, except for Table 2.6.

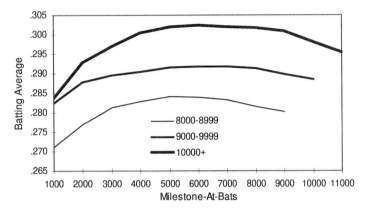

Figure 2.2 Batting Averages of Longtime Players at Milestone-At-Bats

Figure 2.2 shows cumulative batting averages of the 96 retired longtime players, who are placed into three groups based on their career at bats. The overall batting average of all players in each group is given after each milestone-at-bat.

The three at bat groups show the same basic pattern (Fig. 2.3). Players batting averages rise progressively over the first 5000 at bats, remain fairly constant from 5000 to 7000 at bats, and dip slightly at 8000 AB. The dip at 8000 AB depends on the number of career at bats. Players with 10,000+ AB don't drop, those with 9000–9999 AB decline 1 point, and those with 8000–8999 AB drop 2 points.

Let's look closer into what the late career drops signify. Players with 8000–8999 career AB drop 2.3 points. In order for the cumulative

Figure 2.3 Batting Averages of Longtime Players within
Milestone-At-Bat Intervals

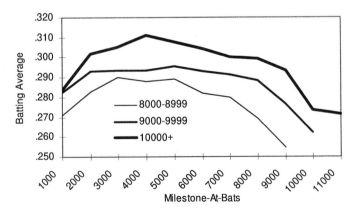

batting average to decline this much, the batting averages for at bats 7000–8000 must be 16 points lower than the average for the first 7000 AB. Thus, the batting average for these 39 players has clearly dropped.

What about milestone-at-bats beyond 8000 AB? For the 42 players with at least 9000 at-bats, batting average drops an average of 1.6 points from 8000 to 9000 AB. Batting averages decline 2.9 points from 9000 to 10,000 AB for the 14 players with at least 10,000 at bats.

Best Single Season Batting Averages by Player Age

We have seen how batting averages first rise, then hold fairly constant, and finally drop in players with long careers. We also noted that cumulative averages of players change less markedly than single season averages. Consequently, we can gain additional insights in batting average ability by looking at the top single season averages by the player's age. The player's age will be defined as his age as of July 1 for the given year. Since these batting averages are fully adjusted, this list gives a sneak preview of how the final rankings will shake out (Table 2.1).

The combined average of the top 10 hitters at each age, given in Table 2.2, is shown in Figure 2.4. From the graph we can see that hitting ability improves rapidly from age 20–22, climbs more slowly at ages 23–27, peaks at age 28, declines 3–4 points per year to age 32, and then remains relatively stable until age 35. The average declines like a rocket at age 38 — a 19-point drop from .332 to .313. A further 19-point drop occurs over the next two years, ending up at .294 at age 40.

At what age have ballplayers reached their 8000th at bat? Robin Yount, at age 32, was the youngest to do it, while Cap Anson, at age 43, was the oldest. Thirty-five players reached it by age 35, 40 at ages 36–37, 20 at ages 38–39, and the final 10 in their 40s. Thus, most of the longtime players locked in their averages before age 38.

While it is not our primary question, it is interesting to know who the top *older* hitters are. Ted Williams, in his book *My Turn At Bat* (page 120), said:

> If in the end I didn't make it as the greatest hitter who had ever lived — that long-ago boyhood dream — I kind of enjoy thinking that I might have become in those last years the greatest *old* hitter who ever lived.

Table 2.1 Top Adjusted Single-Season Batting Averages by Age

	Age 20			Age 21		
1	Pete Browning	1882	.350	Joe Jackson	1911	.347
2	*Alex Rodriguez*	1996	.342	Rogers Hornsby	1917	.334
3	Ty Cobb	1907	.339	*Ken Griffey, Jr.*	1991	.330
4	Al Kaline	1955	.326	Richie Ashburn	1948	.328
5	Rogers Hornsby	1916	.324	Cesar Cedeno	1972	.326
6	Mickey Mantle	1952	.315	Ty Cobb	1908	.325
7	Vada Pinson	1959	.308	Ted Williams	1940	.318
8	Orlando Cepeda	1958	.307	Jimmie Foxx	1929	.316
9	*Ken Griffey, Jr.*	1990	.303	Orlando Cepeda	1959	.314
10	Ted Williams	1939	.295	Frank Robinson	1957	.313
	Average		**.321**	**Average**		**.325**
	Age 22			Age 23		
1	Ted Williams	1941	.377	Ty Cobb	1910	.363
2	Ty Cobb	1909	.362	Arky Vaughan	1935	.346
3	Joe Jackson	1912	.348	Tommy Davis	1962	.345
4	Stan Musial	1943	.343	*Don Mattingly*	1984	.344
5	*R. Henderson*	1981	.341	Ted Williams	1942	.344
6	Pete Reiser	1941	.339	Joe Jackson	1913	.343
7	Eddie Collins	1909	.333	Rusty Staub	1976	.340
8	Tris Speaker	1910	.333	*Gary Sheffield*	1992	.338
9	Sherry Magee	1907	.333	Pete Browning	1885	.336
10	Vada Pinson	1961	.331	Al Simmons	1925	.335
	Average		**.344**	**Average**		**.343**
	Age 24			Age 25		
1	*Tony Gwynn*	1984	.358	Mickey Mantle	1957	.359
2	*John Olerud*	1993	.356	Stan Musial	1946	.356
3	Joe DiMaggio	1939	.353	H. Zimmerman	1912	.354
4	Ty Cobb	1911	.353	Ty Cobb	1912	.353
5	Tris Speaker	1912	.347	*Will Clark*	1989	.353
6	George Sisler	1917	.346	*Don Mattingly*	1986	.352
7	Rogers Hornsby	1920	.346	Tommy Tucker	1889	.347
8	Bill Madlock	1975	.346	Rogers Hornsby	1921	.346
						(continued)

Note: Players with seasons on or after 1980 are italicized and underlined.

THE METHOD

Table 2.1 Top Adjusted Single-Season Batting Averages by Age
(continued)

	Age 24			Age 25		
9	Tommy Davis	1963	.343	Joe Medwick	1937	.346
10	Dave Orr	1884	.343	Bobby Murcer	1971	.345
	Average		**.349**	**Average**		**.351**

	Age 26			Age 27		
1	Nap Lajoie	1901	.372	*George Brett*	1980	.376
2	Norm Cash	1961	.369	*Tony Gwynn*	1987	.365
3	*Willie McGee*	1985	.359	Stan Musial	1948	.360
4	Jeff Bagwell	1994	.356	*Wade Boggs*	1985	.356
5	Ty Cobb	1913	.350	*Kirby Puckett*	1988	.353
6	Cleon Jones	1969	.349	George Sisler	1920	.350
7	Rogers Hornsby	1922	.346	Jesse Burkett	1896	.345
8	Joe DiMaggio	1941	.344	Hugh Duffy	1894	.344
9	*Mike Piazza*	1995	.344	Willie Mays	1958	.343
10	*Frank Thomas*	1994	.343	C. Yastrzemski	1967	.343
	Average		**.353**	**Average**		**.354**

	Age 28			Age 29		
1	Rogers Hornsby	1924	.376	Tip O'Neill	1887	.368
2	Tris Speaker	1916	.364	George Sisler	1922	.364
3	*Mike Piazza*	1997	.362	Nap Lajoie	1904	.359
4	Ralph Garr	1974	.357	Rod Carew	1975	.356
5	Rod Carew	1974	.357	Al Simmons	1931	.354
6	King Kelly	1886	.355	*Tony Gwynn*	1989	.350
7	George Stone	1906	.354	Luke Appling	1936	.348
8	Harry Heilmann	1923	.350	Rogers Hornsby	1925	.348
9	Babe Ruth	1923	.348	*Wade Boggs*	1987	.347
10	Harvey Kuenn	1959	.346	*Edgar Martinez*	1992	.346
	Average		**.357**	**Average**		**.354**

	Age 30			Age 31		
1	*Wade Boggs*	1988	.358	Rod Carew	1977	.372
2	Ty Cobb	1917	.356	Ty Cobb	1918	.349
3	*Paul Molitor*	1987	.352	*Paul O'Neill*	1994	.347
						(continued)

Note: Players with seasons on or after 1980 are italicized and underlined.

Table 2.1 Top Adjusted Single-Season Batting Averages by Age
(continued)

	Age 30			Age 31		
4	Harry Walker	1947	.351	Richie Ashburn	1958	.347
5	Joe Torre	1971	.349	Honus Wagner	1905	.344
6	*Cecil Cooper*	1980	.349	Ed Delahanty	1899	.344
7	Jesse Burkett	1899	.348	Nap Lajoie	1907	.342
8	Tony Gonzalez	1967	.348	Dan Brouthers	1889	.340
9	Rico Carty	1970	.345	*R. Henderson*	1990	.339
10	Bobby Avila	1954	.340	Frank Robinson	1967	.339
	Average		**.350**	**Average**		**.347**

	Age 32			Age 33		
1	Rogers Hornsby	1928	.360	*Tony Gwynn*	1993	.350
2	Cy Seymour	1905	.351	Honus Wagner	1907	.348
3	*Edgar Martinez*	1995	.349	Dixie Walker	1944	.347
4	*C. Lansford*	1989	.345	Hal Chase	1916	.344
5	R. Clemente	1967	.343	Paul Waner	1936	.335
6	*Dave Winfield*	1984	.341	Rogers Hornsby	1929	.329
7	Harry Heilmann	1927	.340	Luke Appling	1940	.328
8	*R. Henderson*	1990	.339	Ed Collins	1920	.325
9	Jesse Burkett	1901	.338	Billy Herman	1943	.325
10	Honus Wagner	1906	.337	*Wade Boggs*	1991	.325
	Average		**.344**	**Average**		**.336**

	Age 34			Age 35		
1	*Tony Gwynn*	1994	.378	Nap Lajoie	1910	.365
2	Honus Wagner	1908	.360	*Tony Gwynn*	1995	.361
3	Cap Anson	1887	.343	Honus Wagner	1909	.350
4	Dan Brouthers	1892	.339	Ty Cobb	1922	.345
5	Tom Paciorek	1981	.338	Lefty O'Doul	1932	.341
6	Earl Averill	1936	.337	*Al Oliver*	1982	.334
7	Ed Delahanty	1902	.336	Ted Williams	1954	.333
8	Billy Williams	1972	.334	Elston Howard	1964	.333
9	C. Gehringer	1937	.333	*Paul Molitor*	1992	.327
10	*Paul Molitor*	1991	.332	Tris Speaker	1923	.327
	Average		**.342**	**Average**		**.342**

(continued)

Note: Players with seasons on or after 1980 are italicized and underlined.

Table 2.1 Top Adjusted Single-Season Batting Averages by Age
(continued)

	Age 36			Age 37		
1	*Tony Gwynn*	1996	.346	*Tony Gwynn*	1997	.367
2	Cap Anson	1888	.343	*Rod Carew*	1983	.340
3	Zack Wheat	1924	.340	*George Brett*	1990	.332
4	Luke Appling	1943	.337	Honus Wagner	1911	.330
5	Babe Ruth	1931	.336	*Paul Molitor*	1994	.330
6	Stan Musial	1957	.334	Nap Lajoie	1912	.329
7	*Wade Boggs*	1994	.331	Ted Williams	1956	.326
8	R. Clemente	1971	.330	Tris Speaker	1925	.323
9	*Dave Winfield*	1988	.327	Stan Musial	1958	.320
10	*Paul Molitor*	1993	.326	Hank Aaron	1971	.318
	Average		**.335**	**Average**		**.332**
	Age 38			Age 39		
1	Ted Williams	1957	.373	*Paul Molitor*	1996	.322
2	Pete Rose	1979	.323	Ted Williams	1958	.320
3	Ty Cobb	1925	.319	*Eddie Murray*	1995	.315
4	Nap Lajoie	1913	.315	Luke Appling	1946	.308
5	Honus Wagner	1912	.307	*Dave Parker*	1990	.296
6	Cap Anson	1890	.304	Jimmy Ryan	1902	.292
7	Eddie Collins	1925	.302	Tris Speaker	1927	.290
8	Jake Daubert	1922	.297	Willie Mays	1970	.290
9	Sam Rice	1928	.296	Sam Rice	1929	.289
10	*Wade Boggs*	1996	.296	Cap Anson	1891	.289
	Average		**.313**	**Average**		**.301**

		Age 40		
	1	*Pete Rose*	1981	.326
	2	Ty Cobb	1927	.316
	3	Sam Rice	1930	.307
	4	Luke Appling	1947	.306
	5	*Dave Winfield*	1992	.294
		Paul Molitor	1997	.289
		Cap Anson	1892	.280
		Willie Mays	1971	.278
		Nap Lajoie	1915	.277
		Lave Cross	1906	.271
		Average		**.294**

Note: Players with seasons on or after 1980 are italicized and underlined.

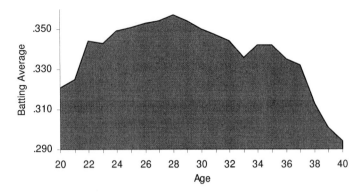

Figure 2.4   Average of Top 10 Single-Season Batting Averages by Age

Certainly his adjusted .373 year at age 38 in 1957 stands as a stunning accomplishment. It was 50 points higher than the next best year, .323, by Pete Rose. To find the best *older* hitters, let's look at batting averages at age 35 or older.

Batting averages drop off dramatically with age for older players. Thus, for Tables 2.2 and 2.3 — which show the adjusted top 10 hitters starting at age 35 — players must have had at least 400 at bats over the final two ages in the age range. For example, for the age 35–38 list, the player must have a total of 400 AB for ages 37 and 38. I allowed one exception — for Roberto Clemente, who died in a plane crash while on a humanitarian mission to Nicaragua on New Year's eve, 1972. Cle-

Table 2.2   Adjusted Top 10 Hitters Starting at Age 35

	Ages 35–36		Ages 35–38	
1	Tony Gwynn	.354	Tony Gwynn	.359
2	Nap Lajoie	.349	Ted Williams	.344
3	Zach Wheat	.339	Nap Lajoie	.335
4	Ted Williams	.336	Rogers Hornsby	.326
5	Honus Wagner	.333	Roberto Clemente	.324
6	Roberto Clemente	.331	Rod Carew	.321
7	Cap Anson	.328	Zach Wheat	.317
8	Paul Molitor	.326	Pete Rose	.314
9	Babe Ruth	.326	Cap Anson	.313
10	Ty Cobb	.321	Paul Molitor	.312
	Average	.334	**Average**	.326

Table 2.3   Top *Older* Hitters — Batting Average from Age 35–40

	Player	AB	BA
1	Ted Williams	2209	.328
2	Nap Lajoie	2728	.314
3	Rod Carew	2131	.314
4	Ty Cobb	2845	.311
5	Paul Molitor	3422	.311
6	Honus Wagner	3047	.310
7	Pete Rose	3689	.308
8	Luke Appling	2270	.306
9	Eddie Collins	2685	.305
10	Cap Anson	3108	.303
	Average		**.311**

mente had 378 AB as a 37-year-old. Even if Clemente were credited with no hits in 22 additional at bats (to make 400 AB), he would still place 6th on the list with a .319 average.

Gwynn, with three batting titles from age 35–37, tops the 35–38 year-old hitters list. With his great year at age 38, Williams ranks second.

Table 2.3 lists the greatest *older* hitters, with Williams indeed on top. Every player on the list is in the Hall of Fame, except for Paul Molitor, who is still active, and Pete Rose, who is currently not eligible.

Figure 2.5 shows the cumulative batting average starting at age 35

Figure 2.5   Cumulative Batting Average of Older Players

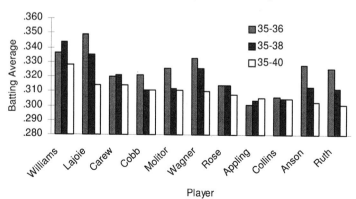

of the top 11 older hitters. We can see the difficulty that each one had in maintaining a high batting average. Notice, in particular, the dramatic declines of Lajoie, Wagner, Anson, and Ruth.

Choice of the Longevity Adjustment

As noted earlier in this chapter, the first adjustment will be to limit batting average comparisons to a player's first 8000 at bats. This adjustment—the *longevity adjustment*—only affects the 105 players with more than 8000 at bats.

I have four principal reasons for choosing 8000 at bats and not, say, 6000 or 7000 AB, the milestone-at-bats at which the overall batting average of longtime players peaked? First, using the 8000 at bat cutoff, the longevity-adjusted batting average includes as many at bats as possible while avoiding a strong late-career downturn. Second, many players had higher batting averages at the end of their career than they did at 6000 or 7000 at bats. However, Roberto Clemente is the only fully adjusted top 100 hitter (after all four adjustments in this book are made) whose batting average rose at least one point from 8000 AB to career end. Third, 8000 at bats are exactly twice the amount needed to be a qualifying player. Finally, players with the longest careers (10,000+ AB) were able to maintain their average through 8000 at bats.

What about stopping at some age between 34 and 37 instead of using a fixed number of at bats? This has problems as well. Tony Gwynn's average climbed throughout those ages. Luke Appling, Paul Molitor, Zach Wheat, and other players also improved their averages during most of these years. Ted Williams had one of the greatest years ever at age 38. In contrast, Ty Cobb, who had his 8000th at bat by age 34, saw his average drop 6 points by age 38. Hank Aaron and many other hitters who reached 8000 at bats earlier, declined earlier as well. While today's players tend to have fewer at bats by a given age than earlier in the game's history, with modern sports medicine they often play better at older ages. While no choice is perfect, some choice is needed for a fairer comparison of players; the 8000 at bat cutoff is mine.

Longevity-Adjusted Batting Average

The *longevity-adjusted* batting average is applied to players with more than 8000 at bats. There are two methods for calculating it: an *exact* method and an *approximate* method.

The *exact* method divides the number of hits in the first 8000 at bats by 8000. To use this method, however, one would need to research the number of hits in the first 8000 at bats from box scores. Consequently, the *approximate* method below is more practical.

The *approximate* method first totals the number of hits, H_1, obtained in seasons prior to the one with the 8000th at bat. Then, in the season with the player's 8000th at bat, the approximate number of hits up to the 8000th at bat is given by

$$H_2 = \text{hits} \times N \div \text{at bats}$$

where hits and at bats are those of the full season and N is the number of at bats in that season up to the 8000th at bat. The longevity-adjusted batting average then equals $(H_1 + H_2) / 8000$.

All longevity adjustments applied in this book use the approximate method, except for the final-adjusted averages of the top two hitters, Ty Cobb and Tony Gwynn.

Applying the Longevity Adjustment

Let's see how this adjustment would be applied to Hank Aaron's batting average. Aaron's lifetime average is .3050. From 1954–66, Aaron had 2434 hits in 7683 at bats, for a .317 batting average. In 1967, Aaron hit .3067 in 600 at bats, which gave him 8283 career at bats. To obtain the longevity-adjusted batting average, we assume that Aaron batted consistently over the entire 1967 season. Thus, in his first 317 at bats (which took him to 8000 AB), he "got" $.3067 \times 317 = 97.2$ hits. Thus, his batting average is $(2434 + 97.2) / 8000 = .3164$. Aaron "gained" 11.4 points by the adjustment, moving him into 55th place in the "longevity-adjusted" top 100, slightly ahead of Van Haltren.

Table 2.4 Players with the Greatest Gains in Batting Average
Due to the Longevity Adjustment

Player	AB Rank	Change
Eddie Murray	5	9.6
Honus Wagner	11	9.6
Carl Yastrzemski	3	9.6
Ty Cobb	4	9.1
Hank Aaron	2	8.9
Reggie Jackson	21	8.7
Willie Mays	9	8.6
Nap Lajoie	26	8.3
Tris Speaker	15	7.4
Frank Robinson	18	7.2

Notes:

AB Rank is the ranking of the player in career at bats.

Change in batting points due to the longevity adjustment, with the other three adjustments also applied.

Table 2.4 shows the 10 players helped most by the longevity adjustment. All of the players are Hall of Famers and all rank among the top 26 for career at bats. Thus, the longevity adjustment clearly helps those players with the longest careers.

Only 6 retired players, shown in Table 2.5, were "hurt" by the longevity adjustment, since their averages improved from 8000 AB to their career ends. Only Clemente and Aparicio were hurt by more than 1 batting point.

Changes in the Top 100 with the Longevity Adjustment

What changes occur in the list of top hitters after adjusting for player longevity? Six players join the top 100 — Hank Aaron (55th), Willie Mays (67th), George Brett (79th), Mel Ott (85th), Pete Rose (89th), and Jimmy Ryan (96th). Five players at the bottom of the traditional batting average list — George Burns, Matty Alou, Hack Wilson, Johnny Pesky, and George Kell — drop off. Paul Molitor, whose average im-

Table 2.5   Players Hurt by the Longevity Adjustment

Player	AB Rank	Change
Roberto Clemente	31	−3.5
Luis Aparicio	14	−1.5
Doc Cramer	44	−0.4
Fred Clarke	71	−0.3
Richie Ashburn	79	−0.2
Jimmy Dykes	96	−0.1

Notes:

AB Rank is the ranking of the player in career at bats.

Change in batting points due to the longevity adjustment, with the other three adjustments also applied.

proved past 8000 at bats, also drops off the list. (Don't worry Molitor fans — he'll be back!) The new players on the longevity-adjusted list combined for 10 batting titles and 32 top 5 finishes while the six dropped from the list had 2 batting titles and 23 top 5 finishes.

Several changes occur among the top 10 hitters. Ty Cobb, Rogers Hornsby, and Joe Jackson retain the top three spots. Nap Lajoie jumps from 18th to 4th, Tris Speaker inches up from 7th to 5th, and Willie Keeler climbs from 12th to 6th. Ed Delahanty, Babe Ruth, Ted Williams, and Billy Hamilton all move around among the top 10, while Dan Brouthers and Harry Heilmann slip out of the top 10 (Table 2.6).

Table 2.6   Top 10 Hitters before and after the Longevity Adjustment

	Player	Trad.	Player	Long.
1	Ty Cobb	.366	Ty Cobb	.370
2	Rogers Hornsby	.358	Roger Hornsby	.360
3	Joe Jackson	.356	Joe Jackson	.356
4	Ed Delahanty	.346	Nap Lajoie	.351
5	Ted Williams	.344	Tris Speaker	.347
6	Billy Hamilton	.344	Willie Keeler	.347
7	Tris Speaker	.344	Ed Delahanty	.346
8	Dan Brouthers	.342	Babe Ruth	.346
9	Babe Ruth	.342	Ted Williams	.344
10	Harry Heilmann	.342	Billy Hamilton	.344

Notes:

Trad. = traditional unadjusted batting average.

Long. = longevity-adjusted batting average.

Rod Carew

Second Base —— Adjusting for Hitting Feasts and Famines 3

Suppose that an archaeological dig tomorrow reveals that caveman Rocky batted .452 over 5000 at bats in some Stone Age baseball game. Would you immediately believe that he was the greatest hitter of all time? No—you'd ask all kinds of questions. What kind of bat and ball was used? How did the pitchers throw the ball? How good were the fielders? Were there nine of them? What did the ballfields look like? Just because "major league baseball" officially started in 1876, should you ask any fewer questions?

In 1876, pitchers pitched underhanded from a distance of 45 feet away. Nine balls were needed for a walk and four strikes for a strikeout and fouls were not called strikes. Not only that, the batter indicated to the pitcher whether he wanted a high pitch or a low pitch and the pitcher was required to comply. There were "foul hits"—hits that landed in fair territory but bounced or rolled foul, even on the near side of the bases. Does that sound like baseball to you?

On the other hand, why does major league baseball only officially recognize batting records starting in 1876? The National Association played from 1871–75 and batting average records were kept. However, the National Association was *not* designated as a "major league." Why not? Many of the stars of 1875 were the stars of 1876—pitchers like Al Spaulding and George Bradley and batters like Ross Barnes and Hall of Famer Cap Anson. Sure the National Association folded and the National League was formed in 1876, but why does 1876 count while 1875 does not? Anson batted .352 from 1871–75 and .356 in 1876. Meanwhile, Barnes and Cal McVey had .379 and .362 averages for 1871–75 and posted .429 and .347 averages in 1876, respectively.

During the first quarter century of major league baseball, 1876–1900, many changes occurred, making the game quite close to the one we know and love. These changes both kept an interesting balance between pitcher and hitter and made the game more exciting to watch. In 1887, when the pitcher was allowed to pitch overhand wherever he wanted to in the strike zone, the number of balls needed for a walk was dropped from 7 to 5. Many of the most significant changes made are shown in Table 3.1.

Rule changes were made less frequently after 1900. However, changes in equipment, pitching, ballparks, and training continued to occur. Night baseball was introduced, relief pitchers became more prominent, and designated hitters replaced pitchers in the American League lineups. Sometimes these changes were dramatic, sometimes

Table 3.1 Major Nineteenth-Century Rule Changes
in the National League

Year	Distance	Balls	Strikes	Other Changes
1876	45	9	3–4	Pitcher — must pitch underhand
				Batter — requests location
				Strikes — batter misses
				Strikeout — batter must be thrown out at first base
				Foul balls — outs if caught on
1880		8		Strikeout — batter out if strike held
1881	50			
1884		6		Pitcher — can pitch overhand
1887		5		Batter — can't request location
1888			3	
1889		4		
1893	60.5			
1894				No at bat for sacrifice
				Foul hits — strikes on bunts

Notes:

Distance in feet from the pitcher's box to home plate.

Balls needed for a walk.

Strikes needed for a strikeout.

In 1876, if a batter with two strikes does not swing at a well-pitched ball, the umpire calls "good ball." If the batter fails to swing at another well-pitched ball, the umpire calls "strike three."

gradual. They have resulted in "eras" of the game — periods of hitting feasts and famines. Adjustments for these changes must be made in order to compare hitters from different eras fairly.

Later in the chapter we will compare Bill Terry's 1930 season, when he led the National League with a .401 average, to George Brett's .390 AL batting title half a century later in 1980. After adjusting for the era of play, Brett's year will wind up 45 points better than Terry's.

Batting Average over the Years

Let's reexamine Figure 1.5 from chapter 1, presented here as Figure 3.1. This figure shows how the batting averages of players with 4000 or

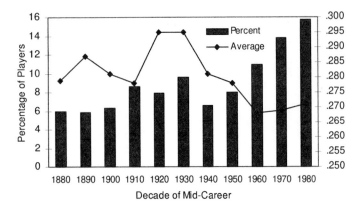

Figure 3.1 Batting Average by Decade of Mid-Career

more at bats vary by the decade of mid-career. The batting averages peak at .295 in 1920–39 and ebb to around .269 from 1960–89. This spread of 26 points in batting average is considerable and, as a result, 48 of the traditional top 100 hitters were in mid-career during 1920–39.

Figure 3.2 shows the league batting average year by year in the National League. The solid curved line, called a *loess curve*, shows the general trend by "smoothing" the data. The dashed line at .255 will gauge the feast and famine periods, with averages above .255 representing feasts. A small famine occurred from 1904 to 1920 followed by a tremendous feast that lasted from 1921 until 1939. Between 1940 and 1960, a modest feast occurred followed by a 32-year period which hugged the .255 line. Since 1993, the league batting average has been about .262.

The American League batting averages, displayed in Figure 3.3, show basically the same pattern. However, the hitting famine was particularly severe during the 1960s when hitting stars Rod Carew, Al Kaline, Mickey Mantle, Tony Oliva, Frank Robinson, and Carl Yastrzemski played. The jump in the dashed line from .255 to .2635 in 1973 reflects the introduction of the designated hitter. This increase is discussed in greater detail later in this chapter.

Having 48 of the top 100 hitters in mid-career during a twenty-year stretch — 1920–39 — looks highly suspicious. This skepticism, of course, relies on a healthy dose of baseball knowledge and requires that the numbers not be treated as timeless things. Let's see where the investigation leads.

THE METHOD

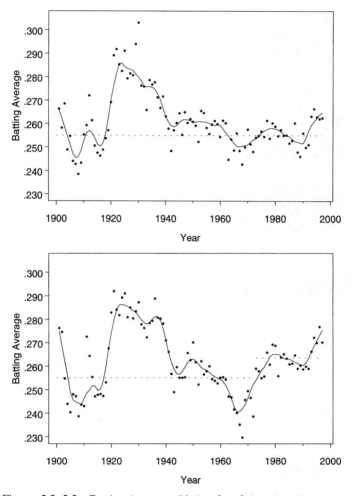

Figures 3.2, 3.3   Batting Average—National and American Leagues
Batting averages are shown for 1901–97 for the National League (*top*) and
American League (*bottom*). The curved lines (loess curves) provide
"smoothed" trends for the data. The straight dashed line, at .255, is used to
gauge feast and famine periods. The dashed line jumps to .2635 for the
American League in 1973, due to the increase in batting averages attributed
to the designated hitter (explained later in this chapter).

In track and field, swimming, and a host of other athletic events,
we have seen consistent improvements in performance. Baseball is not
an *absolute* sport measured with a clock or a measuring stick, it is a
relative game. If a great new pitcher arrives on the scene, batting aver-

ages will drop even if the players are not *absolutely* worse than before. Stephen Jay Gould made this basic observation in a 1986 *Discover* magazine article, "Entropic Homogeneity Is Not Why No One Hits .400 Anymore," and later extended it in his book *Full House*. Consequently, batting averages should not be considered as absolutes.

It would be quite strange if some very important aspect of hitting ability which couldn't be taught, was lost around 1940, leading to the major decline in batting average seen then. It would be even more surprising if the league batting average *never* changed over time, as if it were a timeless constant like the speed of light. Consequently, the changes that do occur should not *all* be attributed to player ability. They may be the result of rule changes, night baseball, or other changes already mentioned.

Ted Williams, in *My Turn At Bat* (p. 234), attributes some of the decline in batting average after World War II to the introduction of the slider.

> The big thing the slider did was to give the pitcher a third pitch right away. With two pitches you might guess right half the time. With three your guessing goes down proportionally.

Still, some fans may desire more convincing data — say where dramatic changes in hitting occurred over a very short stretch of time. Well . . . those data exist!

The Great Batting Average Rise of 1893 – 94

Something occurred in major league baseball during the years 1893 and 1894 that had neither occurred before nor since. In two short years, the league batting average rose 65 points. What happened?

In 1890 there were 24 major league teams in three 8-team leagues — the National League, the American Association, and the Player's League. The Player's League folded after a single season despite recruiting some talented ballplayers, including future Hall-of-Fame hitters Jake Beckley, Dan Brouthers, Roger Connor, Hugh Duffy, Buck Ewing, Jim O'Rourke, and Monte Ward. The American Association, after rivaling the National League for a decade, folded after the 1891 season. In order to accommodate the best players from the now-defunct rival leagues, the National League expanded from 8 to

12 teams in 1892. In 1891, the league batting averages were .252 and .255 in the National League and American Association, respectively, but dropped to .245 for the expanded National League in 1892.

Then something surprising happened! The National League batting average jumped to .280 in 1893 and to .309 in 1894, with the 1894 average being the highest in major league history. What could have happened during these two years to account for such a major gain in average? Were the pitchers on strike? All 18 pitchers who pitched at least 300 innings in 1892 and pitched at least 100 innings in each of the following two years yielded higher batting averages in 1893 and 1894 than in 1892. Except for Sadie McMahon, whose opposing batting average went up a "mere" 21 points, the increase ranged from 51 to 128 points from 1892 to 1894. This includes Hall of Famers Amos Rusie (+51), Jack Clarkson (+57), Kid Gleason (+68), Kid Nichols (+69), and Cy Young (+78). Notably, the average change of this elite list is +65 points, equaling the average change of the entire league.

Was it the hitters? Table 3.2 shows all 19 Hall of Famers or traditional top 100 hitters who had at least 200 at bats in each of the three seasons.

In 1894, seventeen of the 19 (89%) batted as well as or better than they had in 1892 and 15 (79%) improved their averages successively over the three years. Contrast this with the players from 1926–28 when the greatest concentration of top 100 hitters in baseball occurred (Table 3.3).

Only 20 of 34 (59%) players batted higher in 1928 than 1926 and only 10 of 34 (29%) players improved their averages successively over the three years. Yet the players of 1926–28 — led by Ruth, Gehrig, Cobb, Hornsby, and Sisler — is a much more impressive list of hitters than those from 1892–94. So how did the hitters of 1892 do it? Did they all work out during the off-season?

The Philadelphia Outfield of 1894

Billy Hamilton, Sam Thompson, and Ed Delahanty shared the outfield for the Philadelphia Phillies in 1894, as they had since 1891. These were the only years in major league history when three Hall of Fame teammates shared the same outfield. Hamilton was the batting champion in 1891 (.340) and finished second in 1892 (.330), but re-

Table 3.2 Batting Averages of Hall-of-Famers or
Top 100 Hitters in 1892–94

Player	Team	Age	1892	1893	1894	Rise
Dan Brouthers	Bkn	35	.335	.337	.347	Y
Billy Hamilton	Phi	26	.330	.380	.404	Y
Cupid Childs	Cle	23	.317	.326	.353	Y
Buck Ewing	Cle	32	.310	.344	.251	
Ed Delahanty	Phi	25	.306	.368	.407	Y
Sam Thompson	Phi	32	.305	.370	.404	Y
George Van Haltren	Pit	26	.302	.338	.331	
Hugh Duffy	Bos	25	.301	.363	.438	Y
Roger Connor	NY	34	.294	.309	.321	Y
Jimmy Ryan	Chi	29	.293	.299	.361	Y
Mike Tiernan	NY	25	.287	.309	.276	
Jesse Burkett	Cle	23	.275	.348	.358	Y
Elmer Smith	Pit	24	.274	.346	.356	Y
Cap Anson	Chi	41	.272	.314	.395	Y
Monte Ward	NY	32	.265	.328	.265	
Denny Lyons	Pit	26	.257	.306	.323	Y
Tommy McCarthy	Bos	27	.242	.346	.349	Y
Joe Kelley	Bal	20	.239	.305	.393	Y
Jake Beckley	Pit	24	.236	.303	.343	Y

Notes: Hall of Fame players are in italics.

Age = player age in 1892.

Team = team with whom the player had the most at bats from 1892 to 1894.

Y indicates that the player's average rose each year from 1892 to 1894.

bounded to beat his two teammates for the title in 1893, hitting .380. In 1894, Hamilton topped that performance with a .404 mark. Unfortunately, he didn't win the batting title. In fact, he was outhit by his three outfield teammates. Thompson and Delahanty both hit .407 and the backup outfielder, Tuck Turner, bettered them all, hitting .416 with 339 AB!

While no major leaguer has hit .400 since 1941, the 1894 Philadelphia Phillies had four outfielders who broke .400. Even so, Boston's Hugh Duffy, who sported a .440 average, the highest in major league history, beat them all. Adding insult to injury, Philadelphia even failed to win the championship, finishing 18 games behind Baltimore!

Table 3.3   Batting Averages of Hall-of-Famers or
            Top 100 Hitters in 1926–28

Player	Team	Age	1926	1927	1928	Rise
Heinie Manush	Det	24	.378	.298	.378	
Babe Ruth	NYA	31	.372	.356	.323	
Harry Heilmann	Det	31	.367	.398	.328	
George Burns	Cle	33	.358	.319	.254	
Goose Goslin	Was	25	.354	.334	.379	
Bibb Falk	ChiA	27	.345	.327	.290	
Al Simmons	PhiA	24	.343	.398	.351	
Ty Cobb	PhiA	39	.339	.357	.323	
Riggs Stephenson	ChiN	28	.338	.344	.324	
Sam Rice	Was	36	.337	.297	.328	
Paul Waner	Pit	23	.336	.380	.370	
Travis Jackson	NYN	20	.327	.318	.270	
Joe Sewell	Cle	27	.324	.316	.323	
Bing Miller	StLA	31	.322	.325	.329	Y
Kiki Cuyler	Pit	26	.321	.309	.285	
Hack Wilson	ChiN	26	.321	.318	.313	
Babe Herman	Bkn	23	.319	.272	.340	
Rogers Hornsby	StLN	30	.317	.361	.387	Y
Pie Traynor	Pit	26	.317	.342	.337	
Bob Meusel	NYA	29	.315	.337	.297	
Frank Frisch	StLN	27	.314	.337	.300	
Lou Gehrig	NYA	23	.311	.373	.374	Y
George Kelly	Cin	30	.303	.270	.296	
Fred Lindstrom	NYN	20	.302	.306	.358	Y
Earle Combs	NYA	27	.299	.356	.320	
Jim Bottomley	StLN	26	.299	.303	.325	Y
George Sisler	StLA	33	.289	.327	.340	Y
Bill Terry	NYN	27	.289	.326	.326	Y
Ken Williams	StLA	36	.280	.322	.303	
Charlie Gehringer	Det	23	.277	.317	.320	Y
Gabby Hartnett	ChiN	25	.275	.294	.302	Y
Mickey Cochrane	PhiA	23	.273	.338	.293	
Chick Hafey	StLN	23	.271	.329	.337	Y
Max Carey	Bkn	36	.222	.266	.247	

Notes: Hall of Fame players are in italics.

Age = player's age in 1926.

Team = team with whom the player had the most at bats from 1926 to 1928.

Y indicates that the player's average rose each year from 1926 to 1928.

The Smoking Gun — Pitching Distance from Home Plate

It seems highly unlikely that all the hitters simultaneously improved their "true" batting ability by about 65 points over the course of two seasons. The contrast between the 1892–94 and 1926–28 hitters is just too extreme to believe that the nineteenth-century hitters mastered some great secret that eluded the great players of Babe Ruth's and Ty Cobb's day. A more reasonable explanation is that something about the game changed that made it easier to get hits in 1893 and 1894 than in 1892.

I suspect that you are haunted now by the *why* question. *Why* questions are among the most difficult to answer in life. Mankind long accepted the idea that the sun would rise every day before a convincing theory of why this is so was developed. Still . . . it is interesting to speculate why batting averages rose so much during this time. *Total Baseball* provides an appendix describing playing and scoring rule changes, some of which have already been identified in Table 3.1. In 1892, the near edge of the pitcher's box was 50 feet away from home plate. In 1893 a white rubber plate was set in the ground 60 feet 6 inches from the outer corner of home plate. This additional distance allowed hitters more time to react to the pitch. It seems reasonable that this rule change was largely responsible for the 35-point jump in batting average that occurred in 1893. Not surprisingly, strikeouts also went down by one-third — from 3.3 to 2.2 per team per 9 innings. Remember caveman Rocky?

So what about the additional rise in 1894? A scoring change was made: batters would not be charged with an at bat on a sacrifice bunt that advanced a baserunner. Could this have contributed to the 30-point increase? Let's estimate what effect this rule change had on batting averages.

From 1891–93 there was an average of 2.98 "unsuccessful" at bats (calculated as at bats minus hits) per inning pitched. The number is slightly less than three because of double plays and other situations where an out is registered against the team but not as an extra at bat for the player.

From 1894–96, there were 2.88 unsuccessful at bats per inning pitched. This suggests that there were .10 sacrifices per inning pitched, or slightly less than one per 9-inning game per team.

In 1893, there were 1.15 hits per inning. Thus, by these numbers, the batting average (which equals hits/(hits + at bat outs)) would change from $1.15/(1.15 + 2.98) = .278$ to $1.15/(1.15 + 2.88) = .285$ — a 7-point increase in batting average.

This rule change, then, explains only part of the increase seen. What about the other 23 points? I'm not sure — perhaps the hitters made some batting adjustments that allowed them to take even greater advantage of the pitching distance change made in 1893.

Lowering the Pitching Mound in 1969

In 1969, a change was made in baseball with the deliberate goal of raising batting averages. The urgency of the decision was readily apparent in the aftermath of the so-called "year of the pitcher" in 1968. Denny McLain, who won 31 games for the Detroit Tigers, was the dominant pitcher in the American League. Bob Gibson, a 22-game winner with the St. Louis Cardinals, owned the National League with 13 shutouts and a stellar 1.12 ERA. The league batting average in the National League (.243) slipped to the lowest level in 60 years and the fourth lowest in the league ever. The American League average, .230, was the all-time lowest. Carl Yastrzemski, the batting champion with a .301 average, was the only AL player to exceed .300 in 1968.

The baseball owners voted to lower the height of pitching mound from 15 to 10 inches above the level of home plate and to narrow the strike zone. In 1969, batting averages rose 7 points in the National League and 16 points in the American League.

There have been other large changes in batting average from one year to the next as well. Table 3.4 shows the years in which the greatest changes in batting average occurred, with possible explanations for the changes. Note that 7 of the 13 years were in the nineteenth century. Also note that, although lowering of the mound height in 1969 led to a significant increase in batting average, it is not even one of the largest.

Relative Batting Average

John Thorn and Pete Palmer, in *The Hidden Game of Baseball* (chap. 6), define the *Relative Batting Average* (RBA) as the batting average of

Table 3.4 Largest Single-Season League Batting Average Changes

Year	League	Change	Possible Explanation
1893	NL	+35	Pitching mound moved back 10 feet
1888	AA	−35	Three strikes = strikeout
1894	NL	+30	Sacrifices are not charged as at bats
1887	AA	+30	Five balls = walk
1888	NL	−30	Three strikes = strikeout
1911	AL	+30	Cork-centered balls allowed
1931	NL	−27	Baseball deliberately "deadened"
1889	AA	+24	Four balls = walk
1898	NL	−21	
1903	AL	−20	Strikes given for foul bunt attempts
1973	AL	+20	Designated hitters hit for pitchers
1904	NL	−20	Strikes given for foul bunt attempts
1921	NL	+20	"Lively ball" era, spitball outlawed, frequent replacement of baseballs

Note: Change = difference in batting points from the previous year.

the player divided by the batting average for the league for that year times 100. They credit the RBA to David Shoebotham ("Relative Batting Averages," *Baseball Research Journal*, 1976) and Merritt Clifton ("Relative Baseball," Samisdat, 1979). Bill Terry's RBA for 1930 is

$$.401/.303 \times 100 = 132.3,$$

while George Brett's RBA for 1980 is

$$.390/.269 \times 100 = 145.0.$$

An RBA of 100 represents a batting average that equals the league average. Using the RBA, we can say that Terry's year was 32.3% better than average (100 + 32.3%). Meanwhile, Brett's year was 45% better than average. Extending this formula year by year we can obtain a career relative batting average, which Thorn and Palmer present in *The Hidden Game of Baseball* and their subsequent encyclopedia, *Total Baseball*.

Baseball fans seem to understand batting averages much more easily than some new statistic, such as RBA. The RBA can be multiplied by some "standard" league batting average to get a "standardized" batting average. From 1969–92, the National League batting average hov-

THE METHOD

ered around .255 (it is .264 now), so .255 will be used as the standard. Recent American League averages have been about 8 points higher since 1973 when "designated hitters" began to hit for the weak-hitting pitchers (a further adjustment for the effect of the designated hitter on batting averages is discussed next). Thus, rather than obtaining a "relative" batting average, we obtain a *Mean-Adjusted Batting Average* (MABA) by dividing the player's batting average by the league average and multiplying by .255. Thus, we get MABAs of

$$(.401 \div .303) \times .255 = .337$$

for Terry and

$$(.390 \div .269) \times .255 = .370$$

for Brett. Using these adjusted averages, we rate Brett's performance 33 batting points better than Terry's. (In the next section, we will make an additional adjustment and rate Brett's performance as even better.)

The choice of the "standard" batting average is not critical. Had we used .303 as the standard, Terry's average would remain .401 but Brett's would be .439. The "standard" batting average "lowers" the batting averages of most years since the league batting average usually exceeded .255.

The relative batting average represented an attempt to *level the playing field*. As important a concept as relative batting average is, if it were completely satisfactory I wouldn't have written this book. We will see now that RBA undervalues the performance of AL players who played after 1972. In the next two chapters we will see further limitations of the RBA and refine it even further. Only then will we have a fully developed system for comparing performances across baseball history.

The Effect of the DH on Batting

When the American League introduced the designated hitter (DH) in 1973, the promise that the relative batting average could be a fair way of adjusting batting average to a common standard average across time ended. Why? Its principal weakness lies behind its primary assumption—that the "average hitter" is an equally good hitter throughout baseball history. The batting average of this "average hitter" would be the league batting average. But where does this average come from?

The league batting average is composed of the combined batting experience of individual players, who have different hitting abilities. It includes starters and benchwarmers, outfielders and infielders (remember the poor hitting shortstops and catchers?), Hall of Famers and average players. Most important, it includes pitchers as well as non-pitchers.

As any seasoned or current National League fan knows, pitchers generally hit much worse than non-pitchers. Yes, Babe Ruth began his career as a pitcher and he was quite a good one. Given his Ruthian hitting abilities, however, he was moved from the mound to the outfield. Indeed, a basic rationale for the designated hitter was to increase offensive production by replacing poor-hitting pitchers with good-hitting hitters!

How much did the DH rule change the batting average in the American League? In 1973, batting went up 20 points in the AL (from .239 to .259), but it also went up 6 points in the NL, where no rule change occurred. As we have already seen, changes in the league batting average are constantly occurring and many changes lack obvious explanations. Hence, it is problematic to assume that the 20-point change was solely due to the designated hitter rule. A more direct measure is to look at the effect that pitchers had on batting average just prior to 1973.

From 1969–72, pitchers averaged .145, while non-pitchers averaged .253. Pitchers had 1 of every 13.5 at bats. If pitchers are left out of the batting averages, the averages would be 7.4–8.3 points higher (average change = 8.0 points), as Table 3.5 shows. So this is the effect of the rule change, right? Not quite.

The rule change substituted designated hitters for pitchers in the batter's box. These DHs were generally older players who were outstanding batters for average and/or power when they were in their prime, but were less able fielders than other players at their positions due to age or chronic injury. In 1973 the average non-pitcher was 28 years old, while the average DH was 31. Designated hitters often played at some position, while many position players also played as DH.

All at bats of every player who was the principal DH for his team or who played more as DH than at any other position were used for Table 3.5. The designated hitters hit a little better than the other hitters, raising the league average slightly by 0.5 points. Thus, the overall

Table 3.5   Changes in the AL Batting Average
            Due to the Designated Hitter

Year	BA	BA w/o Pitchers	Diff
1969	.2460	.2542	.0082
1970	.2498	.2581	.0083
1971	.2469	.2550	.0081
1972	.2390	.2464	.0074
Average	.2454	.2534	.0080

Year	BA	BA w/o DH	Diff
1973	.2594	.2585	−.0009
1974	.2583	.2576	−.0007
1975	.2553	.2556	.0003
1976	.2560	.2552	−.0008
Average	.2572	.2567	−.0005

effect of the designated hitter rule is to boost the league average by 8.5 points (8.0 for dropping the pitchers and 0.5 for adding the designated hitters).

The DH was also estimated in a second way—by comparing the NL to AL batting averages. From 1969–72, the NL batting average was 6.7 points higher, but was 2.4 points lower from 1973–76—a 9.1-point shift.

The two estimates agree fairly well. Since the first is more direct, the "standard" batting average for the American League after 1972 will be .255 + .0085 = .2635. George Brett played for Kansas City in the American League in 1980. Thus Brett's 1980 average should be

$$(.390 \div .269) \times .2635 = .382.$$

His performance is now rated 45 points better than Bill Terry's 1930 year. Two more adjustments, the subjects of the next two chapters, are needed to compare fully Brett's and Terry's stellar years.

Applying the Mean-Adjustment

1. Get the hits and at bats for a player in the year of interest from a baseball encyclopedia or other source. As an example, we'll use Ty Cobb's 1910 season. Cobb had 194 hits in 506 at bats, for an unadjusted .383 average.

2. Compute the number of *adjusted hits* using the appropriate formula below:

Adjusted hits = hits × .255/league batting average
for years without DH (all years except for AL 1973–present)

Adjusted hits = hits × .2635/league batting average,
for years with the DH (AL 1973–present).

The league batting average is found in Appendix III. For Cobb's 1910 season, we get 194 × .255/.2431 = 203.5 adjusted hits. It may seem strange to have a fractional number of "hits." However, this avoids biases due to rounding adjusted hits to the nearest whole number.

3. Divide adjusted hits by at bats to get the MABA. For Cobb's 1910 season MABA = 203.5/506 = .4022, which can be rounded to .402.

The procedure is summarized in the technical note below.

TECHNICAL NOTE

Mean-Adjusted Batting Average

The mean-adujsted batting average is:

MABA = hits/at bats × .255/ league batting average
(for years without a DH)

and

MABA = hits/at bats × .2635/league batting average
(for years with DH),

where .255 is the standardized batting average for years without a DH (all years except 1973–present in the AL, for which .2635 is the standardized BA).

To obtain the career MABA, the yearly MABA values are multiplied by the at bats for the years to get adjusted hits. The adjusted hits are then totalled and divided by total at bats. The longevity adjustment is also applied to obtain the career MABA.

The league batting averages are given in Appendix III.

Why should we multiply for feast and famine periods rather than add or subtract? When the batting average jumps 10 points, do pitchers and poor hitters improve their hitting to the same degree as the great hitters? Think about this — if all the stadium fences were moved in 10 feet, would all the hitters get, say, 4 more home runs? No, the sluggers would have a field day and the weak hitters would still have trouble reaching the fences. It is more likely that the *percentage* change would remain constant. This is the rationale behind using a multiplicative factor.

Calculating a mean-adjusted batting average for a player's entire career takes a little care since players have different numbers of at bats in different years. Career batting averages are **not** obtained by averaging batting averages from individual years. Instead, career totals of hits and at bats are obtained and calculated directly. The same thing needs to be done to mean-adjusted batting averages. Perhaps the simplest way to do this is to add a player's adjusted hits for his career and divide by the total number of at bats.

The building blocks for determining the career MABA are given in Table 3.6 for Ty Cobb. Since we are applying the adjustments sequentially as we go, the MABA for a player's career will be longevity-adjusted as well. (Note: The term "MABA" also applies to single season averages, for which no longevity-adjustment is needed). To get Cobb's career MABA, then, one applies the longevity adjustment described in chapter 2, but using mean-adjusted hits instead of hits. Cobb's 8000th at bat was his 271st at bat in 1921. To get his total adjusted hits in his first 8000 at bats, simply add the adjusted hits for years 1905–20 (2872.3) to 91.8 (= 171.8 × 271 / 507) from 1921 to get 2964.1 adjusted hits, giving him a career MABA of 2964.1/8000 = .371.

Confusion over Mean-Adjustment

There are a number of different mean-adjustment procedures in use. Most are relegated to appendices and are not completely described. Thus, it is not surprising that confusion remains.

The original formula for computing the "relative batting average" was given by Bill Shoebotham in a 1976 *Baseball Research Journal*

Table 3.6 Calculation of the Mean-Adjusted Batting Average
(MABA) for Ty Cobb

Year	AB	Hits	Raw BA	AL Avg	Adj Hits	MABA
1905	150	36	.240	.2408	38.1	.2540
1906	358	113	.316	.2487	115.9	.3237
1907	605	212	.350	.2474	218.3	.3608
1908	581	188	.324	.2390	200.6	.3453
1909	573	216	.377	.2438	225.9	.3942
1910	506	194	.383	.2431	203.5	.4022
1911	591	248	.420	.2731	231.6	.3919
1912	553	226	.409	.2648	217.6	.3935
1913	428	167	.390	.2558	166.5	.3890
1914	345	127	.368	.2475	130.8	.3791
1915	563	208	.369	.2482	213.7	.3796
1916	542	201	.371	.2485	206.3	.3806
1917	588	225	.383	.2477	231.6	.3939
1918	421	161	.382	.2535	162.0	.3848
1919	497	191	.384	.2680	181.7	.3656
1920	428	143	.334	.2835	128.6	.3005
1921	507	197	.389	.2924	171.8	.3389
1922	526	211	.401	.2848	188.9	.3591
1923	556	189	.340	.2823	170.7	.3070
1924	625	211	.338	.2898	185.7	.2971
1925	415	157	.378	.2915	137.3	.3308
1926	233	79	.339	.2814	71.6	.3073
1927	490	175	.357	.2855	156.3	.3190
1928	353	114	.323	.2809	103.5	.2932
Total	11434	4189	.366			

article. In his definition, the player's hits and at bats are subtracted
from the league totals. Although this definition requires more computing, it seems, at first glance, to be a more accurate version of RBA.
After all, why should a player's own numbers be used in the league
totals to adjust his relative average? However, the RBA definition given
in this chapter is simpler and is better for three reasons. First, it is
preferable to view each player as part of a population of hitters, not as
apart from it. Second, using Shoebotham's RBA definition, the ranking
of hitter can change. For example, Chick Hafey narrowly edged out

Bill Terry for the 1931 batting title. Using Shoebotham's formula, however, Terry had the higher relative batting average because he had 611 at bats compared to Hafey's 450, and lowered the "rest-of-the-league" average enough to slip past Hafey. Finally, today there are almost twice as many teams as there were from 1901–60, so we can reasonably expect there to be twice as many outstanding players. Thus, to avoid disadvantaging modern players when using Shoebotham's formula, we should also subtract out one equally good peer with an equivalent number of at bats.

In a July 28, 1997 cover story, while Tony Gwynn was pursuing the elusive .400 batting average, *Sports Illustrated* called Gwynn "The Best Hitter Since Ted Williams" and ranked him sixth in major league history. Their method differs from the one presented here in four ways. First, they did not make any adjustment for the introduction of the designated hitter. Second, they used a single "era" average for the American and National Leagues combined. These two differences had the effect of hurting all players after 1972 by about 4 points each (half of the 8.5 point shift identified earlier). Third, they apparently did not weight the single-season averages by at bats, since they dropped out years in which the player had less than 100 at bats. Finally, they subtracted the league average, rather than dividing by it. If *SI* recalculated the averages using the mean-adjusted batting average formula given here, Gwynn would rank second to Ty Cobb, slightly ahead of Williams.

Changes in the Top 100 after Mean-Adjustment

Applying the MABA adjustment really shakes up the top 100 list! Forty players are replaced and major ranking changes occur among those who remain. Let's look at these changes.

Earle Combs, the 30th ranked player for longevity-adjusted batting average, drops completely off the list. Meanwhile, Tony Oliva, who played during the great AL famine of the late 1960s and early 1970s, and who was unranked on the longevity-adjusted list, ranks 23d on the MABA list. Other top batters dropping off the list are Babe Herman, Kiki Cuyler, Chuck Klein, and Frankie Frisch while Matty Alou (33d), Al Kaline (40th), Ralph Garr (44th), Frank Robinson (46th), Paul

Molitor (49th), and Al Oliver (50th) jump onto the top half of the MABA list.

Overall, the forty players who dropped off the longevity-adjusted top 100 list played in two distinct time periods. Thirty-three of them were in mid-career from 1918–40, while the other seven had mid-careers ranging from 1893–99. The players who joined the list are from four time periods: 1884–88 (5 players); 1905 (2 players); 1946–50 (3 players); and 1956–91 (30 players).

The MABA hitter list is a considerable improvement over the longevity-adjusted list. Only four of the players dropped from the list won batting championships. By contrast, 19 of the newcomers won batting titles, including three each by Bill Madlock, Tony Oliva, and Carl Yastrzemski, and two each by Tommy Davis and Paul Hines. Additionally, only 7 of the dropped players had 3 or more top 5 finishes compared to 25 of the added players.

Ty Cobb remained on top, but most other top 10 batters changed positions, as Table 3.7 shows. Cobb's closest competition is coming from his contemporaries—Joe Jackson, Nap Lajoie, and, a couple of spots further back, Tris Speaker. Five new players join the top 10 list—Pete Browning (from 16th to 4th); Rod Carew (25th to 6th); Tony Gwynn (22d to 7th); Honus Wagner (14th to 8th); and Dan Brouthers (13th to 10th). Meanwhile, Rogers Hornsby, Willie Keeler, Ed De-

Table 3.7 Top 10 Hitters before and after Mean-Adjustment

	Player	Long.	Player	MABA
1	Ty Cobb	.370	Ty Cobb	.370
2	Roger Hornsby	.360	Joe Jackson	.349
3	Joe Jackson	.356	Nap Lajoie	.344
4	Nap Lajoie	.351	Pete Browning	.343
5	Tris Speaker	.348	Tris Speaker	.340
6	Willie Keeler	.347	Rod Carew	.339
7	Ed Delahanty	.346	Tony Gwynn	.338
8	Babe Ruth	.346	Honus Wagner	.336
9	Ted Williams	.344	Ted Williams	.336
10	Billy Hamilton	.344	Dan Brouthers	.335

Notes:

Long. = longevity-adjusted batting average.

MABA = career mean-adjusted batting average.

THE METHOD

lahanty, Babe Ruth, and Billy Hamilton drop out. Even with the loss of Hornsby's 7 batting titles, the MABA top 10 had 18 more batting titles than the longevity-adjusted top 10!

If *Sports Illustrated* had obtained their top hitter list using MABA, Tony Gwynn would have placed second. So why does he rank 7th here? First, *SI* also required that the hitter have at least 2500 hits, which eliminates Joe Jackson and Pete Browning from consideration. Second, the ranking presented here in Table 3.7 adjusts for *both* the league batting average and longevity. The remaining players ahead of Gwynn, other than Cobb, fall short if the longevity adjustment is not applied as well.

We now have a much more balanced profile of top batters by decade, as Figure 3.4 shows. The huge concentration of top 100 hitters in the 1920s and 1930s is gone after applying the mean-adjusted batting average adjustment. The percentage of top 100 MABA players is now about 12% for each decade except for the first decade, 1880–89, where nearly a quarter of the qualifying players make the top 100 and the last decade, 1980–89, where only 7% of the players make it. The chi-square test *p*-value = .55, indicating that these imbalances could be due to chance. However, the decade percentages will become even closer after the next adjustment, based on hitting talent.

Figure 3.4 Percent of Players from Decade in the Top 100 —
Traditional List vs. MABA List

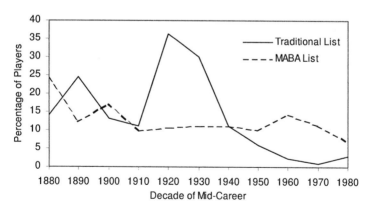

Joe Jackson

Third Base —— Adjusting for League Batting Talent

4

It is fun to look at the performance of batting champions. After all, they are the premier hitters of their championship years. When we look at them over time, we see something surprising—the best years ever achieved occurred early in baseball history. Remember caveman Rocky?

Were Early Batting Champions Better?

Ross Barnes, a second baseman, played in the National Association in 1871–75, batting a mean-adjusted .361 with 1425 at bats during those years. Not bad! However, the baseball powers decided that the averages from 1871–75 don't count. Too bad, Ross. But there's good news too. Batting averages *do* count, starting in 1876. In 1876, the owner-run National League replaced the player-run National Association. Barnes's mean-adjusted batting average in 1876 was .412, the second best single season average of all-time! Let's hear it for underhanded pitching thrown where the batter wants it! Barnes played in only three seasons after 1876, batting a mean-adjusted .264 with a total of 710 at bats. (For the remainder of this chapter, all batting averages will be mean-adjusted unless otherwise specified.)

If Ross Barnes posted the second best season, who was best? Ty Cobb? Rogers Hornsby? Wee Willie Keeler? Nap Lajoie? Ted Williams? Tony Gwynn?

No. How about Fred Dunlap?

Fred Dunlap, second baseman for the St. Louis Maroons, hit .429 in the only year of the Union Association. Fred Dunlap totaled at least 300 at bats in the National League in each of 4 seasons before and 4 seasons after 1884. He finished third in batting in 1881 (.318) and sixth in 1883 (.317). In the other years he averaged .268 over 2778 at bats. In 1881, there was a single league with only 8 teams playing at least 80 games. By 1884, there were three leagues and 26 such teams. Baseball playing talent was spread quite thin. The top 5 batters in each of the three leagues in 1884 are shown in table 4.1. The least established league, the Union Association, had the highest averages while the most established league, the National League, had the lowest.

How did the top 5 hitters of the Union Association do in 1885? Dunlap and Orator Shaffer both moved to the NL and batted .285 and .206, respectively. Jack Gleason only had 7 at bats in 1885 and batted .196 over 299 at bats in the AA in 1886 before retiring. Buster Hoover

Table 4.1 Top Batters in 1884 by League

National League		American Association		Union Association	
Player	MABA	Player	MABA	Player	MABA
King Kelly	.366	Dave Orr	.377	Fred Dunlap	.429
Jim O'Rourke	.358	John Reilly	.361	Buster Hoover	.379
Ezra Sutton	.357	Pete Browning	.358	Orator Shaffer	.375
Cap Anson	.346	Harry Stovey	.347	Harry Moore	.350
Dan Brouthers	.338	Fred Lewis	.344	Jack Gleason	.337

Note: MABA = mean-adjusted batting average.

did not play in 1885 and batted .217 in 208 at bats over the rest of his career. Harry Moore's only big league year was 1884.

None of the top 5 hitters for the Union Association ever batted .300 again. None of them ever attained 4000 career at bats.

Meanwhile, the top 5 hitters in 1884 in the National League all had at least 4000 at bats. More significantly, all but Ezra Sutton are in the Hall of Fame! Three of the American Association's top hitters reached 4000 at bats, although none made it into the Hall. Even so, Dave Orr and Pete Browning are recognized by baseball buffs as being outstanding hitters of their day.

From the data in Table 4.1 and discussion above, it should be clear that the Union Association was not as good a league as either the National League or the American Association. Consequently, Dunlap's mean-adjusted batting average is overrated. That means that mean-adjustment by itself is not enough to "level the playing field." Later in this chapter, we will develop a measure for league talent, and show that the 1884 Union Association had the weakest players in the history of major league baseball!

What about other top single-season, mean-adjusted batting averages? Table 4.2 gives all mean-adjusted averages of at least .380. Five players topped .400, with Tip O'Neill, Nap Lajoie, and Ty Cobb joining Barnes and Dunlap. Both Lajoie and Cobb had their .400 mean-adjusted seasons in 1910, when they were in a tight batting race. A rich businessman provided an added incentive by promising a car to the winner. The championship came down to the final day. Cobb officially won the race, although the winner wasn't declared for weeks, due to a controversy. Lajoie's average is higher in Table 4.2, following a scoring error correction. The controversy regarding who really won the batting

Table 4.2   Single-Season Mean-Adjusted Batting Averages
of .380 and Above

Rank	Player	Team	League	Year	MABA
1	Fred Dunlap	StL	UN	1884	.429
2	Ross Barnes	Chi	NL	1876	.412
3	Tip O'Neill	StL	AA	1887	.407
4	Nap Lajoie	Cle	AL	1910	.402
5	Ty Cobb	Det	AL	1910	.402
6	Tris Speaker	Cle	AL	1916	.397
7	Pete Browning	Lou	AA	1882	.396
8	King Kelly	Chi	NL	1886	.395
9	Ty Cobb	Det	AL	1909	.394
10	Ty Cobb	Det	AL	1917	.394
11	Ty Cobb	Det	AL	1912	.394
12	Nap Lajoie	Phi	AL	1901	.393
13	Nap Lajoie	Cle	AL	1904	.392
14	Roger Connor	NY	NL	1885	.392
15	Ty Cobb	Det	AL	1911	.392
16	Cap Anson	Chi	NL	1881	.392
17	Ty Cobb	Det	AL	1913	.389
18	Ted Williams	Bos	AL	1941	.388
19	Ted Williams	Bos	AL	1957	.388
20	Ty Cobb	Det	AL	1918	.385
21	Rod Carew	Min	AL	1977	.384
22	Rogers Hornsby	StL	NL	1924	.382
23	George Brett	KC	AL	1980	.382
24	Joe Jackson	Cle	AL	1911	.381
25	Ty Cobb	Det	AL	1916	.381
26	Joe Jackson	Cle	AL	1912	.380

title is discussed further in chapter 6. Fortunately, the businessman was
not part of the controversy, since he gave cars to both players.

The lofty batting averages in Table 4.2 are heavily weighted toward the early years of baseball. Seven of the averages were attained in
the nineteenth century: 4 in the first 11 years of the National League, 2
in the first 6 years of the American Association, and one in the only
year of the Union Association.

Fourteen top batting averages occurred during the first 18 years of the American League, with Cobb garnering 8 of the top averages, La-joie — 3, Jackson — 2, and Speaker — 1. Interestingly, Joe Jackson's two great years (1911 and 1912) were both overshadowed by better years of Ty Cobb. In 1916, Tris Speaker hit .396, becoming the only man to officially beat Ty Cobb for a batting championship between 1907 and 1919 — in spite of the fact that Cobb had a .381 average in 1916, the 25th best mean-adjusted batting average of all time.

Only 5 of the top mean-adjusted batting averages given in Table 4.2 occurred after the first 18 years of the given league's existence. These were led by Ted Williams's fine 1941 and 1957 seasons. The other occasions were: Rogers Hornsby in 1924, Rod Carew in 1977, and George Brett in 1980.

This heavy concentration of top hitters in the early years of base-ball indicates to me that MABA alone is not enough. However, I've heard a contrary argument by some baseball fans. The argument ba-sically goes like this: Not many home runs were hit early in the game's history. The primary focus of the hitter, then, was to hit for a high average. Now, many players sacrifice batting points for home runs. Thus, it would not be surprising that the best hitters played early in the game's history. An adjustment for rule changes that raise and lower batting averages is OK, but that's all that is needed.

I first began to adjust players' batting averages while in high school in order to play the ultimate baseball fantasy game with my brothers — managing teams of the all-time best players. We adjusted for home runs, doubles, ERA, and many other batting and pitching statis-tics. A similar pattern emerged — the early players were better than modern players for most of the statistics, including home runs — but that's where the modern players are supposed to excel!

Two areas where modern players *do* dominate the adjusted lists are stolen bases and triples, which were much more common *early* in baseball history. Thus, a strange twist of fate has occurred. For many baseball events, the game's best players are those playing when the event is rare! Let's see a little of that evidence.

Mean-Adjusted Home Runs — A Flawed Method

From 1993 to 1997, the National League home run average was a constant .028; that is, an average player hit 14 homers per 500 AB. The

NL home run champions from 1993–97 had between 40 and 48 home runs. We'll use .028 as our standardized home run average.

The AL home run average in 1961 was also .028, so Roger Maris had 61 *mean-adjusted* home runs the year he broke Babe Ruth's home run record. However, Babe Ruth had 54 home runs in 1920 when the home run average was only .0088, resulting in 172 *mean-adjusted* home runs! The curious thing is that Ruth only had 155 *mean-adjusted* hits in 1920. Altogether, on 15 occasions ballplayers hit at least 100 *mean-adjusted* home runs by current standards — with Ruth accounting for 9 of them.

Besides Ruth, the other top seasons were: Lou Gehrig — 127 in 1927; Gavvy Cravath — 122 in 1915; Tilly Walker — 106 in 1918; Tim Jordan — 105 in 1906; Harry Davis — 102 in 1906; and Jimmy Foxx — 100 in 1932. It's true that many of the mean-adjusted totals are heavily inflated. For example, Tilly Walker only hit 11 homers in 1918, but homers were so rare then that each one counts as 9.7 homers by to-day's standards. That year Ruth tied Tilly for the home run title, in spite of having only 317 at bats as a pitcher and part-time outfielder. Imagine what Ruth would have done if he had played every day!

The AL home run champ had more than 61 mean-adjusted home runs in 42 seasons, all of which were *before* 1950, including years by Cobb and Lajoie. There were 39 such years in the NL and all but 5 were before 1950. Such players as Hank Aaron, Willie Mays, Mickey Mantle, Ken Griffey Jr., or Mark McGwire attained none of these top years. It should be clear by now that the concept of *mean-adjusted home runs* **doesn't** work.

To a lesser, but still significant extent, mean-adjusted doubles favors the early years — the 6 largest AL totals all occurred by 1914 and 5 of the 10 best NL totals occurred between 1901 and 1910.

Since mean-adjusted performance doesn't work for either doubles or home runs, its use for comparing batting averages should also be questioned. Merritt Clifton noted the problem and decided to make comparisons across eras based on the batting champions, not the average player. His approach is described briefly in *The Hidden Game of Baseball* (p. 108).

Mean-adjustment shows *relative* performance. The fundamental problem of *relative* methods is that they are . . . well, *relative*. One of the best ways to look good on the golf course is to play with three lousy partners. This is especially true if your golf ranking at the club is only based on how many strokes better than (the foursome) average you shot. This is basically what the RBA (or, equivalently, MABA) does. When comparing players from different years, a basic assumption is being made when using RBA: Average hitters from the two years are equally good. We will now investigate whether this assumption is likely to be true.

Do New Leagues or New Teams Dilute the Talent Pool?

There is a basic feeling among many baseball fans who pore over stat sheets that expanding the number of major league teams dilutes the talent pool. This results in better *relative* performances in the years directly following expansions. When a new league forms or is expanded, many roster spots are added. If the management for the teams existing the year before expansion did a good job in identifying talent, new rookies would not be as good as the established players. Thus, in expansion years it is logical that the average batting ability drops. With time, new talent is nurtured and average batting ability improves. How much is the talent pool weakened and how long does it take to recover (assuming it does)? To investigate this further, we'll need to take a brief tour of baseball history.

Nineteenth-Century Baseball

The first quarter century of baseball, 1876–1900, was not very stable. Leagues came and went. The number of teams in a league was frequently increased and decreased, often depending on its financial stability. Figure 4.1 profiles the number of major teams year by year (ignoring teams that folded in mid-season).

In 1882, a 6-team American Association formed to rival the 8-team National League. Expanding to 8 teams the next year, the American Association survived until 1891. This upstart league attracted some talented players, led by Pete Browning, Dave Orr, Tip O'Neill, Denny Lyons, Oyster Burns, and Chicken Wolf.

Two other expansion leagues lasted but single years — the Union Association in 1884 and the Player's League in 1890. When the Ameri-

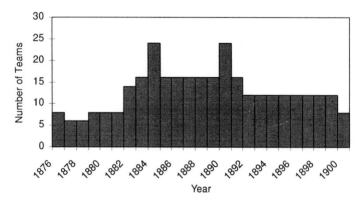

Figure 4.1   Number of Teams during the Nineteenth Century

can Association folded after the 1891 season, the National League was expanded from 8 to 12 teams in order to absorb the best players.

The Birth of the American League

In 1900, the National League trimmed down from 12 to 8 teams. This shakedown of talent was even sharper than had occurred in 1892, since there had been at least 12 major league teams since 1882. Ban Johnson formed the American League in 1900 — with team owners picking up many of these released players. Yes, that's right — 1900. You will not find this year in most standard baseball encyclopedias since the American League was not considered to be a "major" league until 1901 — who decides these things? Player listings and batting statistics from the eight teams — Chicago (managed by Charlie Comiskey), Milwaukee (managed by Connie Mack), Indianapolis, Detroit, Kansas City, Cleveland, Buffalo, and Minneapolis — are given in *Nineteenth Century Baseball* by Marshall Wright. In the book's introduction, Wright says:

> In my mind, the truest definition of a major league is a league that contains the highest level of baseball being played. Both the National Association, and the American League's first year fit the description. . . . Over half the players participating in the first year of the American League were former major league stars. This certainly measures up to the record of the "major" American Association in 1882, and the Union Association of 1884.

League Expansions

From 1901 to 1960, both the National League and the American League had 8 teams, in spite of the fact that the number of U.S. men of baseball age had tripled. Expansion finally came in 1961. The American League added two new teams, the Los Angeles (later California, now Anaheim) Angels and the Washington Senators, replacing the existing Senators team, which became the Minnesota Twins. The schedule was correspondingly enlarged from 154 to 162 games. The eight extra games led to an asterisk after Roger Maris's 61 homers in 1961, because he needed those last 8 games to break Babe Ruth's record. The NL added two teams in 1962, the Houston Colt 45's (now Astros) and New York Mets.

In 1969, both leagues went from 10 to 12 teams, splitting each league into two 6-team divisions. The Kansas City Royals and Seattle Pilots (now Milwaukee Brewers) joined the AL, while the Montreal Expos and San Diego Padres were NL expansion teams.

In 1977, the AL again beat the NL in the expansion business by adding the Seattle Mariners and Toronto Blue Jays. The NL waited 16 years before keeping pace by adding the Colorado Rockies and Florida Marlins in 1993.

Recent League Expansions Match the Population Growth

Let's see how the number of major league baseball teams compares to the U.S. population over the history of the game (Fig. 4.2).

Figure 4.2   Number of Teams Compared to the Population Size

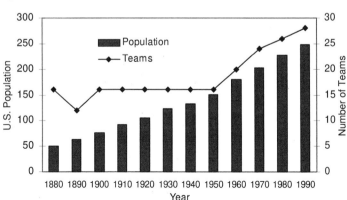

Several things stand out immediately from Figure 4.2. First, in the early years of baseball, there were many more teams per capita than there were in 1950. Second, from about 1950 on, the expansion of teams has kept pace with the population growth.

The Geography of Baseball

One shouldn't look at the population size alone to gauge the talent pool from which baseball players are drawn. It also matters how effectively talent is recruited from the population. Many interesting insights emerge from examining where ballplayers originate. It's difficult to gather information on where ballplayers were raised, but most baseball encyclopedias contain their birthplaces, which are often the same.

I have divided the geography of baseball players into 6 regions (using the official state two-letter code) as follows:

Mid-Atlantic	NJ, NY, PA
New England	CT, ME, MA, NH, RI, VT
Rim	DE, DC, IL, IN, IA, KY, MD, MI, MO, OH, WV, WI
South	AR, AL, FL, GA, MS, LA, NC, SC, TN, TX, VA
California	CA
Other	AK, AZ, CO, HI, ID, KS, MN, MT, NE, NV, NM, ND, OK, OR, SD, UT, WA, WY.

The "Rim" states border the Mid-Atlantic states and extend to the northern Midwest, and include half of the eight major league teams in 1876. The "Other" states include the western states except for California and the midwestern states not included in the "Rim" group.

A series of charts over baseball history will now be shown comparing the number of players from the different regions to the expected number, given the population sizes. The expected number of players is based on the U.S. census nearest to 28 years before the year being studied, because the average age of ballplayers is about 28 years old. For example, the expected number of players for 1876 is based on the 1850 census. Certain years were chosen because of interesting league happenings or particular player performances. These reasons will be given with each chart.

Let's think about the starting players, except for pitchers, for each team. Thus, there will be 8 players per team.

1876

In 1876, the first year of major league baseball, there were 8 teams, so we're talking about 8 × 8 = 64 players (Fig. 4.3). Forty-one of them came from either New York, Pennsylvania, or New Jersey. Seven others came from New England. On the other hand, only one came from the traditional south. Of the eight New York Mutuals starters, seven were born in New York and one in Ireland. Would you call this a "national" league?

The chart clearly shows the large excess of players from the Mid-Atlantic states compared to other regions of the country. Mid-Atlantic states were home to the New York and Philadelphia teams. Boston and Hartford were New England teams. The Rim states border the Mid-Atlantic states and extend west to the states that border Illinois. These states were home to the remaining 4 teams: Chicago, Cincinnati, Louisville, and St. Louis.

There was no major league baseball team in the South. Excluding the Negro Leagues, Houston and Atlanta became the first "Southern" cities to have major league baseball teams in the 1960s—about 90 years later! A scant 11 years after the Civil War ended in 1865, the National League was formed. Although baseball helped to heal the nation's wounds, it was too early yet.

There were no players and almost no people in California and the

Figure 4.3   Geographic Region of Players — 1876 NL

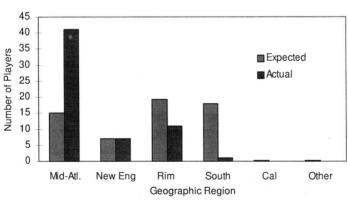

remaining western states (the "Other" category). These regions will show up in later graphs, though.

1900

The National League downsized from 12 to 8 teams. The 1900 American League was not yet a "major league." While picking up some released players, the AL did not yet lure NL players with big contracts like they did in 1901.

Twenty-four years later than in 1876, only 23 of the players came from the Mid-Atlantic states, although this was still 50% more than we would expect given their population size (Fig. 4.4). The New England and Rim states also provided more players than expected, while only one came from the South.

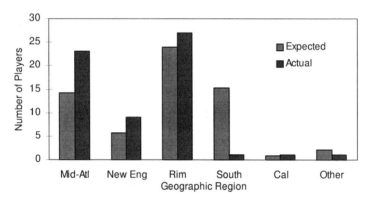

Figure 4.4   Geographic Region of Players — 1900 NL

1912

The five top hitters in the American League during its first two decades — Ty Cobb, Joe Jackson, Tris Speaker, Nap Lajoie, and Eddie Collins — were the 5 top hitters in 1912 (Fig. 4.5).

The regional balance improved in 1912, although the American and National Leagues still only had 7 and 5 players from the South, respectively. One would expect 16 players from the South in each league, based on population size. The players who did break in were standout players, especially in the American League. The seven players included Ty Cobb

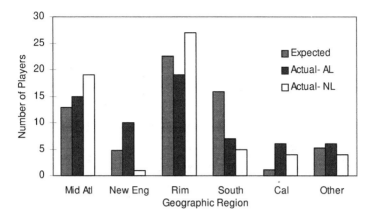

Figure 4.5   Geographic Region of Players — 1912

from Georgia, "Shoeless" Joe Jackson from South Carolina, and Tris Speaker from Texas, who finished 1-2-3 in the batting race, respectively. Clyde Milan from Tennessee and Del Pratt from South Carolina led their clubs in batting. Also noticeable is that California produced 10 major leaguers, compared to the 2 expected from their population size.

1941

In 1941 (Fig. 4.6), Ted Williams became the last player to hit .400, finishing with a .406 unadjusted average. Surprisingly, he failed to win

Figure 4.6   Geographic Region of Players — 1941

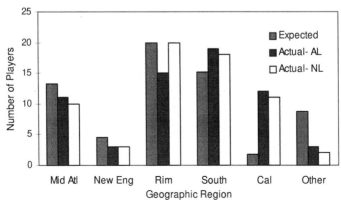

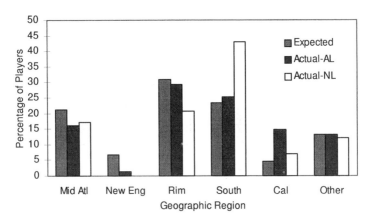

Figure 4.7   Geographic Region of Players — 1961

the most valuable player award. The MVP went to Joe DiMaggio, who had a 56-game hitting streak and .357 unadjusted average.

By 1941, the geographic distribution had changed again (Fig. 4.7). Now, the Mid-Atlantic states were producing less than their share of players, while the South was producing more, even though there were still no Southern major league teams. More dramatically, California was the birthplace to three times as many players as expected. Guess what — both Williams and DiMaggio were born in California!

1961

In 1961, the American League expanded to 10 teams and the New York Yankee M & M boys, Mickey Mantle and Roger Maris, assaulted Babe Ruth's single-season home run record. Ruth had hit 60 home runs in 1927. Maris did break the record, hitting 61 homers. With the first expansion in the American League since its inception in 1900, however, the number of games was increased from 154 to 162. Since Maris only had 59 homers after 154 games, his record season was placed alongside that of Ruth's with an asterisk, indicating that the expanded season had helped him. Mantle wound up with 54, giving them a combined 115 home runs, a teammate duo record which still stands.

Southerners took the National League by storm, accounting for 43% of the U.S.-born starting players. Over half of the Southerners came from Alabama (8 players) and Texas (6 players).

Table 4.3   All-Alabama National League "Team" of 1961

POS	Name	City	Team
1B	Willie McCovey	Mobile	SF
2B	Frank Bolling	Mobile	Mil
SS	Alex Grammas	Birmingham	StL
3B	Jim Davenport	Siluria	SF
OF	Hank Aaron	Mobile	Mil
	Willie Mays	Westfield	SF
	Billy Williams	Whistler	Chi
PH	Lee Maye	Tuscaloosa	Mil

Alabama could have supported an outstanding team by itself — except for a catcher (Table 4.3). Look at the power in the lineup with McCovey, Aaron, Mays and Billy Williams!

Texas also had an outstanding birth-state "team," after getting a little help from the American League (Table 4.4). They would need a catcher and another outfielder, but what a lineup!

With the talent from Alabama and Texas, is it any wonder that the National League began to dominate the All-Star games over the American League, winning 23 of 25 games from 1960–82?

1980

In 1980, George Brett won the AL batting title with a .390 unadjusted batting average. After all adjustments are made, it is the third best single-season average of all-time.

Table 4.4   All-Texas Major League "Team" of 1961

POS	Name	City	Team
1B	Norm Cash	Justiceburg	Det
2B	Pete Runnels	Lufkin	BosA
SS	Ernie Banks	Dallas	ChiN
3B	Eddie Matthews	Texarkana	Mil
OF	Curt Flood	Houston	StLN
	Frank Robinson	Beaumont	Cin
UT	Charlie Neal	Longview	LA

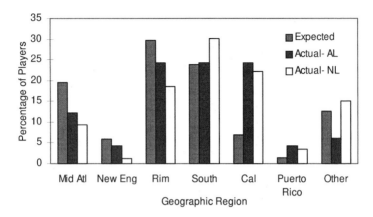

Figure 4.8   Geographic Region of Players — 1980

The Mid-Atlantic, New England, and Rim states produced fewer players than expected, while California continued to provide many more (Fig. 4.8). Puerto Rico, a U.S. commonwealth, is also shown in the graph. It had almost three times as many players as expected from its population, demonstrating some of the shift to the Caribbean as "home" to major leaguers.

1995

This year the baseball strike ended. It is halfway between the league expansions of 1993 and 1998 and brings us close to the present day. It

Figure 4.9   Geographic Region of Players — 1995

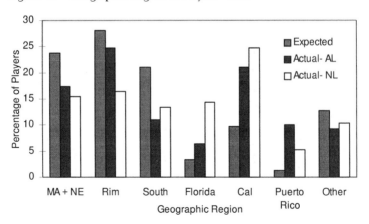

THE METHOD

also features the 18th best single-season average — by Tony Gwynn from San Diego.

The geographic pattern of major league player birthplaces shows a further shift to the south. California, Florida, and Puerto Rico produced more than their population's share of major leaguers (Fig. 4.9). Puerto Rico, expected to have 3 major leaguers, contributed 16. Meanwhile, after pulling Florida out, the rest of the South produced fewer players than expected. Most of the shortage was due to 2 states: Texas and Virginia. The northern states also produced fewer major leaguers than expected.

Geographical Summary

A basic geographic pattern has emerged over time from the charts. The game began as a northeastern game, particularly popular in the Mid-Atlantic states. There were very few southern players. Gradually, however, the game did move south and west to sunny California. Now it is even moving offshore to Puerto Rico in the Caribbean. Could it be that the earlier springs in the South, California, and the Caribbean allow young ballplayers more time to develop their skills?

Foreign-Born Players

Further evidence of the shift "south" can be seen in the percentage of foreign-born players (Fig. 4.10). In the early days of baseball, the foreign-born players were primarily from Ireland, Great Britain, or Canada. In 1941, only one foreigner, .325-hitting Canadian-born Jeff Heath, was able to secure a starting role in the majors.

By 1980, the Caribbean had become a hotbed of players. Besides Puerto Rico (a U.S. commonwealth mentioned above), several foreign countries contributed players: Dominican Republic (6 players), Cuba (1), and Virgin Islands (1). Other Central and South American countries, Mexico (4), Venezuela (3), Panama (3), and the Canal Zone (1), also contributed players.

By 1995, 13% of all major league starters were foreign-born. The principal countries represented were the Dominican Republic (16) and Venezuela (6).

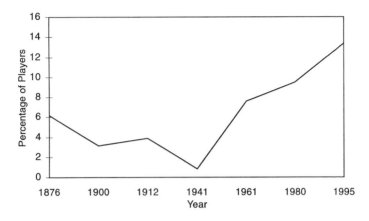

Figure 4.10   Foreign-Born Starters in Baseball

African-American Players

Jackie Robinson became the first twentieth-century African-American to play major league baseball when he joined the Brooklyn Dodgers in 1947. Integration was fairly slow in the early years. Many of the greatest early African-American stars were standout players on the 1961 Alabama- and Texas-born teams (Hank Aaron, Ernie Banks, Willie Mays, Willie McCovey, Frank Robinson, and Billy Williams). Since then, many other top black hitters have donned major league uniforms, including Rod Carew, Kirby Puckett, Tony Gwynn, and Junior Griffey. According to a *Sports Illustrated* Special Report, "Whatever Happened to the White Athlete?" (December 8, 1997) 17% of the major league baseball players in 1997 were black. This is slightly higher than the 13% of blacks in the population.

Why Mean-Adjusted Averages Don't Work

Let's review the observations presented in this chapter so far:

1. Using mean-adjusted averages, the top early hitters were better.
2. There was a smaller population per team in the early years than today.
3. Early players came primarily from the northeastern states, while

today's players are more likely to come from California, the South, or the Caribbean.

4. African-Americans were excluded from baseball until 1947.

Observations 2–4 suggest that the top hitters ought to be better today, contradicting observation 1. Why is that? Early in the game's history, baseball didn't draw from the entire population, especially from the South and from African-Americans. Moreover, the mean-adjustment yields some ridiculous findings when applied to home runs. My conclusion is that MABA does not adequately reflect who the top hitters truly are. Perhaps the flaw in MABA lies in choosing a single standard batting average across the whole of baseball history (except for our designated hitter adjustment, of course). Stating it more directly, maybe an *average* hitter today is better than an *average* hitter from the nineteenth or early twentieth century was.

If the average hitter is better now than early in the game's history, then many difficult questions need to be raised. What was the *true* batting ability of average players over the years? Did it drop when new leagues were introduced or expanded? Was there a rapid rise after leagues folded? I don't see an obvious way to answer these questions. I did develop an adjustment system in which the standard batting average was lower in the early years of baseball, but I wasn't very satisfied with it. As a graduate student in statistics, I came up with a more satisfying solution. However, we'll need to talk a little bit about statistics in order to get there.

The Science of Statistics

Statistics is the branch of science that tries to make sense of data that vary. If you measure your weight five times one day and get 130 pounds each time, you don't need statistics to help you. On the other hand, if you get 130, 121, 142, 132, and 153 — now that's interesting! Maybe the scale is broken, maybe you should stop jumping up and down on it, or maybe you should put a lock on the refrigerator.

Measurement of a process, like hitting, produces data that vary — batting averages — called a *variable*. Batting averages vary from year to year for the same player and between players in the same year. If they didn't, games wouldn't be so much fun to watch.

Statistically, we understand a variable when we know its *distribution*. A distribution is a pairing of the set of possible outcomes and the probability of their occurrence. In other words, we don't know what's going to happen every time, but we *do* know the *probability* that a given outcome will happen. When Mets catcher Mike Piazza comes up to the plate, we are excited by the probabilities. When Braves pitcher Greg Maddux bats, we moan if we're Braves fans. Maddux is a great pitcher, but he isn't much of a hitter (even though he hits well for a pitcher). We don't know what *will* happen, but we have some idea of the *probabilities* of what will happen. From a statistical point of view, the best we can do is to *know the probabilities* . . . unless the outcome is fixed of course.

What will the distribution of batting averages of players with, say, 500 or more at bats be next year? While all averages between .000 and 1.000 are possible, baseball fans know that averages around .250 are common, while averages around .350 are rare. Unfortunately, with real data we almost never completely know what distribution we have — but we *can* estimate it. A *histogram* is a good way of estimating and seeing a distribution of a variable.

Let's take another look at the distribution of batting averages of qualifying players — those with 4000 at bats (Fig. 4.11). In chapter 1, we saw that they ranged from .218 for George McBride to .366 for Ty Cobb, and averaged .279 overall. Averages between .260 and .279 are the most common. The distribution is basically bell-shaped, although high averages are more distant from the peak than low averages. It is important to understand the *spread* of batting averages, which is measured by the *standard deviation*.

Figure 4.11   Batting Average Profile of Qualifying Players

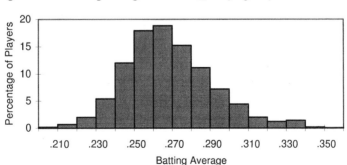

THE METHOD

A Moment to Learn

The information from a distribution can be summarized by a series of numbers called *moments*. There are an infinite number of moments, which have boring names and interesting names. The boring names are: first moment, second moment, third moment, etc. Their interesting aliases are: mean, variance, skewness, kurtosis, etc. The number of the moment is the power to which a certain mathematical expression is raised. If you haven't had or can't remember high school algebra, don't worry — I'm done talking about powers.

The standard deviation is a very important statistical concept. It is the square root of the variance. Statisticians usually have a better feeling for it than they do for the variance because it is in the same units as the mean. As a baseball fan, you probably know that it is 90 feet from home plate to first base. You probably haven't thought about the fact that the area between the base paths is 8100 ($= 90 \times 90$) *square* feet. Similarly, the variance is in *square* units. Thus, we will use the standard deviation *form* of the second moment.

The point of talking about moments is that, after adjusting batting averages for the mean, the next most logical statistical adjustment to make is the one for the standard deviation, because it is a form of the *second* moment. It is definitely a moment to learn! When teachers grade on "a curve," they are applying a mean- and standard deviation-adjustment to the test scores, where the "curve" is assumed to be the normal ("bell-shaped") distribution — at least that was the original use of the term.

Each moment is less important than the previous one in gaining an understanding of the distribution. The first four moments for the distribution of batting averages shown above are:

$$\text{mean} = .279$$

$$\text{standard deviation} = .023$$

$$\text{skewness} = .54$$

$$\text{kurtosis} = .56$$

These four numbers, when said to an experienced statistician, bring to mind a picture of the histogram. Find a statistician and try this out! This is not too different from the brief way a baseball situation is described: 3-0 count on the clean-up hitter, bases loaded, bottom of the ninth, one out. Do you have an image now? This time, find a person who knows nothing about baseball. Then ask them what image comes to mind.

So how do we interpret these four numbers?

The first one, .279, is simply the average batting average of players with 4000 or more at bats.

The standard deviation gives us good information about the spread of the averages. Take the mean and subtract 2 times the standard deviation to get .233 [= .279 − (2 × .023)]. Now take the mean and add 2 times the standard deviation to get .325. About 95% of the averages will be between these two numbers, as is the case for bell-shaped distributions.

The skewness basically tells us whether the distribution is symmetric around the middle. A symmetric distribution looks the same if you hold it in front of a mirror. A skewness value of zero suggests symmetry. A positive number tells us that the extreme averages are farther away from the peak for high averages than for low averages.

Our skewness value is positive and this is just what the histogram shows. It makes sense that batting averages should have positive skewness. If a player is hitting well, the manager plays him. If a player hits poorly, the manager benches him. It's hard to get 4000 at bats — the minimum number to qualify for the histogram — from the bench.

The kurtosis is used to compare the distribution to an ideal bell-shaped distribution, called the *normal distribution*. The normal distribution has a kurtosis value of zero. A positive kurtosis value indicates that there are more extreme scores than the *normal distribution* has, while a negative kurtosis indicates fewer extreme scores. For the distribution of batting averages, there are more extreme scores. Since the kurtosis is less than 1, the departure from a normal distribution is not very great.

Statisticians adjust for skewness and kurtosis as well, when they judge that to be necessary. I see no need to in our case, but perhaps someday someone will.

This side trip into statistics has given us a game plan. We will use histograms to visualize the distributions of batting average year by year and compute both the means and standard deviations to better compare players from different leagues or eras.

Creating a Histogram

We want to get a quick image of the player batting averages year by year. But whom should we include? In any given year the range in the number of at bats among players is huge, ranging from 1 to the 500s or 600s. We are not very interested in batting averages that are based on very few at bats. The choice of 200 at bats, which will be used here, restricts attention to roughly 10 players/team, while accounting for 78% of the at bats for the season (both numbers are slightly higher for the AL since 1973).

Figure 4.12 shows histograms of two years: the 1884 Union Association and 1910 American League. The height at each batting average shows the number of players with batting averages in the given interval (the batting average shown gives the lower bound of the interval). The box at .420 for the 1884 histogram represents Fred Dunlap's all-time best mean-adjusted batting average. The box at .400 for the 1910 histogram represents the mean-adjusted batting averages for Nap Lajoie and Ty Cobb.

The 1884 histogram is quite spread out compared to the 1910 histogram. The histogram, which peaks at .240 (representing batting averages from .240 to .249), does not have a nice bell shape. The 1910 histogram also peaks at .240 but has relatively high numbers of players at .220, .260, and .270 as well.

Both histograms present the mean-adjusted averages. Players with at least 200 at bats, however, typically bat better than the league average. The mean batting average is .275 for 1884 and .270 for 1910.

The standard deviation "captures" our sense of the greater spread in the 1884 histogram compared to 1910. The standard deviation (SD) for 1884 is .054, whereas the SD for 1910 is .043.

Next, we compare the 1910 AL and 1980 AL histograms. In 1980, George Brett had a mean-adjusted batting average of .382, one of best single-season averages ever.

The 1980 histogram, based on 167 hitters, is much more bell shaped than the 1910 histogram. The averages are also more concentrated between .220 and .300; that is, the spread is less. For 1980, SD = .031.

Histograms smooth out as the number of data points increases.

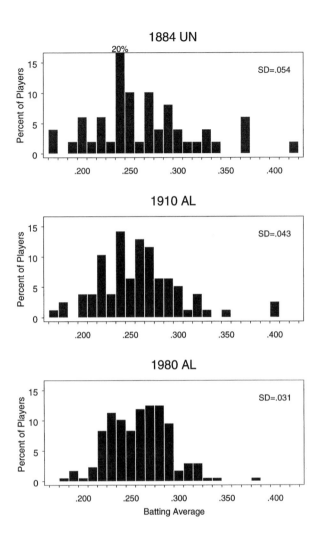

Figure 4.12   Histograms of Batting Averages

Histograms of mean-adjusted batting averages of players with at least 200 at bats are shown for the 1884 Union Association, 1910 American League, and 1980 American League. The standard deviations (SD) reflect the spread of the histograms.

Taking data from 5 consecutive years is one way to increase the data size. Table 4.5 summarizes results from four histograms: 1910–14 AL, 1980–84 AL, and the corresponding years from the National League.

There are three things to note from Table 4.5.

First, 4% of 1910–14 AL hitters batted at least .350, compared to

Table 4.5   Percentage of Hitters with Various Batting Averages

BA	1910–14 AL	1980–84 AL	1910–14 NL	1980–84 NL
.130–.219	12	6	6	6
.220–.349	84	94	94	94
.350+	4	0.2	0	0.5
SD	.043	.031	.030	.028

less than 1% for the other three periods. This means that, while still rare, hitters in the 1910–14 American League were 14 times more likely to hit .350 or more than were hitters from the other periods!

Second, 12% of the 1910–14 AL hitters batted less than .220, compared to 6% for the other three periods.

Third, since 1910–14 AL had more hitters with very high and very low averages, they had fewer in the center of the distribution.

The histograms and table have shown us what is going on and the standard deviation summarizes it with a single number. The standard deviation measures league talent, with a smaller number indicating more talent. Early in the game's history a number of weak hitters played major league baseball and made the good hitters look awesome.

Who were these weak hitters? In the AL from 1910–14, players hit below .220 with 400+ at bats seven times. One player appears on this list three times and hit .220 in a fourth year. Who was he? George McBride—the worst unadjusted hitter in baseball and "contrasting bookend" to Ty Cobb—the all-time best unadjusted hitter and best hitter of the period. McBride's poor hitting made Cobb's hitting look *relatively* better. The overevaluation of Cobb certainly did not depend *solely* on McBride. Many of Cobb's American League compatriots would likely have ridden the National League bench during the same era and would not make the major leagues today. It's interesting, though, that the two unadjusted batting averages that are the farthest apart are somehow linked together.

Calculating the Standard Deviation

The standard deviation, abbreviated SD, is a number measuring how much a variable varies. Since a variable's essence is to vary, it is a fundamental thing to measure. An SD of 0 means that all the values

Standard Deviation and Variance

Suppose that you have n data points labeled X_1, X_2, . . ., Xn, with mean equal to MN and weights w_1, w_2, . . ., w_n. (The definition below is for the *weighted* variance. The standard definition of variance sets all the weights equal to 1). Let $W = w_1 + w_2 + \ldots + w_n$. Then, the weighted variance is

$$VAR = [w_1(X_1 - MN)^2 + w_2(X_2 - MN)^2 + \ldots + w_n(X_n - MN)^2] / W.$$

The weighted standard deviation, SD, is the square root of the weighted variance, that is,

$$SD = \sqrt{VAR}.$$

are the same — that is, the variable *doesn't* vary. The larger the SD, the more the variable varies.

We want to calculate standard deviations for the histograms we have just seen. The histograms only include players with at least 200 at bats. It is not right, however, to count batting averages based on 200 AB as much as those based on 600 AB. Thus, we need to calculate a *weighted* standard deviation for the histograms, where the at bats are the weights.

The Standard Deviation over Time

The batting average standard deviation for the American League is shown year by year in Figure 4.13. The standard deviations range from a low of .0234 in 1935 to a high of .0427 in 1911. From the figure we can clearly see variation from year to year. An overall tendency can also be seen, however. The standard deviations rose from 1901 to 1911, declined gradually to about .029 (the dashed line) in 1933 and have been bobbing up and down around it ever since. The irregular solid line is a 5-year moving average, which is an average of nearby data and is described in more detail later in this section.

The pattern for the NL standard deviation is somewhat different,

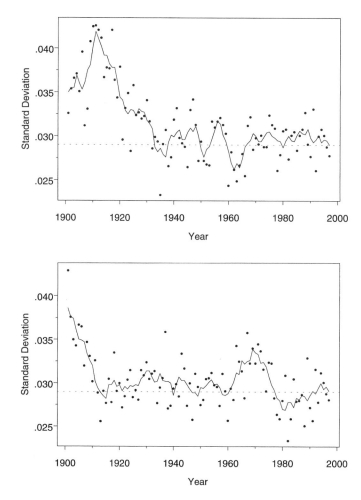

Figures 4.13, 4.14 Batting Average Standard Deviation — AL and NL
The standard deviation of the batting average of all AL (*top*) and NL (*bottom*)
players with at least 200 at bats (weighted by the number of at bats) are shown
for 1901–97. The irregular lines give the 5-year moving averages for the data.
The dashed lines are at .029, a value which reflects recent moving average
values.

as Figure 4.14 shows. The long-term trend, given by the 5-year moving
average (solid line) shows a decreasing trend from about .038 in 1901
to about .029 in 1913. Since 1913, the long-term pattern has been
reasonably constant except for an increase in the 1960s.

Why is the American League pattern different from that of the National League? Remember that the NL is 25 years older than the AL. Overall, the NL had better players in the early years of the AL. When outstanding hitters — Ty Cobb, Eddie Collins, Tris Speaker, and Joe Jackson — joined the American League between 1905–8, the variability increased because they outshone the rest of the league. Each year from 1910 to 1916, at least three of these four players were among the league's top 5 hitters. As the league became stronger, the SD dropped.

The batting average SD will be used as a measure of the hitting talent of the league for that year. The ups and downs of the yearly points would then indicate that the league got worse, got better, got worse, etc., in fairly dramatic ways over a few years' time. This seems quite unlikely to *really* be true. It is more likely that the standard deviation data are *noisy*, with some part of the ups and downs indicating real differences and the other part random fluctuations. To separate the *signal* from the *noise*, we have to do some averaging of data, often called *smoothing*. A very simple procedure called a *moving average* provides the smoothing.

Let's calculate a 5-year moving average of the American League SD for 1910. We first obtain SDs for 1910, the two years before and the two years after — a total of 5 years of SD data, with 1910 in the middle. We then average the 5 numbers together. For 1910, the 5-year average SD is

$$(.0332 + .0409 + .0426 + .0427 + .0422) / 5 = .0403.$$

What makes it a *moving* average? It is that when calculating the 5-year average SD for 1911, the 1908 SD is dropped out and the 1913 SD is added to the remaining four SDs above.

Why average 5 years? Well, an odd number of years provides an equal number of years on each side of the year being smoothed. Adding more years into the average reduces the noise, but may not reflect the right average if true standard deviation is really changing over the size of the period chosen. Thus, a tradeoff results. A 5-year moving average balances the two needs.

Why the Standard Deviation Declines over Time

In his book *Full House*, Stephen Jay Gould, an evolutionary biologist, presents a very similar figure to Figures 4.13 and 4.14. For his purposes, he combined the American and National League data and doesn't provide the detailed observations that the use of moving averages allows. Still, his basic point is fairly similar to mine. Gould imagines that there is a "wall" of human ability. The best players at the turn of the century may have been close to the "wall," but many of their peers were not. Over time, progressively better hitters replace the weakest hitters. As a result, the best current hitters do not stand out as much from their peers.

Gould and I believe that the reduction in standard deviation demonstrates that there has been an improvement in the overall quality of major league baseball today compared to nineteenth-century and early twentieth-century play. This fits well with the geographic and ethnic expansion of players, the stability and desirability of a career in baseball, and the relative scarcity of positions per capita. This phenomenon is not unique to baseball, but is quite common in evolving systems. The standard deviation allows us to quantitate these changes.

Applying the Standard Deviation Adjustment

In this section we will work through the calculation of the standard deviation–adjusted batting average (SDABA). For those interested, the following two technical notes indicate the basic ideas.

Use of the standard deviation in adjusting batting averages has been proposed before. In *The Hidden Game of Baseball* (p. 108), Thorn and Palmer state that "a more sophisticated approach to Relative Batting Average was proposed in 1982 by Ward Larkin in *The Baseball Analyst*. This method employs the standard deviation of batting average from the norm rather than a simple ratio of individual to league norm or to league leader."

Calculating the standard deviation–adjusted batting average (SDABA) begins with the mean-adjusted batting average developed in chapter 3. Table 4.6 provides the calculation for Ty Cobb, using the formula in the previous technical note. To get a better feel for it, let's calculate it for 1910.

1. Start with Cobb's MABA of .4022 from Table 3.6.
2. Subtract from it the 5-year moving average of the mean batting average of the players with 200 or more at bats, .2693, given in

Standardization

Standardization of a variable, which consists of subtracting the mean from the variable and dividing it by its SD, is used quite often in statistics. In our case, we define

$$Z = (MABA - MN)/SD,$$

where MABA is a player's mean-adjusted batting average and MN and SD are the mean and standard deviation of the MABA values, respectively, for all players with at least 200 at bats for the year.

Z is the number of standard deviations that a player's average is up or down from the mean and is often called the Z-score. If Z is positive, the player is above average; if Z is negative, the player is below average.

Standard Deviation–Adjusted Batting Average

The standard deviation–adjusted batting average is:

$$SDABA = MN + .029 \times Z$$
$$= MN + .029/SD \times (MABA - MN),$$

where .029 is the standardized standard deviation and Z is as described in the standardization technical note.

The longevity adjustment is also applied to obtain the career SDABA.

In the formula above, .029/SD is a multiplier term to MABA, which has the effect of lowering above average batting averages whenever SD is greater than .029 and raising them when SD is less than .029.

THE METHOD

Table 4.6, to get .1329. (Thus, Cobb hit 132.9 batting points above the mean in 1910.)

3. Rescale that difference to the *standardized* SD value of .029 as follows:

$$.1329 \times .029 / .0403 = .0956,$$

Table 4.6   Calculation of the Standard Deviation–Adjusted Batting Average (SDABA) for Ty Cobb

Year	AB	MABA	MN	SD	SDABA	Adj Hits
1905	150	.2540	.2671	.0360	.2565	38.5
1906	358	.3237	.2672	.0353	.3136	112.3
1907	605	.3608	.2680	.0361	.3425	207.2
1908	581	.3453	.2688	.0375	.3280	190.5
1909	573	.3942	.2690	.0381	.3643	208.7
1910	506	.4022	.2693	.0403	.3649	184.7
1911	591	.3919	.2701	.0419	.3544	209.5
1912	553	.3935	.2705	.0411	.3573	197.6
1913	428	.3890	.2704	.0402	.3560	152.3
1914	345	.3791	.2707	.0392	.3509	121.1
1915	563	.3796	.2704	.0392	.3512	197.7
1916	542	.3806	.2701	.0382	.3540	191.9
1917	588	.3939	.2696	.0378	.3650	214.6
1918	421	.3848	.2689	.0378	.3578	150.6
1919	497	.3656	.2681	.0362	.3462	172.1
1920	428	.3005	.2675	.0344	.2953	126.4
1921	507	.3389	.2671	.0341	.3282	166.4
1922	526	.3591	.2667	.0329	.3481	183.1
1923	556	.3070	.2666	.0325	.3026	168.3
1924	625	.2971	.2667	.0330	.2934	183.4
1925	415	.3308	.2670	.0329	.3232	134.1
1926	233	.3073	.2669	.0323	.3032	70.6
1927	490	.3190	.2670	.0331	.3126	153.2
1928	353	.2932	.2673	.0328	.2902	102.4
Total	**11434**	**.355**				

Notes:

MABA = career mean-adjusted batting average.

MN = yearly mean needed for the SDABA formula.

SD = yearly standard deviation needed for the SDABA formula.

Adj Hits = standard deviation–adjusted hits.

where .0403 is the 5-year moving average for standard deviation for 1910, as given in Table 4.6. (Cobb's edge has now been re-scaled to be 95.6 batting points above the mean.)

4. Adding back the mean, .2693, we obtain the SDABA:

$$.2693 + .0956 = .3649.$$

In summary, the four steps can be performed on a single line as:

SDABA for $1910 = .2693 + .029/.0403 \times (.4016 - .2693) = .3645.$

The career SDABA is then obtained by adding up the yearly SDABA averages weighted by the number of at bats in each year. One way to do this is to compute the number of adjusted hits, add them up, and divide by the total number of at bats.

As we did in chapter 3, to obtain Cobb's career SDABA, we need to get his total adjusted hits for his first 8000 at bats. We add the adjusted hits for 1905–20 (2675.7) with $271/507 \times 166.4 = 88.9$ from 1921 to get 2764.6 adjusted hits, giving him a career SDABA of $2764.6/8000 = .346$.

The SD-Adjusted Top 100

The standardized standard deviation (.029) was chosen to reflect modern talent pool variability, which has been fairly constant since 1920 in the National League and 1940 in the American League. Thus, nineteenth century and early twentieth century players will have lower averages after this third adjustment, while more recent players' batting averages will not change much.

The changes in adjusting for the standard deviation to the previous two adjustments are nontrivial but not nearly as dramatic as the MABA adjustment changes. Nine players were replaced in the list, as shown in Table 4.7.

Sources of Variability in the Standard Deviation

While I have used standard deviation to reflect the talent pool changes over baseball history, my approach still *assumes* that the best players are

Table 4.7 Changes in the Top 100 after the SD-Adjustment

	Dropped from List		
MABA Rank	Player	Team	Mid Yr
57	Deacon White	—	1884
66	George Gore	ChiN	1886
67	Paul Hines	ProN	1884
77	Hugh Duffy	BosN	1894
83	Fred Clarke	PitN	1902
84	Hardy Richardson	BufN	1886
86	Denny Lyons	Phia	1891
90	Frank Chance	ChiN	1905
94	Bobby Veach	DetA	1919

	Added to List		
SDABA Rank	Player	Team	Mid Yr
80	Keith Hernandez	StLN	1982
81	Tim Raines	Mon	1988
84	Ken Griffey, Sr.	Cin	1981
91	Heinie Zimmerman	ChiN	1914
93	Luke Appling	ChiA	1940
94	Dixie Walker	Bkn	1943
96	Eddie Murray	Bal	1987
97	Billy Goodman	BosA	1953
99	Enos Slaughter	StLN	1948

comparably good over time. My method can be viewed as obtaining a percentile ranking for each player for the era he played in and then combining all the percentile rankings into a single list. While I don't believe this approach works over all percentile rankings (the 10th percentile, for example), it appears to be suitable at the top end (the best 100 hitters place in the 88th percentile or better).

The variability in player batting averages comes from two different sources: random variability and player-to-player difference. A player with a .250 batting average will not get exactly one hit for each four at bats. This variability still exists if a player has 400 at bats. If we had 10 clones of this hypothetical player, whose *true* batting average ability is .250, with 400 AB each, the expected standard deviation is

$$SD = \sqrt{.250 \times (1 - .250)/400} = .022.$$

For distributions that have a normal distribution, 95% of the averages fall within 2 standard deviations of the true average. Thus, the clones might hit for averages as low as $.250 - 2 \times .022 = .206$ and as high as $.250 \times 2 \times .022 = .294$!

Since the standard deviation of players with at least 200 at bats in recent years has hovered around .029, we can see that a significant amount of the variability is due to random variability. The sources of the variability in the batting average standard deviation could be explored further using a statistical method called a *random effects model*, but we will not do that here.

Changes in the Top 100 after Standard Deviation Adjustment

Six of the hitters dropped from the list played from 1884–91, while most of the hitters added played in the 1940s and 1980s. The player shift increased the number of batting titles among the top 100 hitters by 4 and top 5 finishes by 8. More significantly, as Figure 4.15 shows, the percentage of hitters in the SDABA top 100 is now almost perfectly balanced across the decades.

Now that we are finishing our slide into third base, the competition for the top spots is becoming intense (Table 4.8). The standard deviation-adjusted averages of Ty Cobb, Joe Jackson, Tris Speaker, and Nap Lajoie dropped 17–21 points. Nineteenth century stars Pete Browning and Dan Brouthers also dropped about 20 points and fell off the top 10 list.

Cobb retains the top spot, although his edge over the second place hitter, now Tony Gwynn, is much narrower than after the MABA adjustment. Like Gwynn, the batting averages of Carew, Musial, Boggs, Williams, and Hornsby did not change much, allowing them to slip past several of the turn-of-the century players. In fact, Musial, Boggs, and Hornsby, with 19 batting titles to their names, replaced

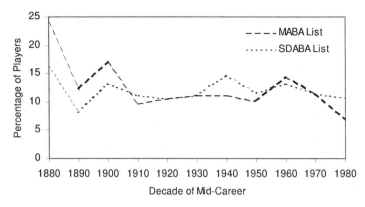

Figure 4.15 Top 100 Hitters by Mid-Career Decade MABA List vs. SDABA List

Browning, Speaker, and Brouthers in the top 10, who had 10 batting titles combined.

For the first time, our current top 10 list contains all seven hitters in major league history with at least seven batting titles!

Let's round the bag and head for home!

Table 4.8 Top 10 Hitters before and after SD-Adjustment

	Player	MABA	Player	SDABA
1	Ty Cobb	.370	Ty Cobb	.346
2	Joe Jackson	.349	Tony Gwynn	.339
3	Nap Lajoie	.344	Rod Carew	.337
4	Pete Browning	.343	Stan Musial	.333
5	Tris Speaker	.340	Wade Boggs	.333
6	Rod Carew	.339	Ted Williams	.333
7	Tony Gwynn	.338	Rogers Hornsby	.330
8	Honus Wagner	.336	Joe Jackson	.329
9	Ted Williams	.336	Nap Lajoie	.327
10	Dan Brouthers	.335	Honus Wagner	.325

Rogers Hornsby

Home —— Adjusting for Ballpark 5

Coors Field. These two words conjure up images of home runs, high scoring games, frazzled pitchers, and hits, hits, hits. Coors Field — home of the expansion Colorado Rockies team. Home and road batting statistics of Rockies players remind us of the fictional extremes of Superman and Clark Kent, of Mr. Hyde and Dr. Jekyll. Unlike these fictional characters, however, the batting numbers they produce are duly tabulated on official scoring sheets and are being placed in books alongside hitters scratching out a meager existence in San Francisco. What's going on here?

In 1997, the Rockies and their NL opponents hit .317 in Coors Field and .268 away from Coors Field. The question of whether batting statistics are affected by the ballpark played in was addressed by Bill James in *The Bill James Baseball Abstract* (1982). James gauged the "park effect" as the average number of runs for both teams at home and on the road for each team for the three previous years. He concluded that "the ballpark that a man plays in has a massive impact on his statistics. What the park effects chart does is to enable you to adjust for that effect."

Seymour Siwoff, Steve Hirdt, and Peter Hirdt then provided detailed data on ballpark differences for batting average, runs, and 9 other batting events in their 1987–93 annual publications of *The Elias Baseball Analyst*. They gave the total number of at bats and hits for *both* teams of all games played at each park for the previous year. They determined the *ballpark difference* by contrasting the combined "home" batting average with the combined "road" average of the team and their opponents. It is quite important that the batting data of both the home and visiting teams be used, since teams usually hit better at home than on the road. This method of determining the effects of a ballpark on batting average works because baseball is a balanced game, with a long-standing tradition that any pair of teams play half of their games at each other's ballparks. Starting with the American League expansion in 1977, slight imbalances have occurred, but their impact is quite minimal and will be ignored in the ballpark adjustment.

The ballpark differences for batting averages for 1983–92 from *The Elias Baseball Analyst* are shown in Table 5.1. Players batted 20 points better at Fenway than at the average of the other American League ballparks. Since Boston players accumulated half of their at bats at Fenway Park (actually players receive 48.8% of their bats at home), this would seem to give them about a 10-point advantage over

Table 5.1 Home-Away Batting Average Differentials for 1983–92

Team	Ballpark	1983–92	1983–87	1988–92
Boston	Fenway Park	20	18	21
Atlanta	Atlanta Stadium	17	19	15
Chicago NL	Wrigley Field	12	10	15
Minnesota	Metrodome	11	9	14
Cleveland	Cleveland Stadium	8	11	6
Cincinnati	Riverfront Stadium	8	10	6
Texas	Arlington Stadium	6	9	3
Chicago AL	Comiskey Park	5	5	
Kansas City	Royals Stadium	2	1	3
Seattle	Kingdome	2	0	4
Toronto	Exhibition Stadium	2	2	
Philadelphia	Veterans Stadium	1	3	−2
Pittsburgh	Three Rivers Stadium	−2	3	−6
St. Louis	Busch Stadium	−2	−1	−3
New York AL	Yankee Stadium	−2	−4	0
Los Angeles	Dodger Stadium	−2	−5	1
Montreal	Olympic Stadium	−4	−8	−1
San Diego	Jack Murphy Stadium	−5	−8	−1
Milwaukee	County Stadium	−5	−1	−9
Houston	Astrodome	−7	−8	−6
California	Anaheim Stadium	−7	−8	−6
New York NL	Shea Stadium	−8	−4	−11
Baltimore	Memorial Stadium	−8	−8	
San Francisco	Candlestick Park	−8	−10	−7
Detroit	Tiger Stadium	−12	−15	−10
Oakland	Oakland-Alameda	−16	−18	−14

Sources: The 1988 Elias Baseball Analyst, The 1993 Elias Baseball Analyst.
Notes:

The numbers shown are the differences in the home and away batting averages by both teams for the given stadium.

Blanks are given for teams who changed ballparks from 1988 to 1992.

a player at an average hitting ballpark. (The advantage was actually only 8 points, because the rest of the league was slightly underaverage. This is calculated later in the chapter.)

The data in Table 5.1 should spice up discussions comparing

Wade Boggs and Don Mattingly, recent stars for Boston and New York, respectively, before Boggs joined Mattingly in New York in 1993. Of special interest is the 1986 season when Boggs beat Mattingly by 5 points to win the AL batting championship. Assuming that Table 5.1 shows the "true" ballpark differences, Mattingly should be considered the batting champion since Boggs was helped 8 points, while Mattingly was hurt by 1 point.

Apparently, the poorest hitter's park from 1983–92 was Oakland-Alameda County Stadium, where players batted 16 points lower than average. Imagine the struggles that Carney Lansford must have undergone when he moved from Boston to Oakland in 1983. If Lansford's batting averages are adjusted using the ballpark differences given in Table 5.1, Lansford would have lost the batting title in Boston in 1981 to Seattle's Tom Paciorek, but would have won in Oakland in 1989 instead of Kirby Puckett. Thus, if these ballpark differences are *real*, that is, the differences are attributable to the ballpark played in and not some short-lived random difference, they have important consequences.

According to Table 5.1, the American League does not enjoy a monopoly on sizable ballpark differences. National League ballfields Atlanta Stadium and Wrigley Field also seem to be strong hitter's parks, yielding 17 and 12 point advantages, respectively. If these differences are real, they cannot be safely ignored, since many players play most or all of their careers with a single ballclub (although this is becoming increasingly rare with free agency).

Ballpark Differences Are Real

The differences of home and road batting averages change from year to year. The combined batting average of the Boston Red Sox and their opponents from 1983–92, both at Fenway and at their opponents' parks are given in Table 5.2. Each year, the home and road batting averages are based on about 81 games. Over the 10 years, the differences in the home and away batting averages varied from 9 to 33 points.

The yearly differences might be due to different weather conditions, number of day versus night games, or perhaps accidental or intentional differences between which players have more at bats at Fenway versus away from Fenway. Some degree of the differences from

Table 5.2 Batting Averages of the Boston Red Sox
and Opponents, 1983–92

Year	Fenway Park	Opponent's Park	Difference
1983	.285	.269	.016
1984	.291	.258	.033
1985	.286	.261	.025
1986	.273	.264	.009
1987	.286	.274	.012
1988	.282	.260	.022
1989	.280	.258	.022
1990	.277	.256	.021
1991	.271	.254	.017
1992	.263	.238	.025

Source: *The Elias Baseball Analyst* (Years 1985–93).

year to year is no doubt due to chance alone. We would like to know, however, whether the differences for Fenway are *completely* due to chance or seasonal events that will average out over time or whether they indicate that some true ballpark difference exists. In spite of the yearly variation, for each year the average was higher at Fenway than away from it. If Fenway were *truly* just like any other ballpark, that would occur with a probability of less than one in 500.

What about the other ballparks? One way to test whether ballpark differences are real is to compare the stability of the home-away differentials obtained from different time periods. Table 5.1 shows home-away batting average differences for consecutive 5-year periods as well as overall. The differences are fairly consistent for the two periods. These data are shown graphically in Figure 5.1.

Three technical notes describe some of the basics of linear regression.

Figure 5.1 shows a roughly increasing linear relationship between the paired differences, where parks with high home-away differences in 1983–87 also have high differences for 1988–92. The strength of this relationship can be measured by the Pearson correlation coefficient, $r = .85$, with p-value $< .0001$. The very low p-value (which is much less than .05 — our benchmark for "evidence") provides a convincing argument that the *ballpark differences are real.*

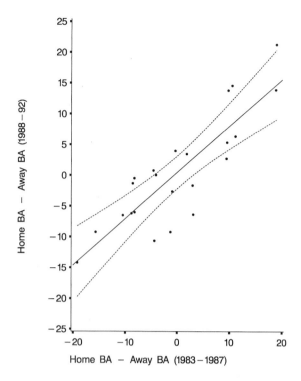

Figure 5.1 Comparing Home-Away Batting Average Differences in Successive 5-Year Periods

The home-away batting average differences for back-to-back 5-year periods are plotted for each ballpark (data are in Table 5.1). The linear regression line shows that the differences in 1983–87 are roughly the same as in 1988–92. The dashed lines show the 95% confidence band, indicating the range of lines that are consistent with the data.

TECHNICAL NOTE

Linear Regression

Linear regression methods allow one to test for the linear association between two variables. The line that minimizes the sums of squared differences in the vertical direction between the points and itself is the best fitting line.

THE METHOD

TECHNICAL NOTE

Confidence Band for Linear Regression

The 95% confidence band specifies a region in which any line could arguably represent the "true" relationship between the two variables given the data and assumptions. The best fitting line is considered to be the best single choice and is in the center of the region. If no horizontal line can be drawn within the confidence band, this allows one to reject the presumption that there is *no* association between the variables with 95% confidence.

In Figure 5.1, the 95% confidence band region is between the curved dashed lines. The straight solid line is the best fitting line.

TECHNICAL NOTE

Pearson Correlation Coefficient (r)

Along with the best fitting line, the degree of linear association, called *correlation*, can be given. A number — the *Pearson correlation coefficient* or simply r — describes this correlation. It is a number between -1 and 1, with the following interpretation:

$r = -1$,   as one variable goes up the other goes down *and* all the points are on the best fitting line

$r < 0$,   as one variable goes up the other goes down

$r = 0$,   the best fitting line is horizontal

$r > 0$,   as one variable goes up the other goes up

$r = 1$,   as one variable goes up the other goes up *and* all the points are on the best fitting line

A *p*-value is used to test whether or not the true correlation differs from zero.

OK, they're real. But do they matter? Changes of 5–10 points can have a significant impact on ranking a ballplayer in the very competitive batting event called *batting average*. Consider Wade Boggs, who played the first half of his career in Boston. He ranks 5th on the SD-adjusted batting average list (Table 4.8). If his average were dropped 9 points, the Fenway Park effect during his time there, he would slip to 9th place. For players farther down the list of the top 100 hitters, a 9-point drop would cost a player 30 or 40 places in the ranking. So it's clear that the effect can be quite substantial. Keep in mind, however, that Boggs hasn't played his entire career for Boston and other players need their own ballpark adjustments as well.

How does the effect of the ballpark on batting average compare to that of home runs and other batting events? On a percentage basis, batting average is the most consistent batting event from park to park of the 12 shown in Table 5.3. Hits were up 8% in Atlanta and down 7% in Oakland from 1983–87. By contrast, some other events have extraordinary differences. Triples were 62% higher in Kansas City and 54% lower in Los Angeles! Home runs also showed considerable variability, being up 44% in Chicago's Wrigley Field and 44% down in the Houston Astrodome.

From 1983–87, Kansas City averaged 46 triples per year, 31 at

Table 5.3   Spread in Batting Events among the 26
          Major League Ballparks, 1983–87

Batting Event	SD	Min	Team	Max	Team
Triples	31.6	−54	LA	62	KC
Home Runs	18.3	−44	Hou	44	ChiN
Doubles	14.1	−28	LA	28	Bos
Extra Base Hit %	13.2	−30	LA	23	Tor
Runs	8.1	−14	Oak	16	ChiN
Stolen Bases	6.2	−10	Bos	12	KC
Slugging Pct.	5.7	−12	Oak	10	ChiN
Errors	5.6	−13	Cin	15	Atl
Strikeouts	5.6	−14	KC	12	SD
Walks	5.1	−10	LA	11	ChiA
Singles	4.2	−7	Tor	9	LA
Batting Average	3.7	−7	Oak	8	Atl

Source: The 1988 Elias Baseball Analyst.

Notes:

SD = the standard deviation between ballparks in percent.

Min and Max = minimum and maximum percentage changes of extreme parks compared to the "average" park for that event.

home and 15 on the road. Baltimore, the poorest triples park in the AL, averaged 20 triples, hitting 6 at home and 14 on the road. An average American League team hit 36, with 20 at home and 16 on the road. In the National League, the Chicago Cubs averaged 163 home runs, with 97 at home and 66 on the road. Houston averaged 112, 41 at home and 71 on the road. An average National League team averaged 126 home runs, 62.5 at home and 63.5 on the road. You can see that the differences between Baltimore and Kansas City for triples and Houston and the Chicago Cubs for home runs are almost exclusively a result of the ballpark effects.

You might be surprised by the spread of some batting events, like walks and strikeouts. Shouldn't these depend only on the pitcher, the batter, and the umpire, all of whom move from park to park? Differences between ballparks may have to do with ball visibility or different pitch count strategies, where players swing at or hold off on pitches depending on the hitting success they anticipate.

Errors are more common in grass parks, while extra-base hits and stolen bases are more common in astroturf stadiums. This book is primarily focused on batting average, but the impact of ballparks on these other events is certainly noteworthy. Batting average is the most consistent batting event and taking account of ballpark effects is still important!

In order to adjust for the effect of the ballpark on batting average, we would like to have these data throughout baseball history. Unfortunately, the home and road data are not readily available before 1980 and they are painstakingly tedious to obtain. They would have to be amassed game by game, year by year from box scores. There is a massive amount of work involved, which is being undertaken by the Retrosheet group of the Society for American Baseball Research.

A statistician faced with a huge data collection problem looks for a good estimate requiring far less effort. Is that possible here? The answer is yes, but a little more statistical savvy is needed.

Estimating Ballpark Effects

The trivial estimate of the effect of a ballpark on batting average is a zero effect. When we calculate the usual batting average, we effectively make this assumption. The estimated effects of ballparks proposed in this book are admittedly imperfect. However, they are vastly better than the trivial estimate of a *zero effect* and we have already seen that the effects are too important to ignore in our search for the 100 best hitters.

Since a ballclub plays half of its games at home, we could estimate the ballpark effect by subtracting the league batting average from the team batting average. The basic idea here is that if a team consistently hits better than the league average, it must be because it is somewhat easier to get hits in its ballpark.

The avid baseball fan will see an obvious problem with this approach since some teams have better hitters than others (like the Yankees — they've been good forever!). Thus, a higher team batting average may reflect superior hitting, not an easier ballpark in which to hit. I can hear the counterarguments as I write: "Why identify superior hitting as a ballpark effect?" I have a question of my own: "How do you know that one team is superior to another?" Superior teams should win more ballgames. Therefore, the regression analysis I propose will adjust the mean-adjusted team batting average for team winning percentage and attribute the *remaining* difference between it and the standardized league batting average to the ballpark effect.

The method is somewhat involved, so it will described in detail for one team, the Philadelphia to Kansas City to Oakland Athletics. The Athletics were one of two franchises that have played for three different cities in the twentieth century — the other being the Boston to Milwaukee to Atlanta Braves.

The first step is to apply mean-adjustment to the team batting average for each year from 1901–92 (we'll use a better method from 1993 on). To gain some insight, we plot the mean-adjusted team batting average against the team winning percentage for the year, as Figure 5.2 shows. The plot shows that higher batting averages are associated with higher winning percentages and $r = .69$. Since the p-value is below .0001, the association is highly significant. The regression analysis gives .254 as the batting average for the team when it wins half of its games — one point below average.

There's only one problem. The Athletic franchise played in four stadiums in three different cities — so one ballpark effect won't do. The team played in two parks while in Philadelphia from 1901–54, in Columbia Park from 1901–8, and in Shibe Park from 1909–54. The franchise then moved to Kansas City, playing in Municipal Stadium from

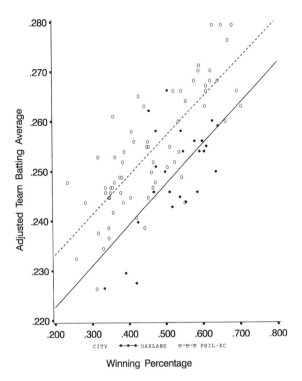

Figure 5.2   The Philadelphia to Kansas City to Oakland Athletics
The mean-adjusted batting averages are plotted against the team winning
percentages for the Philadelphia and Kansas City Athletics (1901–67, open
circles) and Oakland Athletics (1968–92, closed circles). The dashed and
solid lines are the linear regression for the two groups, respectively. The lines
show that team batting average increases with team winning percentage. The
lines are nearly parallel but are 10 points lower when the team was in
Oakland for the same winning percentage.

1955 to 1967. In 1968, the team finally completed its westward trek,
landing in Oakland-Alameda County Stadium in Oakland.

The adjusted team batting averages for the years 1901–67 are
given by dots and from 1968–92 by "O"s, to represent Oakland. The
solid line gives the linear regression for the years 1901–67. We can see
that the Oakland years were below this line for 22 of the 25 years,
illustrating that ballpark effects need to be calculated separately for
each stadium. The dashed line shows the linear regression for the Oakland years, which is nearly parallel to the solid line but 10 points lower.

Several changes were made to Shibe Park while the Athletics played there from 1909 to 1954. Perhaps the greatest came in 1922, when the left field fence was shortened from 380 to 334 ft. and the right field fence was shortened from 502 to 468 ft. Also, during the 46-year period, all the other AL teams moved into new stadiums. There-fore, we should not expect the ballpark effect to remain constant throughout. Thus, I divided the Shibe Park years into three eras: 1909–21, 1922–34, and 1935–54. The choice of 1935 as the second break year will be discussed later.

The Kansas City years are divided into 1955–60 and 1961–67, and the Oakland years are divided into 1968–82 and 1983–92. The break years, 1961 and 1983, will also be explained later.

Altogether, ballpark effects for the Athletics were estimated by multiple regression for 8 different eras. The new correlation coefficient, $r = .82$, is closer to a perfect fit than the value obtained previously before estimating separate ballpark effects for different eras.

League Change Years

In modeling a given ballpark's effect, it became clear that it changed over time. This should not be too surprising. The league batting aver-age changed significantly over the years, so why shouldn't a ballpark's effect change as well? Perhaps the biggest factor is the introduction of new ballparks elsewhere in the league. If a great hitter's park is sud-denly replaced by a park favorable to the pitcher, the ballpark effects elsewhere in the league will change as well. On the other hand, we wouldn't want to re-estimate the ballpark effect for each park every time a new one is built somewhere in the league. Fortunately, it ap-pears that we don't *have* to. (If we did, the regression model would not be very stable and couldn't be used reliably.)

So when should we reestimate a given ballpark's effect given changes that occur elsewhere around the league? I chose seven such years — *league change years* — for the American and National Leagues. The American League change years are 1920, 1935, 1950, 1961, 1970, 1983, and 1993, while the National League change years are 1910, 1921, 1938, 1950, 1962, 1970, 1983, and 1993. The rationale for these choices is given below.

1910 — NL

Between 1909 and 1915, all 8 American League teams and 5 of the 8 National League teams moved into new stadiums. Additionally, in 1909 Robison Field, home to the St. Louis Cardinals, had a major renovation—the left field fence was moved in from 470 ft. to 380 ft. and the center field fence was moved in from 500 ft. to 435 ft. The other two NL teams who did not have a stadium change were the Chicago Cubs and the Philadelphia Phillies. The Cubs played in West Side Grounds from 1893 to 1915, while the Baker Bowl was home to the Phillies from 1895 to 1938 (except for a few scattered months). Since the other NL teams either changed stadiums or had a renovation, a league change year of 1910 was used from which to obtain new ballpark effects for Chicago and Philadelphia.

1920 — AL, 1921 — NL

Around 1920, a baseball mystery occurred. No, I'm not speaking about whether "Shoeless" Joe Jackson helped to throw the 1919 World Series—which may indeed be the greatest of baseball's mysteries. The mystery I'm referring to is this—batting averages and home runs suddenly jumped. The mound wasn't moved back or lowered, and the number of balls for a walk and strikes for a strikeout remained the same. So what happened?

Many sportswriters over the years have attributed the rise in averages and home runs around 1920 to a "livelier" ball. other writers however dispute this claim. Regardless of where the truth lies, the period from 1901–19 became known as the "dead ball" era and the new era, which perhaps extends to the U.S. involvement in World War II in December 1941, became known as the "lively ball" era.

Two men personified these two eras: Ty Cobb and Babe Ruth. Cobb was the preeminent "dead ball" hitter who got on base and scratched for runs with his base stealing exploits. Babe Ruth was emerging as the preeminent "lively ball" slugger, slamming balls out of ballparks. Table 5.4 shows the batting in both the AL and NL before and after 1920. In both leagues, there was a transition year (1919 in the AL, 1920 in the NL) with numbers that were roughly halfway between the numbers for before and after periods.

In both leagues, the league batting averages went up a whopping 37 points, home runs went up by 3 per 500 at bats (a typical season

Table 5.4 Average Batting Totals for a Player with 500 At Bats

Years	League	BA	2B	3B	HR	SB	R
1915–18	AL	.249	18	7	1.7	16	57
1919	AL	.268	22	7	3.2	12	61
1920–24	AL	.286	25	7	5.2	9	71
1915–19	NL	.251	18	7	2.6	15	54
1920	NL	.270	19	8	3.1	12	58
1921–24	NL	.288	22	7	5.9	9	68
1993–97	AL	.271	26	3	15.6	10	73
1993–97	NL	.264	24	3	13.7	11	67

total for a full-time player), while runs scored went up by 14. Doubles also went up, triples remained constant, and stolen bases declined. The home run changes were particularly dramatic, since they represent two- to threefold increases.

Averages from the NL and AL for 1993–97 are presented for comparison. These recent averages show a different profile. Doubles, stolen bases, and runs are like lively ball era players, while batting averages are over 20 points lower (remember that the DH boosts the 1993–97 AL batting average by 8 points). Triples are halved while home runs are more than double the lively ball era rates.

1935 — AL, 1938 — NL

There were several ballpark changes in the American League during the 1930s. Cleveland split time between two stadiums starting in 1932. Two other teams had major stadium renovations — Fenway Park in Boston in 1934 and Navin Field in Detroit in 1938, which was renamed Briggs Stadium. Since these changes center around 1935, this was chosen as the league change year.

In the National League only one stadium change occurred around this time. In 1938, the Philadelphia Phillies moved from Baker Bowl to Shibe Park, beginning their 17 years of sharing it with the Philadelphia Athletics of the American League. There was a 10-point drop in mean-adjusted batting averages following the move from the Baker Bowl, but the drop in home runs was stunning. The Baker Bowl was one of the most distinctive ballparks in major league history. Often called a "bandbox," its right field fence was only 280 ft. from home plate. Although home run averages are not the subject of this book, the league change years were chosen with all offensive averages in mind, hence 1938 was used for the NL.

1950

In 1947, Cleveland began playing all their home games in Municipal Stadium. In 1954, the St. Louis Browns became the Baltimore Orioles. In the National League, the dimensions in Ebbets Field were shortened in 1948 and the Boston Braves moved to Milwaukee in 1953. For both leagues, 1950 is a central year to use to obtain new ballpark effects.

1961 — AL, 1962 — NL

In 1961, baseball was expanded for the first time in 60 years (aside from the ill-fated Federal League of 1914–15). Washington and Los Angeles joined the American League.

The National League was expanded in 1962, when the Houston Colt 45's and New York Mets were added. Two erstwhile New York teams moved to California in 1958. The Brooklyn Dodgers became the Los Angeles Dodgers, a move that still irritates Brooklynites 40 years later. The New York Giants moved to San Francisco. Both the Dodgers and Giants played in temporary stadiums before inhabiting their permanent stadiums in 1962 and 1960, respectively.

1970

In 1969, the second expansion in less than a decade occurred. This time, both the American and National Leagues added two teams. The AL added the Kansas City Royals and the Seattle Pilots, while the Montreal Expos and San Diego Padres joined the NL. Other changes also occurred in both leagues.

In 1968, the Kansas City Athletics team became the Oakland Athletics. In 1970, the Pilots became reestablished as the Milwaukee Brewers. In 1972, the Washington Senators donned new uniforms as the Texas Rangers. A year later, the Kansas City Royals moved into their permanent stadium. In the National League, three established teams moved to new stadiums: Cincinnati and Pittsburgh in 1970 and Philadelphia in 1971. Thus, 1970 is a central league change year for these ballpark changes for both the American and National leagues.

1983

From 1983 on, home and away ballpark data will be used to determine the ballpark effect. I would like to compare the regression estimates to these more accurate data. Thus, a break at 1983 allows for the transition. Also, there have been league change years about every 10–15 years, except around 1910 when nearly every franchise moved into a new stadium. Thus, it allows for smaller shifts that might be going on among the ballparks.

Even though the AL expanded in 1977, when the Seattle Mariners and Toronto Blue Jays were added, no league change seems necessary. Both were very average ballparks for batting average and the relative impact of adding 2 teams was much less than it was in 1961.

1993

In 1993, the Colorado Rockies and the Florida Marlins joined the National League. We have already examined the "mile"-high batting averages being obtained in Colorado. Since Colorado is such a strong hitter's park, the park effects should be recalculated for the National League. Several American League teams — Toronto ('89), Chicago ('91), Baltimore ('92), Cleveland ('94), and Texas ('94) — moved into new ballparks, so we will recalculate park effects for the remaining AL teams in 1993 as well.

Ballpark Effects for Post-1900 Clubs

Regression models were obtained separately for each team from 1901 (or the first year of the team franchise if later than 1901) to 1992. A new ballpark effect was estimated every time the team moved into a new stadium, had a major stadium change, or was at a league change year. Note that these models include ballpark estimates for 1983–92 to compare with the direct home-away data given in Table 5.1.

Figure 5.3 compares the batting average *predicted* from the regression model to the *actual* batting average determined from the data in Table 5.1. The relationship, with $r = .75$, is fairly strong. Fenway Park has both the highest predicted and the highest actual home-away difference, while Oakland has the lowest predicted and actual differences.

Only Atlanta-Fulton County Stadium is poorly fit by the model.

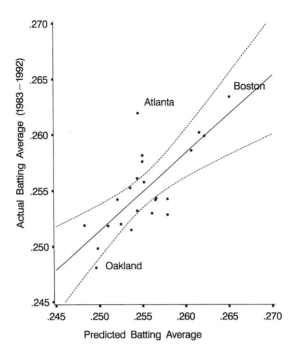

Figure 5.3   Predicted vs. Actual Ballpark Batting Averages
The predicted ballpark batting averages based on regression analysis are
plotted against the actual ballpark batting averages for 1983–92, derived from
the data in Table 5.1. The ballpark data for Atlanta, Boston, and Oakland are
identified. The linear relationship and 95% confidence band shows that the
predicted batting averages roughly correspond to the actual batting averages.

The actual batting average was .262, while the predicted average was
.254. If Atlanta is removed from the comparison, r jumps to .84.

Ballpark Effects for Pre-1901 Clubs

Unfortunately, the linear regression method will not work well with
pre-1900 ballpark data because the teams did not remain in the same
ballpark long enough then for reliable estimates to be obtained. For
the twentieth-century teams, the regression adjusted the mean-adjusted
team batting averages for the team's winning percentage. Thus we have
estimates of winning percentage on hitting.

For the 16 original twentieth-century teams, batting average always increased with winning percentage in the regression model. The *winning percentage effect* gives the number of points that the batting average rises per 10% increase in winning percentage. Except for the outlying value of 3.8 for the Boston-Milwaukee-Atlanta Braves, the winning percentage effects ranged from 5.8 for the Cleveland Indians to 9.5 for the Detroit Tigers. They cluster around the *median* value, 7.4. meaning that half of the effects were less than 7.4 and half were more.

What does a median winning percentage effect of 7.4 imply? Say a team that wins 50% of its games bats .255. If it wins 60% of its games the following year, we would expect it to bat .2624 (=.255 + 1 × .0074), where 1 = (60% − 50%) / 10%. On the other hand, if it only wins 45% of its games, its expected batting average is .2513 (= .255 − 0.5 × .0074). This median effect was used to adjust for the effect of winning percentage for pre-1901 teams, and the Federal League.

The median winning percentage — 7.4 points per 10% increase in winning percentage — was applied "backward" to obtain ballpark effects for the nineteenth-century teams, as the following example illustrates. From 1892 to 1899, the NL Baltimore Orioles played in Orioles Park. The team had a mean-adjusted batting average of .2753 and won 59.4% of their games. If Baltimore had a neutral ballpark, we would have expected them to bat .2620 (= .255 + 0.94 × .0074). Thus, we can see that Orioles Park helps the hitters by 13.3 (= .2753 − .2620) points.

What Causes the Ballpark Effects?

We have seen that ballpark effects are real and have obtained estimates for each field throughout major league history. In doing so, we did not look at ballpark dimension (such as the length to the outfield fences), type of field (natural grass versus artificial turf), percentage of games played at night, visibility of the ball to the hitter, temperature at game time, wind patterns, humidity, or a host of other factors. What was observed was simply that batters hit better at Fenway than away from Fenway, and so on for the other parks.

The *why* questions are quite interesting, but they are also very difficult to answer in most cases. Thousands of research papers have been written, showing that smokers are much more likely to get lung cancer than nonsmokers. We have yet to figure out *exactly* how smoking causes lung cancer. Still . . . it is interesting to speculate a little . . . about ballpark effects, that is.

When speaking with friends, the first factor usually suggested is ballpark dimension. While older ballparks were sometimes quite dissimilar, however, today's parks are fairly similar. The typical dimensions are 330 ft. to the foul poles, 375–85 ft. to the power alleys, and 400–410 ft. to the center. The fences are usually from 7 to 12 ft. high. There are some exceptions to this, of course, and some parks are asymmetric, like Fenway Park and Tiger Stadium. However, I found no obvious relationship based on distances to the fences.

What about the field surface? The three most favorable ballparks to the hitter from 1983 to 1992 (Table 5.1) have grass fields — but the six least favorable ballparks also have grass fields, with the nine astroturf parks sandwiched in between. It is interesting that all five California ballparks favor the pitcher.

One ballpark feature that *does* seem to be related to batting average is the size of the foul territory. The foul territory is the part of the playing field outside the foul lines. Table 5.5 lists the ballparks in decreasing order of hitting advantage. Also shown is the size of the foul territory, as rated by Philip Lowry in *Green Cathedrals* and Bill James in the *1983 Bill James Baseball Abstract*. Notice that the best hitter's park (Fenway) has the smallest foul territory, while the worst hitter's park (Oakland-Alameda) has the largest. Could there be a connection?

Lowry and James largely agree in their ratings. The definite disagreement is with the foul territory of Atlanta-Fulton County Stadium, which Lowry considered "huge" but which James rated as "a little small." Neither person "rated" the foul territory sizes of some stadiums — often the same ones. Presumably, they considered these foul territories to be of "normal" size. Both rank the foul territories of at least 6 of the top 10 hitter's parks as small, whereas only one of the remaining 16 parks (Tiger Stadium) has a small foul territory.

Why should the size of the foul territory make a difference in the batting average at a ballpark? Well, . . . players often hit foul balls. Many of these go into the stands and are nonplayable. Foul balls that are caught are all outs. Therefore, ballparks with small foul territories give the batter more chances to hit the ball into fair territory, resulting in higher batting averages. It would be interesting to have foul territory square footage and stadium overhang information to investigate this apparent association further.

Table 5.5   Size of Ballpark Foul Territories

Team	Ballpark	BA Diff	Turf	Lowry Rating	James Rating
Bos	Fenway Park	20	N	Smallest	Tiny
Atl	Atlanta Stadium	17	N	Huge	A Little Small
ChiN	Wrigley Field	12	N	Very Small	Very Small
Min	Metrodome	11	A	Small	Small
Cle	Cleveland Stadium	8	N	Large	
Cin	Riverfront Stadium	8	A	Small	Small
Tex	Arlington Stadium	6	N	Small	
ChiA	Comiskey Park	5	N	Large	Large
KC	Royals Stadium	2	A	Small	Small
Sea	Kingdome	2	A	Large	Small
Tor	Exhibition Stadium	2	A		
Phi	Veterans Stadium	1	A	Large	Large
Pit	Three Rivers Stadium	−2	A	Large	Fairly Large
StL	Busch Stadium	−2	A	Large	Large
NYA	Yankee Stadium	−2	N	Large Backstop	Large
LA	Dodger Stadium	−2	N	Large	Large
Mon	Olympic Stadium	−4	A	Large	Large
SD	Jack Murphy Stadium	−5	N	Normal	
Mil	County Stadium	−5	N		
Hou	Astrodome	−7	A		
Cal	Anaheim Stadium	−7	N		
NYN	Shea Stadium	−8	N	Very Large	Extremely Large
Bal	Memorial Stadium	−8	N	Large	Normal to Large
SF	Candlestick Park	−8	N	Large	Large
Det	Tiger Stadium	−12	N	Small	Small
Oak	Oakland-Alameda	−16	N	Largest	Immense

Notes:

Turf types: N = natural grass; A = astroturf.

Blanks — ratings not provided in the publications.

So what about Coors Field? Baseball pundits and physicists both seem to agree that the superior hitting seen there is a result of the thinner air. Colorado is the highest ballpark in the major leagues — 5,282 ft. above sea level (the next highest in 1997 was Atlanta at 1,030 ft.). *STATS Baseball Scoreboard 1997* shows that the average outfield fly ball went 19 ft. further (338 ft. vs. 319 ft.) in Colorado than elsewhere in the major leagues. In spite of having fences that are 10–20 ft. farther back than the average distances, batting averages were 65 points better at Coors (.319 vs. .254) from 1995 to 1997 — with triples and home runs over 50% higher.

In *Diamond Diagrams*, Oscar Palacios gave the altitudes for all ballparks. Of the top 9 hitting ballparks given in Table 5.5, only Fenway (21 ft.) had an altitude below 500 ft. Of the remaining 17 stadiums, only 3 were above 500 ft. (Det, Mil, and Pit).

In mid-season 1997, Tony Gwynn of the San Diego Padres and Larry Walker of the Colorado Rockies were locked in a tight batting race near the elusive .400 mark. When the Rockies came to San Diego, several fans held up a sign saying, "Welcome to sea level"!

Calculation of the Ballpark Effect from Home and Away Data

From 1983 onward, the ballpark effects used for adjusting batting average are determined from the home and away ballpark data. Table 5.2 shows the home and away batting averages for Fenway Park from 1983 to 1992. Using the total hits and at bats over the ten-year period, the batting average was .2793 at Fenway and .2593 away from Fenway, giving a *ballpark difference* of .2793 − .2593 = .0200. A Red Sox player plays half his games at Fenway and half away. If he is an average hitter in the games involving the Red Sox, he could expect to hit:

$$(.2793 + .2593) / 2 = .2693.$$

If Boston played each opponent around the league equally, for example by playing one game against each opponent in each of the 14 ballparks, the ballpark effect would be removed. It is doubtful that baseball will ever do this because there would then be no hometown teams — but it *would* remove the ballpark effects on averages! Even though the players aren't going to do it, statistically we can get there by mixing the home and away batting averages as one part home, thirteen parts away, getting:

$$(.2793 + 13 \times .2593) / 14 = .2607.$$

The ratio of these two numbers, .2693/.2607 = 1.033, is the *park factor*. Thus, batting averages of Red Sox players was boosted 3.3% from 1983 to 1992. We can put this in batting average terms. Using

.255 as the standardized batting average, an average hitter would hit $1.033 \times .255 = .2634$. Thus, their averages have been boosted by the *ballpark effect*—8.4 points.This average, .2634, will be referred to as the *ballpark effect batting average*.

The bottom number of the park factor ratio, .2607, is *not* the overall league average since Boston players make up half of both the "home" and "away" batting averages. Consequently, this must be calculated separately for each ballpark.

The general formula for the park factor (PF)is:

$$ PF = \frac{[(Home\ BA\ +\ Away\ BA)/2]}{[(Home\ BA\ +\ (K-1) \times Away\ BA)/K]}\ , $$

where K is the number of teams in the league.

Ballpark Terms Summarized

Several ballpark terms have been defined and used in this chapter, and all were mentioned in the previous section. They are summarized here to clarigy their usage.

ballpark difference = home batting average − away batting average for both teams.
> *Example*: For Fenway Park from 1983 to 92, it is .2793 − .2593 = .0020.

ballpark effect batting average = batting average of an "average hitter" playing for the team whose ballpark is being evaluated, standardized to .255.
> *Example*: For Fenway Park from 1983 to 92, it is .2634.

ballpark effect = the ballpark effect batting average − .255.
> *Example*: For Fenway Park from 1983 to 92, it is .0084, or equivalently, 8.4 points.

park factor = the ball park effect batting average ÷ .255.
> *Example*: For Fenway Park from 1982 to 93, it is 1.033.
> (Note: in the previous section, the park factor was determined by a different formula first, from which the ballpark effect batting average was determined.)

Applying the Ballpark Adjustment

The fully adjusted batting average, which includes the ballpark adjustment, only inserts a park factor term to the SDABA formula from chapter 4. However, the means and standard deviations of the batting averages need to be recalculated after both mean- *and* ballpark effect adjustments have been applied.

As before, we will apply the new adjustment to Cobb's 1910 season.

1. Obtain the ballpark effect from Appendix IV. Since Cobb played for Detroit in 1910, the ballpark effect is .2597. Thus, the park factor is .2597 / .255 = 1.1084.

2. Get the 5-year mean and standard deviation of mean-adjusted batting averages from Appendix III. Be sure to use the ones that have been adjusted for ballpark effects. For the 1910 American League, MN = .2685 and SD = .0387.

TECHNICAL NOTE

Fully Adjusted Batting Average

The fully adjusted batting average is:

$$FABA = MN + .029/SD \times (MABA / PF - MN),$$

where .029 is the chosen standardized standard deviation and PF is the park factor. MABA = (hits/AB) × [SBA/(league batting average)], where SBA, the chosen standardized batting average, is .255 for years without the DH and .2635 for years with the DH.

The longevity adjustment is also applied to obtain the career FABA.

FABA looks just like the standard deviation–adjusted batting average (SDABA) except for the insertion of the park factor, PF. However, MN and SD are the 5-year moving averages for the mean and standard deviation of the batting averages of players with at least 200 at bats for the year after *both* the mean- and ballpark effect adjustments have been applied, respectively. Thus, they differ slightly from the MN and SD used in the SDABA formula.

---

3. Use the FABA formula given in the technical note. The FABA for Cobb's 1910 year is:

.2685 + (.029/.0387) × (.4022/1.0184 − .2685) = .3632.

Table 5.6 contains the information needed to calculate the career FABA for Cobb. As before, the most reliable way to compute the career FABA is to first compute adjusted hits by multiplying each single-sea-

Table 5.6   Calculation of the Fully Adjusted Batting Average
(FABA) for Ty Cobb

Year	AB	MABA	Park	MN	SD	FABA	Adj. Hits
1905	150	.2540	.2597	.2672	.0353	.2527	37.9
1906	358	.3237	.2597	.2674	.0345	.3098	110.9
1907	605	.3608	.2597	.2678	.0351	.3393	205.3
1908	581	.3453	.2597	.2682	.0361	.3251	188.9
1909	573	.3942	.2597	.2683	.0367	.3621	207.5
1910	506	.4022	.2597	.2685	.0387	.3632	183.8
1911	591	.3919	.2597	.2694	.0402	.3527	208.4
1912	553	.3935	.2634	.2702	.0394	.3518	194.5
1913	428	.3890	.2634	.2707	.0389	.3496	149.6
1914	345	.3791	.2634	.2713	.0381	.3443	118.8
1915	563	.3796	.2634	.2713	.0382	.3443	193.8
1916	542	.3806	.2634	.2711	.0377	.3460	187.5
1917	588	.3939	.2634	.2708	.0376	.3561	209.4
1918	421	.3848	.2634	.2701	.0376	.3490	146.9
1919	497	.3656	.2634	.2692	.0358	.3379	167.9
1920	428	.3005	.2601	.2685	.0340	.2908	124.4
1921	507	.3389	.2601	.2678	.0333	.3239	164.2
1922	526	.3591	.2601	.2670	.0319	.3443	181.1
1923	556	.3070	.2601	.2666	.0314	.2984	165.9
1924	625	.2971	.2601	.2665	.0321	.2889	180.6
1925	415	.3308	.2601	.2667	.0321	.3189	132.3
1926	233	.3073	.2601	.2666	.0318	.2982	69.5
1927	490	.3190	.2523	.2667	.0326	.3163	155.0
1928	353	.2932	.2523	.2670	.0323	.2933	103.5
Total	**11434**	**.355**					

son FABA by the number of at bats. The career FABA is then obtained by dividing the total adjusted hits by total at bats (with longevity adjustment also applied, if necessary). Cobb's career FABA is .340.

Ballpark Effects Correspond Well with Superstar Batting Average Records

A considerable amount of attention has been given to understanding ballpark effects in recent years. Older baseball encyclopedias rarely included home and away batting data on the ballplayers. This is now changing. In the 1989 edition of *Total Baseball*, home and away data were provided for 27 superstars. Table 5.7 shows the home and away batting averages and their differences (Diff) for these players. The change in the adjusted batting average (Adj) as a result of the ballpark effect is also given. Players who hit much better at home than away tended to play at good hitter's parks. Consequently, their adjusted averages tended to go down the most. This relationship is shown in Figure 5.4. We will examine the relationship using linear regression.

First, since Chuck Klein is especially unusual because he hit extraordinarily well at home, we'll remove him from the main model. The linear regression relationships obtained was: Diff $= 8.2 - 2.3 \times$ Adj, with $r = .56$.

The formula makes a lot of sense. Players usually hit better at home than on the road — an 8.2-point advantage according to the formula. Secondly, since a player plays half of his games on the road, the difference should be twice the size of the adjustment needed.

Changes in the Fully Adjusted Top 100

Unlike the mean and standard deviation adjustments, the ballpark does not raise or lower the averages of one era compared to another. This adjustment boosts the averages of hitters who played primarily for teams with pitcher's parks and lowers the averages of players from hitter's parks.

Fourteen players drop out of the top 100 after the ballpark adjustment is made, as Table 5.8 shows. Some of the changes are quite substantial. Jim Rice, who played his entire career in Boston, drops 8

Table 5.7 Unadjusted Home and Away Batting Averages of Some Superstars

Player	Team	Home	Away	Diff	Adj
Chuck Klein	PhiN	.354	.285	69	−5.7
Carl Yastrzemski	BosA	.306	.264	42	−8.2
Tris Speaker	Cle	.365	.325	40	−1.8
Jimmie Foxx	PhiA	.345	.307	38	−0.1
Ted Williams	BosA	.361	.328	33	−4.5
Nap Lajoie	Cle	.353	.324	29	−5.0
Frank Robinson	Cin	.307	.283	24	−1.1
Roberto Clemente	Pit	.329	.306	23	−8.9
Mike Schmidt	PhiN	.273	.255	18	−2.4
Sam Crawford	Det	.318	.302	16	−3.5
Honus Wagner	Pit	.335	.320	15	1.9
Mickey Mantle	NYA	.305	.291	14	1.3
Pete Rose	Cin	.310	.296	14	−2.4
Al Kaline	Det	.303	.292	11	−0.9
Stan Musial	StLN	.336	.326	10	−8.3
Babe Ruth	NYA	.347	.338	9	2.7
Ty Cobb	Det	.370	.363	7	−4.4
Joe Morgan	Cin	.275	.268	7	1.5
Harmon Killebrew	Min	.259	.253	6	−4.2
Eddie Collins	ChiA	.333	.332	1	0.8
Rogers Hornsby	StLN	.359	.358	1	0.2
Willie Mays	SF	.302	.301	1	5.4
Hank Aaron	Atl	.303	.306	−3	−4.6
Reggie Jackson	Oak	.255	.268	−13	6.7
Mel Ott	NYN	.297	.311	−14	0.2
Joe DiMaggio	NYA	.315	.333	−18	5.6
Lou Gehrig	NYA	.329	.351	−22	2.1

Source: Total Baseball, First Edition, 1989.

Notes:

Diff = 1000 × (Home BA − Away BA).

Adj = change in batting average due to the ballpark effect (that is, 1000 × (FABA − SDABA)). See Technical Notes for formulae.

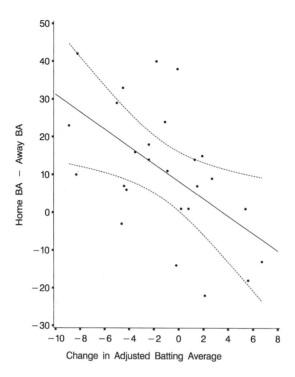

Figure 5.4 Home-Away BA Differences of Superstars
by Change in Adjusted Batting Average
The home-away batting average differences of superstar hitters (except Chuck
Klein) are plotted against the change in the players' adjusted batting averages
due to the ballpark effect. The linear regression line and 95% confidence
band (dashed lines) shows that players who hit much better at home tended
to have their batting averages lowered by the adjustment (since their ballparks
were identified as being favorable to hitters).

points from .300 to .292, falling from 58th place to off the list by a
single hit. On the other hand, Frank McCormick, who played predominantly for the Cincinnati Reds in the 1930s and 1940s, gains 9 points,
from .290 to .299, leaping onto the list in 60th place.

Busch Stadium in St. Louis and Fenway Park in Boston have been
long-standing hitter's parks. Five of the players who dropped off the
fully adjusted list regularly played at one of these two parks. On the
positive side, World Series champion teammates Frank McCormick
and Ernie Lombardi of Cincinnati joined the final adjusted list. Oak-

Table 5.8   Changes in the Top 100 after Ballpark Adjustment

Dropped from List

SDABA Rank	Player	Team	Mid Yr
58	Jim Rice	BosA	1982
71	Joe Torre	MilN	1969
76	Manny Sanguillen	Pit	1970
78	Charlie Gehringer	Det	1933
79	Roger Connor	NYN	1889
83	Jim O'Rourke	NYN	1886
87	Lou Brock	StLN	1970
88	King Kelly	ChiN	1885
90	Cy Seymour	NYN	1905
95	Alex Johnson	—	1970
97	Billy Goodman	BosA	1953
98	Henry Larkin	Phia	1888
99	Enos Slaughter	StLN	1948
100	Curt Flood	StLN	1964

Added to List

FABA Rank	Player	Team	Mid Yr
60	Frank McCormick	Cin	1941
65	Frank Chance	ChiN	1905
78	Rickey Henderson	Oak	1988
80	Ernie Lombardi	Cin	1938
79	Bob Watson	Hou	1975
83	Fred Clarke	Pit	1902
85	Carney Lansford	Oak	1985
87	Babe Herman	Bkn	1931
89	Sherry Magee	PhiN	1911
90	Luis Polonia	Cal	1991
95	Don Mueller	NYN	1953
96	Carl Furillo	Bkn	1952
98	Sam Rice	Was	1925
100	Hugh Duffy	BosN	1894

land Athletics teammates Rickey Henderson and Carney Lansford also place on the list.

Whew! Our hard work is now done. All four adjustments have been made and now a variety of *findings* can be examined. Let's start with the *big* news—the top 100 hitters, especially the top 10.

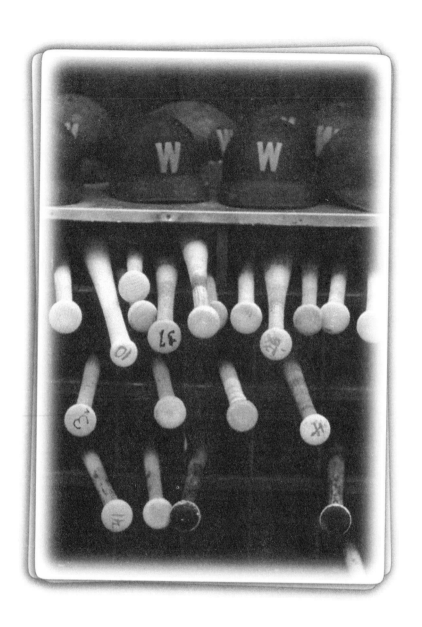

PART II The Findings

Ted Williams

The Adjusted Top 100 Hitters 6

Well . . . we're finally home! The four bases have been tagged, and we're back where we started—home plate. Things aren't the same though. We've *scored* and we have the *right* list of top 100 hitters from 1876 to 1997 (Table 6.1).

Well . . . perhaps, not exactly *right*.

Statistical findings are almost never obtained with certainty and the situation here is not one of those *rare* exceptions. Many modeling assumptions—like the 8000 at bat cutoff and the 200 at bat minimum for including a player in the yearly standard deviation calculation—have been made in this book. Statisticians generally choose an analysis plan from several options, based on different but reasonable modeling assumptions. A random effects model or hierarchical model represent two possible options. Application of these models to batting average comparisons (which are beginning to be published), however, are *much* harder to understand and I believe that the adjusted list of top 100 hitters presented here is the most accurate to date.

Just as in an Olympic event, the competition for the top 100 places has been fierce. Hugh Duffy, the last player on the list, has an adjusted batting average of .2924. Three players—Jim Rice, Joe Torre, and Alex Johnson—just missed with .2923 averages. That's a difference of less than one hit! Altogether, 16 players who missed the list batted within a point of Hugh Duffy's average—a difference of 8 hits or fewer over a career.

The competition has been fierce at the top as well, with Tony Gwynn edging out Ty Cobb by 9 hits over their first 8000 at bats each. Whereas the approximate method of longevity adjustment determination was used for all of the other players who had 8000 or more at bats, the exact method was used for Gwynn and Cobb (see the Technical Note in chapter 2 for details on the methods). Since Gwynn's average dropped in 1997 after his 8000th at bat, the gap would only have been 4 hits if the approximate method were used.

The adjusted averages shown in the table have been standardized to modern play—particularly the years 1973 to 1992, after the introduction of the DH in the American League and before the National League expansion in 1993. This was done by standardizing the league batting average to be .255 in the National League and .2635 in the American League (to account for the DH) and the league standard deviation to be .029. These standardized values reflect the distribution of unadjusted batting averages over the 20-year period.

Table 6.1 The *Adjusted* List of Top 100 Hitters

Rank	Player	Average	Team	Mid Yr	Top 5
1	Tony Gwynn	.342	SD		13
2	Ty Cobb	.340	Det	1916	16
3	Rod Carew	.332	Min	1976	12
4	Joe Jackson	.331	Cle	1915	7
5	Rogers Hornsby	.330	StLN	1923	12
6	Ted Williams	.327	BosA	1949	12
7	Honus Wagner	.326	Pit	1907	13
8	Stan Musial	.325	StLN	1952	16
9	Wade Boggs	.324	BosA		11
10	Nap Lajoie	.322	Cle	1906	7
11	Tris Speaker	.322	Cle	1918	13
12	Pete Browning	.317	Loua	1887	8
13	Willie Mays	.314	SF	1961	7
14	Dan Brouthers	.313	—	1888	11
15	Kirby Puckett	.313	Min	1989	5
16	Babe Ruth	.312	NYA	1926	8
	Tip O'Neill	.312	StLa	1888	5
18	Willie Keeler	.311	NYA	1901	10
19	Joe DiMaggio	.311	NYA	1942	6
20	Tony Oliva	.311	Min	1969	6
21	Jesse Burkett	.310	CleN	1898	7
22	Eddie Collins	.310	ChiA	1917	11
23	George Sisler	.309	StLA	1922	7
24	Lou Gehrig	.308	NYA	1932	9
	Don Mattingly	.308	NYA	1989	4
26	Hank Aaron	.308	Atl	1964	11
27	Billy Hamilton	.308	PhiN	1894	7
28	Paul Molitor	.307	MilA		6
29	George Brett	.307	KC	1983	5
	Paul Waner	.307	Pit	1933	8
31	Bill Terry	.307	NYN	1930	7
32	Al Kaline	.306	Det	1963	7
33	Al Simmons	.306	PhiA	1932	7
34	Pete Rose	.306	Cin	1974	7

(continued)

Table 6.1 The *Adjusted* List of Top 100 Hitters *(continued)*

Rank	Player	Average	Team	Mid Yr	Top 5
35	Cap Anson	.305	ChiN	1888	10
	Tommy Davis	.305	LA	1968	2
37	Joe Medwick	.305	StLN	1939	7
38	Richie Ashburn	.304	PhiN	1955	4
39	Frank Robinson	.304	Cin	1965	9
40	Jackie Robinson	.304	Bkn	1951	4
41	Ed Delahanty	.303	PhiN	1896	9
42	Mickey Mantle	.303	NYA	1959	8
43	Pedro Guerrero	.302	LA	1985	3
44	Ralph Garr	.302	Atl	1974	3
45	Roberto Clemente	.302	Pit	1964	10
46	Bill Madlock	.302	Pit	1980	6
47	Zach Wheat	.302	Bkn	1918	6
	Harry Heilmann	.302	Det	1923	8
49	Edd Roush	.302	Cin	1922	7
50	Matty Alou	.301	Pit	1969	4
51	Tommy Holmes	.301	BosN	1946	3
52	Riggs Stephenson	.300	ChiN	1928	2
53	Ginger Beaumont	.300	Pit	1904	3
54	Sam Crawford	.300	Det	1908	8
55	Barney McCosky	.300	Det	1942	2
56	Sam Thompson	.300	PhiN	1891	5
57	Eddie Murray	.299	Bal	1987	3
	George Kell	.299	Det	1950	7
59	Cecil Cooper	.299	Mil	1981	3
	Frank McCormick	.299	Cin	1942	3
61	Mickey Rivers	.299	NYA	1977	2
62	Billy Williams	.299	ChiN	1968	3
	Al Oliver	.299	Pit	1977	4
	Thurmon Munson	.299	NYA	1975	1
65	Arky Vaughan	.298	Pit	1938	4
66	Frank Chance	.298	ChiN	1905	2
67	Tim Raines	.298	Mon		3
	Heinie Zimmerman	.298	ChiN	1914	2

(continued)

Table 6.1 The *Adjusted* List of Top 100 Hitters (continued)

Rank	Player	Average	Team	Mid Yr	Top 5
69	Jimmie Foxx	.298	PhiA	1935	7
70	Minnie Minoso	.297	ChiA	1956	4
71	Rico Carty	.297	Atl	1973	<u>3</u>
72	Harvey Kuenn	.297	Det	1958	<u>6</u>
73	Luke Appling	.297	ChiA	1940	**3**
	Johnny Mize	.297	StLN	1942	<u>6</u>
75	Steve Garvey	.296	LA	1979	2
76	Orlando Cepeda	.296	SF	1964	2
	Heinie Manush	.296	Was	1930	<u>6</u>
78	Rickey Henderson	.296	Oak		<u>3</u>
	Dick Allen	.296	PhiN	1969	3
80	Ernie Lombardi	.295	Cin	1938	<u>1</u>
81	Bob Watson	.295	Hou	1975	3
	Ross Youngs	.295	NYN	1922	3
83	Fred Clarke	.295	Pit	1902	2
	Ken Griffey, Sr.	.295	Cin	1981	4
85	Carney Lansford	.295	Oak	1985	<u>2</u>
	Dixie Walker	.295	Bkn	1943	**4**
	Babe Herman	.295	Bkn	1931	2
88	Carl Yastrzemski	.295	BosA	1971	**5**
	Sherry Magee	.295	PhiN	1911	<u>4</u>
90	Luis Polonia	.295	Cal	1991	<u>0</u>
91	Elmer Flick	.294	Cle	1903	<u>5</u>
92	Johnny Pesky	.294	BosA	1948	3
93	Lou Piniella	.294	NYA	1974	3
94	Frank Baker	.294	PhiA	1914	3
95	Don Mueller	.294	NYN	1954	2
96	Carl Furillo	.293	Bkn	1952	<u>2</u>
97	Keith Hernandez	.293	StLN	1982	<u>3</u>
98	Sam Rice	.293	Was	1925	0
99	Mike Greenwell	.292	BosA	1991	1
100	Hugh Duffy	.292	BosN	1894	<u>3</u>

Notes: Players are "tied" if their averages agree to 4 decimal places.

Mid-Year = the year that the player was in mid-career (blank for active players).

Top 5 = the number of years that the hitter was among the league's top 5.

Underline = one batting title; **bold** = two or more titles.

Table 6.2   Number of Top 100 Hitters by Franchise—20th Century

Number	Teams
9	NYA, Pit
8	Bkn
7	Det
6	Cin
5	BosA, NYN Giants, StLN, Was
4	BosN, ChiN, Cle, PhiA, PhiN
3	ChiA
2	MilA, StLA
1	Cal, Hou, KC, Mon, SD
0*	Col, Fla, NYN (Mets), Sea, Tex, Tor

Note: *Current franchises only.

See Appendix I for team name abbreviations.

In the traditional top 100 hitters list presented in the introduction, 48 of the players did not win any batting title. Meanwhile, 5 of 21 players with three or more titles were left out. With the fully adjusted list, only 30 top 100 hitters failed to win batting titles and all 21 players with at least three titles are in.

The number of top 5 single-season finishes also goes up dramatically. Whereas 23 players in the traditional list had one or fewer top 5 finishes, only 5 players do in the adjusted list.

Which teams have the most top 100 hitters? Table 6.2 lists the number of players for each franchise. The franchise is listed by the location at which the team played the most years. For example, the Los Angeles Dodgers are listed as Bkn, for Brooklyn.

The New York Yankees and Pittsburgh Pirates lead the charge with great hitters with nine each. An unparalleled five of the Yankees—Ruth, Keeler, DiMaggio, Gehrig, and Mattingly—rank among the top 25! The Dodgers, Detroit, and Cincinnati can also boast of superior numbers of top 100 hitters.

Let's take a closer look at the top 10 . . . I mean top 11 (Table 6.3).

This is a very impressive list of hitters! The elite 11 (Speaker is included since he was less than one adjusted-hit behind Lajoie over 8000 at bats) ranked somewhere among the top 29 players in the traditional list given in the introduction. (Pete Browning, the 12th best hitter,

THE FINDINGS

Table 6.3   The Adjusted Top 11 Hitters

	Player	BA	Top 5	Traditional Rank
1	Tony Gwynn	.342	8/13	16
2	Ty Cobb	.340	10/16	1
3	Rod Carew	.332	7/12	28
4	Joe Jackson	.331	0/7	3
5	Rogers Hornsby	.330	7/12	2
6	Ted Williams	.327	7/12	5
7	Honus Wagner	.326	8/13	29
8	Stan Musial	.325	7/16	24
9	Wade Boggs	.324	5/11	23
10	Nap Lajoie	.322	4/7	18
11	Tris Speaker	.322	1/13	7

Notes:

8/13 = 8 batting titles, 13 times among Top 5 hitters for year.

Traditional rank = rank in the "traditional" unadjusted batting average list.

hit 5 points below Speaker.) The other 18 players from the traditional list all made the top 100 adjusted list, but they were passed by somewhere on the adjustment basepaths.

The top 11 list has all seven players who won at least 7 batting titles. What about the other 4 players? Tris Speaker only won one batting title because Cobb kept beating him. However, he was the only player besides the seven to finish in the top 5 at least 12 times. Nap Lajoie had three *monster* years — 1901, 1904, and 1910 — that are among the best years any player has ever had, to earn his spot. Boggs is still active, but has won 5 titles and has 11 top 5 finishes despite playing in a 14-team league. Joe Jackson was also blocked from winning titles by Cobb and had a shortened career, which limited his number of top 5 finishes.

The stranded players include nineteenth-century stars Ed Delahanty, Billy Hamilton, Dan Brouthers, Pete Browning, Willie Keeler, Jesse Burkett, Sam Thompson, and Cap Anson, Eddie Collins from the 1910s, and Babe Ruth, Harry Heilmann, Bill Terry, George Sisler, Lou Gehrig, Riggs Stephenson, Al Simmons, Paul Waner, and Heinie Manush, who were stars from the 1920s and 1930s. These players were all great batters, but they were *not* top 11 hitters.

Baseball seems to have recognized this distinction already in its Hall of Fame balloting. Three of the top 11 hitters are not in the Hall of Fame: Joe Jackson because of ineligibility (more on this later) and Tony Gwynn and Wage Boggs, because they are still active. All other top 11 hitters were elected in their first or second year of eligibility, except Rogers Hornsby, who needed five ballots (Hall of Fame credentials were less clear back then — he would certainly be selected in a single ballot today).

Ruth and Gehrig, who stood out more for their home run hitting than for batting average, were elected in one ballot. The other 1920s and 1930s players required an average of 9 (range of 4–14) ballots to get in. The nineteenth-century players also need several ballots before being elected. Pete Browning and Riggs Stephenson, both with under 5000 AB, have not been elected to the Hall of Fame.

Tony Gwynn

At the outset of the 1994 season, Gwynn stood as the second best hitter of all time with a .335 average — nearly 6 points behind Ty Cobb's leading .340 mark. With 6190 at bats in the books, first place looked out of reach. Gwynn would have to average .360 over 4 seasons to overtake Cobb. Gwynn was 34 years old and only three players 34 or older even had single-season averages that high. The best adjusted 4-year average for a player starting at age 34 was .340 by Honus Wagner. The real question seemed to be "Would Gwynn be able to hold second place?"

In the strike-shortened season of 1994, the year that cost baseball so dearly in fan support, Tony Gwynn fashioned the best adjusted batting average in baseball history — even better than Ted Williams's famed 1941 season. The distractions of the immanent strike and the season's abrupt end wrested the spotlight from Gwynn's performance, but perhaps allowed him to remain focused on what he does best — hit.

That August, with the baseball strike on, the marquee sign outside the Hall of Fame in Cooperstown, New York, stood frozen on the unchanging league standings. No one seemed to know when or if the strike would end. I overheard a man tell his young son "Look at it. This may be how baseball ends."

That's how the season did end. With no World Series for the first time since 1904, baseball would not end in triumph, but in failure. However, Gwynn's adjusted 1994 batting average — .378 — cut his gap with Cobb by nearly half.

In 1995, Gwynn won his second straight batting title with an adjusted .361 average — becoming the only player other than Cobb to hit above .360 for two consecutive years. Gwynn had closed the gap to 1.3 points — a 9-hit deficit over his career.

In 1996, Gwynn had a partial Achilles heel tear in mid-season, making it painful to put his full weight on it. Gwynn fell 4 at bats short of the minimum number to qualify for the batting title. However, even if those 4 missing at bats were all *outs*, Gwynn's average would still have been the best, and a baseball rule which lay dormant since its approval in 1952, rightly awarded him his third straight title. However, Gwynn had only closed the gap by 2 hits — he was still 7 behind.

Gwynn's 405th at bat in 1997 would bring him to 8000 career at bats. Because of his Achilles heel tear in 1996, *Baseball Weekly*'s March 11th, 1997 cover article raised the question "Can Gwynn Bounce Back — From .353?" He would need to hit .358 to surpass Cobb. Only one player 37 years old or older had done that well over a full season — Ted Williams, with an adjusted .373 average in 1957. The next best was Rod Carew's .340 average in 1983.

Gwynn took the season by storm, batting nearly .400 through July 1 and pushing past Cobb. The University of North Carolina, where I am a professor, sent out a press release. With 100 at bats to go, I wanted to share my excitement about Gwynn's day-by-day performance with fellow fans. The story received TV, radio, and print coverage in North Carolina and at least 3 baseball cities including San Diego.

Gwynn ultimately won by 9 hits. My plan was to be in San Diego for the 8000th at bat. The night before my flight, a friend called with the news that Gwynn was on the cover of *Sports Illustrated* and identified as "The Best Hitter Since Ted Williams." I was traveling to San Diego because I believed him to be "the all-time best."

I met Gwynn the day of his historic 8000th at bat. He is as nice a person as he is a great hitter. He listened to a summary of my batting average adjustment method, thanked me for coming, and gave me a signed and *used* bat! Gwynn became the 105th player to get an 8000th at bat — for him, a single. Perhaps that ball — thrown back to the Padre dugout — will be enshrined in Cooperstown one day.

In his 1990 book *Men At Work*, George Will chose Tony Gwynn as his "featured" hitter in his chapter "The Batter." In it, Will describes the relentless videotaping that Gwynn has done throughout his career in order to maximize his hitting potential. The years of effort seem to have paid off.

Ty Cobb

Ty Cobb won 12 official batting titles — Gwynn has won 8. So, how can Gwynn be a better hitter than Cobb? Well . . . did Cobb truly "win" 12 titles?

Standard baseball reference books provide three different answers. The *Baseball Encyclopedia* says 12, *The Sports Encyclopedia: Baseball* says 11, and *Total Baseball* (1989) says 10. The *World Almanac* for 1993 also gives 12. What accounts for the differences? All sources agree that Cobb won batting championships in 1907–9, 1911–13, 1915, and 1917–19. The years in conflict are 1910 and 1914. In 1910, Cobb, who was not well liked among the players, was in a tight batting title chase with the popular Nap Lajoie. *Total Baseball* (1989, p. 692) describes the episode this way:

> At the end of the season, most people thought Nap had won, based on his getting seven hits in a doubleheader on the final day of the season. There was talk that the opposing [St. Louis] Browns had let him get a number of bunts by playing back, so that the hated Cobb would lose. However, the AL office went over their figures and gave Cobb the title, .385 to .384. Nearly eighty years later, Pete Palmer discovered a critical error: a game in which Cobb had two hits in three at-bats had been entered twice. . . . The League Office discovered this mistake soon after its official announcement that Cobb had won the batting title, because the double entry was corrected for all the other Detroit players. However, Ban Johnson [the Baseball Commissioner] had made a big deal out of how carefully his people had checked the figures in order to settle the controversy, so they kept quiet about the gaffe, leaving Cobb the winner.

Both *The Sports Encyclopedia: Baseball* and *Total Baseball* (1989, edited by John Thorn and Pete Palmer) credit the batting championship to Nap Lajoie. *Total Baseball* (1989) also credits Eddie Collins, rather than Ty Cobb, with the 1914 batting championship. Collins batted .344 while Cobb batted .368. However, Cobb only had 345 AB. Current rules require that a player have a minimum of 3.1 plate appearances per scheduled game. Cobb's total falls short of the current required amount, although that requirement was not in force in 1914. (Ted Williams was not "officially" awarded the 1954 AL championship in spite of having exceeded Cobb's plate appearances.)

For accuracy and fairness across time, *Total Baseball* (1989) lists will be used to determine the number of batting championships and times among the single-season top 5 hitters. Thus, Cobb "had" 10 titles in an 8-team league. If one adjusts for the ballpark effect, Tony Gwynn would have won the 1993 batting title, not Colorado's Andres Galarraga—thereby giving Gwynn 9 titles in a league with 12–14 teams, compared to the 8-team league Cobb played in. Now, suddenly, Cobb and Gwynn again look extremely close to each other.

Rod Carew

Rod Carew is the all-time top hitting second baseman. Overall, Carew won 7 batting titles and finished among the top 5 hitters 12 times. From 1972 to 1978 he won 6 of 7 titles, losing the 7th by a mere 2 points. Rod Carew provides a strong demonstration of the importance of the adjustments. In the "unadjusted" list, Carew places only 28th, behind such players as Riggs Stephenson and Heinie Manush, who have only one batting title between them. Even after mean-adjustment, Carew places but 6th. Only after all adjustments are made is Carew's true batting ability manifest.

Carew's best years were with the Minnesota Twins at hitter-friendly Metropolitan Stadium. Like Carew, 5 other top 11 hitters—Boggs, Cobb, Lajoie, Musial, and Williams—played at very good hitters' parks. How unusual is this? These 6 players all had their averages "lowered" by at least 5 points with the ballpark adjustment. Of the other 253 qualifying players whose fully adjusted batting averages I calculated, only 28 "lost" at least 5 points with the ballpark adjustment. This is a statistically significant finding using the *maximal* chi-square test (it is more involved than the usual chi-square because the *decision* to split the group at the 5-point mark was determined from examining the data—Miller and Siegmund [1982]).

This raises a question. Does a very good hitter, nurtured in the friendly surroundings of a strong hitter's park, develop a confidence that leads him to become a great hitter? The benefits of positive feedback in education are widely known. Can a few extra hits per year do the same for ballplayers — reaping an even larger return from the confidence they exude? The answer appears to be "Yes."

Joe Jackson

Joe Jackson is the only retired top 11 hitter not in the Hall of Fame. Jackson is the somewhat mysterious player who was banned from baseball after he admitted to fixing — along with 7 other Chicago White Sox players — the 1919 World Series against heavy underdog Cincinnati. This expulsion from baseball stopped an outstanding hitting career in its tracks. There have now been questions raised whether Jackson knew what he was signing in his admission of guilt. His mystique has grown with the 1989 movie *Field of Dreams*, where he emerges from the cornfield to play ball again.

Recent questions have been raised about Jackson's actual play during the 1919 World Series. Overall, he hit .375 so questions about his performance center around "key" at bats or plays in the field. In a 1993 *American Statistician* article, Jay Bennett asked the question "Did Shoeless Joe Jackson Throw the 1919 World Series?" Bennett used a system known as "Player Game Percentage," which he and John Flueck had developed, to evaluate the contribution of every play to the probability of the team winning the game. By their system, Jackson was the third best player for the Chicago White Sox in the Series and seventh best overall with a net positive impact for his team. After several additional analyses, Bennett concludes:

> Almost every statistical view of the game data supports the contention that Joe Jackson played to his full potential in the 1919 World Series.

Jackson is also the only top 11 player who didn't win a batting championship. This is largely due to his misfortune of playing at the same time as Ty Cobb, who kept narrowly defeating him. Using adjusted single season averages, Cobb beat Jackson .353 to .347 in 1911, .352 to .348 in 1912, .350 to .343 in 1913, and .338 to .328 in 1919.

Before his expulsion from baseball Jackson finally slipped past an in-jured Cobb, .336 to .291 in 1920, only to finish second to George Sisler, who hit .350.

Rogers Hornsby

Rogers Hornsby is the top right-handed hitter and 2d second baseman in the top 11. As did Rod Carew, Hornsby won 7 batting titles. Six were won consecutively, from 1920 to 1925. Hornsby also showed him-self to be a formidable home run threat, with 11 top 5 finishes. This strong combination of both hitting for average and for the fences is unique among second basemen.

Baseball aficionados know that most of the greatest hitters are left-handed. In spite of the fact that 59% of the players eligible for consid-eration in the top 100 are right-handers, eight of the top 11 hitters are left-handed. In general, left-handed hitters hit better against right-handed pitchers, while right-handed hitters hit better against left-handed pitchers. Managers often use this statistical fact in the late innings when bringing in relief pitchers.

One may want to adjust for player batting handedness in addition to the four adjustments made in this book to obtain "true" batting ability. In the 1980s, left-handed hitters benefited by 6 batting points over right-handed hitters, since 70% of the pitchers were right-handed (see Appendix II). Assuming this advantage to have been consistent throughout this century, Hornsby would slip past Carew and Jackson into third place and Wagner would take fourth behind him.

Honus Wagner

Honus Wagner was an 8-time batting champion who played shortstop, predominantly for the Pittsburgh Pirates. In addition to his superior batting average, Wagner won 7 doubles, 5 RBI, and 5 stolen base titles. Wagner is also considered to have been one of the best defensive short-stops of his era.

The most remarkable thing about Wagner was that he was a *short-stop*. (Wagner became a full-time shortstop in his seventh season of play. Prior to that he split his time between the outfield and sev-

Table 6.4 Top Hitters by Position and Advantage over Other Top Hitters at Position

| | | Points Above | |
Position	Hitter	Next Best	Other Top 10
OF	Tony Gwynn*	15	31
1B	Dan Brouthers	4	10
2B	Rod Carew	2	32
SS	Honus Wagner	28	37
3B	Wade Boggs	16	29
C	Thurmon Munson	4	13
UT	Paul Molitor	3	12

Note: *Because there are three outfield positions, Gwynn is compared to the 4th best and the average of the next best 29 outfielders.

eral infield positions.) His batting average is a whopping 28 points better than the next best hitting shortstop, Arky Vaughan—also a Pirate. No other player so completely dominates the remaining hitters at his position, as Table 6.4 shows.

While in high school in the 1970s, I played simulation baseball with my brothers Kevin and Pat using the all-time greatest players. We adjusted for the league averages and used an ad hoc approach that roughly performed the standard deviation adjustment, so we had a reasonable idea as to who the all-time greats really were.

To be fair in picking players, we randomly determined the order of the first three picks. Each successive three picks then went in reverse order to the previous three. The early picks went:

Kevin—Babe Ruth
Mike—Ty Cobb
Pat—Ted Williams

Pat—Honus Wagner
Mike—Rogers Hornsby
Kevin—Walter Johnson

Kevin—Hank Aaron
Mike—Stan Musial
Pat—Lou Gehrig

Pat, the youngest at age 12, made outstanding choices. He realized the value of acquiring Wagner early because there was no shortstop like him. I sometimes wonder about my own first pick. Should I have chosen Williams over Cobb — or perhaps Wagner over Cobb? Williams certainly provided the best hitting for high average/slugging percentage combination of the three. One feature of our league was that each player was played relative to his career number of at bats. With Cobb, I got almost 50% more playing time than if I had chosen Williams. But . . . back to the point I wanted to make — Wagner is among the very best players in the game, especially considering that he was a shortstop. One other note: four of the original five inductees into the Hall of Fame (Ruth, Cobb, Wagner, and Johnson) were among our first six choices — and Christy Mathewson was picked soon after.

Ted Williams

Except for several war years, Ted Williams played in the Boston Red Sox outfield from 1939 to 1960. Ted won 7 batting titles, narrowly lost one by a fraction of a point, and missed another by lacking the required number of plate appearances. Williams was also a great power hitter, winning 4 home run and 9 slugging titles. Lou Boudreau, manager of the Cleveland Indians, patented an infield shift against him, with the shortstop positioned on the first base side of second base. Fans often wonder what batting average Williams could have batted if he tried for more opposite field hits — which would likely have resulted in more hits overall but fewer extra-base hits. The trade-off between hitting for average and hitting for power is a choice that all players must make during their careers. Williams mostly continued to pull the ball in spite of the shift.

I wonder about an unavoidable disadvantage that Ted Williams faced. Williams spent the better part of 5 years in military service — 1943–45 in World War II and 1952–53 in the Korean War. These years, particularly the first three, were in the prime of Williams's career. What would he have hit during these years and how would that have affected his lifetime batting average? According to my estimates, his average would go up 3 points, pushing him past Hornsby into fifth place. Let's look at the batting average of the top 11 hitters in 1000 AB intervals (Table 6.5).

Based on his average number of at bats in the 3 years prior to and after each of Williams's two military tours of duty, I estimate that Williams would have had 515 AB per year in 1943–45 and 423 AB per year in 1952–53. These "missing at bats" are included in obtaining his average during 1000 AB periods for Table 6.5. From the table, we can see that the missing at bats came between 2001–4000 AB and 6001–8000 AB. For the first 2000 AB and 4001–6000 AB combined, Williams batted 4 points better than the average of the rest of the top 11 (.330 to .326). Assuming the same advantage during 2001–4000, he would have batted .343 during that stretch. This is close to the .3385 average obtained by combining the .344 and .333 averages determined for 104 and 351 AB during the two respective 1000 AB periods. Thus, we will "extend" these batting averages to the full 1000 at bats. The number of AB already in the estimates for 6001–7000 and 7001–8000 are large enough to provide reasonable estimates. Averaging the eight averages gives an estimated overall batting average of .3303. This military service–adjusted batting average would move Williams past Hornsby into 4th place. (If .343 is used instead of .3385 for at bats 2001–4000, Williams's BA would be .3308, leaving him still in 4th place.)

Table 6.5 reinforces the argument that Ted Williams was the greatest older hitter of all time. From 7001 to 9000 AB, Williams aver-

Table 6.5   Batting Averages of Top 11 Hitters during 1000 At Bat Periods

AB	Gwynn	Cobb	Carew	Jackson	Hornsby
1000	.332	.316	.305	.342*	.324
2000	.330	.338	.329	.341*	.303
3000	.352	.360*	.327	.320	.346
4000	.340	.353*	.352	.320	.345
5000	.319	.346	.341		.360*
6000	.332	.347	.354*		.310
7000	.366*	.350	.323		.343
8000	.356*	.314	.321		.306
9000		.329	.318		
10000		.293			

(Continued on next page)

aged over .343, a staggering 27 points over his nearest competitor, Ty Cobb. Tony Gwynn, the best hitter for at bats 6001–8000 is still coming, however!

Stan Musial

Stan Musial played outfield and first base for St. Louis from 1941 to 1963. Musial tied Cobb by having 16 years among the top 5 hitters. Musial had the third best start in baseball history. Let's look at the top hitters after 2000 AB (Table 6.6).

The early success of these players all included winning batting championships, except for Joe Jackson. Five players, including Musial, either maintained their early success (within 3 points) or improved on it at 4000 AB. These 5 players had the highest at bat totals in the list and all made our final top 10.

Wade Boggs

Wade Boggs is still active going into the 1998 season, but already has 8000 AB. Thus, he has already earned his spot as the 9th best hitter.

Williams	Wagner	Musial	Boggs	Speaker	Lajoie
.305	.293	**.332**	**.341**	.306	.292
.356*	.324	**.339**	.333	.317	.300
.344	.314	.319	**.348**	.343	**.349**
.333	.328	**.341**	**.352**	.328	.342
.337	.341	.329	.309	**.351**	.332
.322	**.352**	.327	.300	.292	.295
.304	.341	.309	.296	.314	**.344**
.343	.320	.302	.310	**.324**	**.324**
.348*	.286	.323		.304	.281
.298*	.284	.267		.279	

Notes: Averages in bold in top 40% of group; * = the best.

Underlined averages are based on the estimated at bats and averages had Williams played ball and not served in the military (see text for details). Going down the column, averages shown are based on 104, 351, 641, and 614 AB, respectively.

Table 6.6 Top 10 Hitters at 2000 At Bats

Rank	Player	AB	2000	4000	End
1	Joe Jackson	4981	.341	.331	.331
2	Wade Boggs	8453+	.337	.343	.324
3	Stan Musial	10972	.336	.333	.325
4	Tony Gwynn	8187+	.331	.339	.342
5	Tony Oliva	6301	.330	.322	.311
6	Ted Williams	7706	.330	.333	.327
7	Don Mattingly	7003	.330	.325	.308
8	Pete Browning	4820	.328	.316	.317
9	Tip O'Neill	4255	.327	.314	.312
10	Ty Cobb	11434	.327	.342	.340

Note: End = end of career or 8000 AB for longtime players.

While this is an outstanding ranking, Boggs was ahead of Gwynn and Cobb at the 4000 AB milestone. Let's look at the rest of the top 10 after 4000 at bats (Table 6.7).

Eight players from this list are in our final top 11 (Sisler and Mattingly drop out). Boggs's average at 8000 AB had dropped 19 points from what it was at 4000 AB, causing him to slip to 9th place. This decline happened because Boggs hit 39 points worse (.304 compared to .343) in the second 4000 at bats than he did in the first.

Table 6.7 Top 10 Hitters at 4000 At Bats

Rank	Player	AB	2000	4000	End
1	Wade Boggs	8453+	.337	.343	.324
2	Ty Cobb	11434	.327	.342	.340
3	Tony Gwynn	8187+	.331	.339	.342
4	Stan Musial	10972	.336	.333	.325
5	Ted Williams	7706	.330	.333	.327
6	Joe Jackson	4981	.341	.331	.331
7	George Sisler	8267	.322	.330	.309
8	Rogers Hornsby	8173	.314	.330	.330
9	Rod Carew	9315	.317	.328	.332
10	Don Mattingly	7003	.330	.325	.308

Note: End = end of career or 8000 AB for longtime players.

THE FINDINGS

What about the players from Table 6.7 who failed to make the final top 11? Sisler dropped 21 points to fall off the list. *Baseball's Hall of Fame, Cooperstown, Where the Legends Live Forever* (p. 234) provided the reason for this decline:

> After his great year of 1922, Sisler suffered a violent sinus attack that caused double vision and sidelined him for the entire 1923 season. He rejoined the Browns in 1924 and although he batted .345 one year and .340 another, he was never again — by his own admission — the same player he had been before his illness.

Don Mattingly, who dropped 17 points from the 4000 AB milestone to the end of his career, is the only other player to drop out of the top 11 from the 4000 AB top 10 list. In Mattingly's case a nagging back injury appears to have been the reason.

Nap Lajoie

Just as some players would like to prune the last several years from their careers, Lajoie would be comparatively much better in the standings by dropping a few of his early years. At the 2000 AB mark, Lajoie was 31 points out of the top 10 hitters list. He wasn't even in the top 100! Then, in 1901, he crafted the sixth best batting average of all time, (.372), lifting his average up 16 points. During the next 5 years, Lajoie averaged .338, pulling his overall average up 12 more points to .324. From 1907 to 1909, it dipped 6 points. In 1910, at age 35, Lajoie attained the 12th best single-season batting average in the controversial batting title race with Cobb, regaining 4 of the lost points. Table 6.8 shows the top 11 players after dropping the first 2000 AB.

The players are exactly the same as the final top 11, although the order is slightly different here. Lajoie and Wagner showed the greatest improvement from their early careers. On the other hand Jackson, Musial, and Boggs fell off their early pace. Jackson, Musial, and Boggs were the three best over the first 2000 at bats (Table 6.6), so one might expect their performance to drop off a bit. However, even more than that, they were on the underside of their fellow top hitters from that point on.

To emphasize this point further, say you have 10 equally good hitters on a team and they all play an equal amount of time. You play

Table 6.8 Top 11 Hitters after Dropping the First 2000 AB

Rank	Player	BA	Diff
1	Tony Gwynn	.345	3
2	Ty Cobb	.345	5
3	Rod Carew	.336	4
4	Honus Wagner	.335	9
5	Rogers Hornsby	.329	−1
6	Nap Lajoie	.331	9
7	Ted Williams	.326	−1
8	Joe Jackson	.324	−7
9	Tris Speaker	.325	3
10	Stan Musial	.321	−4
11	Wade Boggs	.319	−5

Note: Diff = change in BA after dropping the first 2000 AB.

an 80-game season (in the analogy representing 8000 at bats for each player). Would you expect that the three leading hitters over the first 20 games to become three of the four worst players from then on? Sure, you may not expect them to continue to be the best, because all the players are very good. If the first 20 games were completely erased and forgotten somehow, you would expect that the three would be average, not subaverage. Given their early success, if they played like an average top 11 player for the final 60 games, Jackson, Boggs, and Musial would have finished 3d, 4th, and 5th, respectively, and not 4th, 8th, and 9th. Thus, something deeper must be going on here. Either pitchers particularly bear down on players with early success in a way that persists compared to the Johnny-come-latelies or the psychological stress of starting out so well and then falling off that pace takes its toll . . . and don't forget the endless questions from the media!

Tris Speaker

Tris Speaker, like Ty Cobb and Joe Jackson, was in his prime in the American League in the second decade of the twentieth century. As a result of Cobb's stranglehold on the batting championship, Jackson

Table 6.9   Yearly Batting Average Ranks for Top AL Players, 1910–22

Year	Cobb	Jackson	Lajoie	Speaker	Collins	Sisler	%LHP
1910	2		1	3	4		23
1911	1	2		10	4		23
1912	1	2	4	3	5		18
1913	1	2	6	3	4		28
1914		3	—	2	1		31
1915	1	7	—	4	2		30
1916	2	3		1	6	8	32
1917	1	10		3	—	2	25
1918	1			4		3	23
1919	1	4		—	10	3	25
1920	10	3		2	5	1	26
1921	2			5	10	4	25
1922	2			4	10	1	20

Notes:

Blanks indicate that the player did not have enough at bats to qualify for the batting title under modern rules.

— indicates that the player failed to make the top 10 that year.

% LHP = percentage of innings pitched by left-handed pitchers.

and Speaker only had a single batting championship between them. A fourth top 11 hitter, Nap Lajoie, was also in the autumn of his career then. Table 6.6 shows the ranking of these players (and two other .300 hitters who played for the AL then).

The dominance of Cobb, Jackson, and Speaker is striking. From 1911 to 1917, each player was always in the year's top 10. (In 1914, Cobb is not ranked because he had only 345 AB. He was the "official" batting champion, with a .368 average, but failed to have at least 3.1 plate appearances per game.) In three of the years, the trio took the top three spots (1912, 1913, and 1916). Second basemen Nap Lajoie and Eddie Collins were also batting standouts during this era. The year 1912 stands out as a classic year in which all 5 players were in the top 5!

The percentage of innings pitched by left-handers is also shown. In 1912, left-handers pitched only 18% of the innings. It's no wonder that this powerful combo of left-handed hitters fared so well (only Lajoie was right-handed)! The managers must have caught on, since the percentage of left-handers jumped to a new American League high of 28% in 1913 and averaged 27% from 1913 to 1922. (Note: left-handers only pitched 20% of the innings in the first three of Cobb's championship years — 1907–9.)

Honus Wagner

Top Hitters by Position

7

In the last chapter we looked at the top 100 hitters overall. Now we will look at them in more detail, position by position. Not surprisingly, the top hitter list is stacked full of outfielders and first basemen because the fielding demands on those positions are much less than for the remaining positions. The top 10 hitters for each position will be shown, even if they were not in the top 100 overall. Thus, 29 additional players, all those with averages below .293 except for Mike Greenwell and Hugh Duffy, are in the lists that follow.

A new player performance summary, the *batting average trend*, which will be used in the lists, will be defined now.

Batting Average Trend

Batting statistics have typically used a single number to assess overall hitting ability—the batting average. This number is just an average though and does not always reflect the player's ability throughout his career. We saw that the combined batting average of longtime players (> 8000 AB) rose for the first 5000 AB, stabilized for 2000 AB, and dropped a little in the final 1000 AB. However, many individual players' patterns differ from this composite trend. Thus, I developed a method, the batting average trend, to get a snapshot for an individual player.

To obtain a player's batting average trend, one must first determine his fully adjusted batting average at 2000 AB, 4000 AB, and at the end of his career (or at 8000 AB for longtime players). Comparisons are then made between the progressive averages (from 2000 to 4000 AB and from 4000 AB to the career end). If the average goes up by at least

Table 7.1 Batting Average Trends of Three Selected Outfielders

		At Bats		
Outfielder	Trend	2000	4000	End
Ken Griffey Sr.	BB	.311	.305	.295
Fred Clarke	RR	.297	.294	.295
Dixie Walker	SS	.272	.287	.295

5 points, the player is given an S for having a *"surging"* average. If the average drops by at least 5 points, the player is given a B for being "good out of the *box.*" If the average changes by less than 5 points in either direction, the player is given an R for being "solid as a *rock.*" (To determine the trend, averages are carried out to 4 decimal places, if necessary.) Carl Yastrzemski's average was .290 at 2000 AB, .301 at 4000 AB, and .295 at the end of his career. Thus, Yastrzemski is a surger-boxer (SB). Table 7.1 shows three other outfielders with the same adjusted average as Yastrzemski with very different trends.

So what good is batting average trend? I use it in three ways myself.

First, it demonstrates that players' careers develop differently. In chapter 2 we saw that the average profile was for a player's average to rise, stabilize, and then perhaps drop somewhat. This profile is consistent with the SR or SB pattern. However, some players do not follow this "average" profile. The 132 players shown in the tables in this chapter have the following distribution of batting average trends: SR (25%); RR (19%); SB (13%); RB (12%); BR (11%); SS (8%); BB (8%); BB (5%); and BS (0%).

Second, it can be interesting to examine individual player trends. Tony Oliva, a BB player, started having a fabulous career. However, knee injuries caused a rapid demise in his hitting ability. On the other hand, Roberto Clemente had a steadily improving career, as indicated by his SS trend.

Finally, it seems to be highly related to election into the Hall of Fame. Players who "surge" somewhere during their career are more likely to have been elected to the Hall of Fame than those who never "surge" as Table 7.2 shows.

Table 7.2   Batting Average Trends and Election into the Hall of Fame

Trend	Trend Categories	Outfielder	Non-Outfielder
"Surge" Somewhere	SB, SR, SS, RS	21/25 84%	19/28 68%
"Box" First	BB, BR	3/8 38%	1/11 9%
Other	RB, RR	9/18 50%	9/22 41%

Note: This table gives the Hall of Fame status of 120 of the 132 top players by position given in this chapter. The remaining players are ineligible for Hall of Fame consideration.

A Guide to the Tables in This Chapter

Player — Hall of Fame players are shown in *italics*.

BA — Fully adjusted batting average.

Team — Team for which the player played the most games. A summary of team name abbreviations is given in Appendix I.

H — Batting handedness, **R** = Right, **L** = Left, **B** = Both.

Top 5 — 8/13 = 8 championships, 13 times in Top 5.

Underline = one championship; **Bold** = two championships.

Trend — Batting average trend of players. This is explained above.

In brief, the first letter is the trend from 2000 at bats to 4000 at bats and the second letter represents the BA change from 4000 at bats to the end of the player's career, or 8000 at bats for longtime players. S is used for a 5 or more point increase in batting average, B for a 5-point or greater drop, and R if the change is less than 5 points in either direction.

Outfielders

The Top 30 Outfielders

Tony Gwynn and Ty Cobb dominate the outfield list, just as they do the top 100 list overall (Table 7.3). Jackson, Williams, Musial, and Speaker, whom we have already discussed, form the second cluster of outfielders. Altogether, these six outstanding hitters combined for 33 batting titles and 77 top 5 finishes. Interestingly, all of them except for Gwynn have finished among the top 5 home run hitters at least 3 times.

The next 10 best hitting outfielders (#7 through #16) include the preeminent singles hitter and the leading home run hitters. Career home run leaders Hank Aaron, Babe Ruth, and Willie Mays and Yankee star Joe DiMaggio combined for 22 home run championships and 49 top 5 home run finishes to go along with their 6 batting titles and 30 top 5 batting finishes. How well could these home run hitters have batted if they had tried to make contact more and swung for the fences less? (Ted Williams, who hit 15–20 points better than Mays, Ruth, and Aaron, is the preeminent hitter-slugger.)

In sharp contrast to the 6′2″, 215-pound Babe Ruth is 5′4″, 140-pound Wee Willie Keeler, the "hit 'em where they ain't" kid, who

Table 7.3 Top Hitting Outfielders

	Player	BA	Years	Team	H	BA Top 5	HR Top 5	Trend
1	Tony Gwynn	.342	1982–	SD	L	8/13		SR
2	Ty Cobb*	.340	1905–28	Det	L	10/16	6	SR
3	Joe Jackson	.331	1908–20	Cle	L	7	3	BR
4	Ted Williams	.327	1939–60	BosA	L	7/12	4/9	RB
5	Stan Musial	.325	1941–63	StLN	L	7/16	4	RB
6	Tris Speaker*	.322	1907–28	Cle	L	13	5	SR
7	Willie Mays*	.314	1951–73	SF	R	7	4/10	SR
8	Kirby Puckett	.313	1984–95	Min	R	5		SR
9	Babe Ruth	.312	1914–35	NYA	L	8	12/16	RR
	Tip O'Neill	.312	1883–92	StLa	R	5	2	BR
11	Willie Keeler	.311	1892–1910	NYA	L	10		SB
12	Joe DiMaggio	.311	1936–51	NYA	R	4	10	SB
13	Tony Oliva	.311	1962–76	Min	L	3/6		BB
14	Jesse Burkett	.310	1890–1905	CleN	L	3/7	1	SR
15	Hank Aaron	.308	1954–76	Atl	R	11	4/13	SR
16	Billy Hamilton*	.308	1888–1901	PhiN	L	7		RR
17	Paul Waner	.307	1926–45	Pit	L	4/8		BR
18	Al Kaline	.306	1953–74	Det	R	7		RS
19	Al Simmons	.306	1924–44	PhiA	R	7	7	SB
20	Pete Rose	.306	1963–86	Cin	B	4/7		SR
21	Tommy Davis	.305	1959–76	LA	R	2		BR
22	Joe Medwick	.305	1932–48	StLN	R	7	3	SR
23	Richie Ashburn*	.304	1948–62	PhiN	L	4		RR
24	Frank Robinson	.304	1956–76	Cin	R	9	10	RS
25	Ed Delahanty	.303	1888–1903	PhiN	R	9	6	SS
26	Mickey Mantle*	.303	1951–68	NYA	B	8	5/9	SB
27	Ralph Garr	.302	1968–80	Atl	L	3		RB
28	Roberto Clemente	.302	1955–72	Pit	R	4/10		SS
29	Zach Wheat	.302	1909–27	Bkn	L	6	2	RS
	Harry Heilmann	.302	1914–32	Det	R	4/8	4	SS
31	Edd Roush	.302	1913–31	Cin	L	7		RB
32	Matty Alou*	.301	1960–74	Pit	L	4		SR
33	Tommy Holmes	.301	1942–52	BosN	L	3	1	SB

(continued)

Table 7.3   Top Hitting Outfielders (continued)

	Player	BA	Years	Team	H	BA Top 5	HR Top 5	Trend
34	Ginger Beaumont*	.300	1899–1910	Pit	L	<u>3</u>	1	RR
35	*Sam Crawford*	.300	1899–1917	Det	L	8	6	RS
36	Barney McCosky*	.300	1939–53	Det	L	2		RR
37	*Sam Thompson*	.300	1885–1906	PhiN	L	<u>5</u>	4	RR
38	Mickey Rivers*	.299	1970–84	NYA	L	2		RR
39	*Billy Williams*	.299	1959–76	ChiN	L	<u>3</u>	5	SR
40	Al Oliver*	.299	1968–85	Pit	L	<u>4</u>		RS
41	Tim Raines	.298	1979–	Mon	B	<u>3</u>		SB
42	Minnie Minoso	.297	1949–80	ChiA	R	4		RB
43	*Heinie Manush*	.296	1923–39	Was	L	<u>6</u>		SR
44	Rickey Henderson	.296	1979–	Oak	R	3		RR
45	*Ross Youngs*	.295	1917–26	NYN	L	3		BB
46	*Fred Clarke*	.295	1894–1915	Pit	L	2		RR
47	Ken Griffey Sr.	.295	1973–91	Cin	R	3		BB
48	Dixie Walker	.295	1931–49	Bkn	L	4		SS
	Babe Herman	.295	1926–45	Bkn	L	2	2	RB
50	*Carl Yastrzemski*	.295	1961–83	BosA	L	3/5	<u>3</u>	SB
	Sherry Magee	.295	1904–19	PhiN	R	<u>4</u>	3	RR
52	*Elmer Flick*	.294	1898–1910	Cle	L	<u>5</u>	1	RR
53	Lou Piniella	.294	1964–84	NYA	R	3		BR
54	Don Mueller	.294	1948–59	NYN	L	2		RR
55	Carl Furillo	.293	1946–60	Bkn	R	<u>2</u>		RR
56	*Sam Rice*	.293	1915–34	Was	L			BR
57	Mike Greenwell	.292	1985–96	BosA	L	1		BR
58	*Hugh Duffy**	.292	1888–1906	BosN	R	<u>3</u>	3	SB

Notes: See Guide to the Tables in the beginning of the chapter.

* indicates that the player was primarily a centerfielder.

Players are "tied" if their averages agree to 4 decimal places.

sprayed singles into the gaps between the fielders. Nineteenth-century stolen base leader Billy Hamilton was also predominantly a singles hitter.

The remaining top 30 outfielders, from Paul Waner down to Harry Heilmann, span the different eras of baseball well, except for the 1980s and 1990s. Pete Rose and Ralph Garr, the most recent players in the group, were in mid-career in 1974. The group includes sluggers Frank Robinson and Mickey Mantle as well as singles hitters Richie Ashburn, Rose, and Garr. It also includes three players — Ed Delahanty, Harry Heilmann, and Roberto Clemente — who had steadily surging careers. Unfortunately, both Delahanty and Clemente met untimely deaths while still playing.

As a whole, the top 30 outfielders are a very impressive group. Altogether, they account for over one-third (82 of 233) of the batting titles in major league history. They averaged 2.7 titles and 7.8 top 5 finishes.

Not all outfield positions were created equal. The centerfield position is typically the most demanding defensively, requiring the greatest range. Of the 58 top hitting outfielders, only 14 were centerfielders. These players have been highlighted with asterisks in Table 7.3. Cobb was the premier hitting centerfielder. Edd Roush, Matty Alou, and Ginger Beaumont, while barely missing the top 30 outfielders list, are among the top 10 *centerfielders*. The three centerfielders who had at least 10 top 5 home run finishes, are among the greatest players of the game — Willie Mays, Joe DiMaggio, and Mickey Mantle.

The Whole Group of Outfielders

There has never been another outfield like the Philadelphia Phillies had in the 1890s. From 1891 to 1895, they had three Hall of Fame outfielders among the top 100 hitters — Ed Delahanty, Billy Hamilton, and Sam Thompson. From 1893 to 1895 all three were among the league's top 5 hitters, while Philadelphia won all three team batting titles. In only three other years was the starting outfield of one team stocked with three top 100 hitters. In 1916, Ty Cobb, Sam Crawford, and Harry Heilmann provided Tiger fans with "hitters in the outfield." In 1923–24, Heinie Manush joined Cobb and Heilmann for the final two times in major league history. Perhaps surprisingly, none of these eight teams won their league's pennant.

The golden period for top hitting outfielders was from 1956 to 1976, when at least 12 players were active and peaking at 15 from 1970 to 1974. The National League was particularly packed with great outfielders. During the 1950s, Stan Musial, Richie Ashburn, Carl Furillo, and Don Mueller were quickly joined by Willie Mays, Hank Aaron, Roberto Clemente, and Frank Robinson, and later by Tommy Davis and Billy Williams. Matty, Alou, Pete Rose, Ralph Garr, and Al Oliver joined the ranks in the 1960s. From 1950 to 1974, 11 different top-hitting NL outfielders accounted for 22 of the 25 batting titles.

Table 7.4 Top Hitting First Basemen

	Player	BA	Years	Team	H	BA Top 5	HR Top 5	Trend
1	*Dan Brouthers*	.313	1879–96	—	L	5/11	6	RR
2	*George Sisler*	.309	1915–30	StLA	L	7	2	SB
3	*Lou Gehrig*	.308	1923–39	NYA	L	<u>9</u>	3/12	RR
	Don Mattingly	.308	1982–95	NYA	L	<u>4</u>	1	BB
5	*Bill Terry*	.307	1923–36	NYN	L	<u>7</u>	2	SR
6	*Cap Anson*	.305	1876–97	ChiN	R	10	4	RR
7	Eddie Murray	.299	1977–97	Bal	B	3	<u>4</u>	SR
8	Cecil Cooper	.299	1971–87	MilA	L	3		SB
	Frank McCormick	.299	1934–48	Cin	R	3	1	BB
10	*Jimmie Foxx*	.298	1925–45	PhiA	R	3/7	4/12	SB
11	*Johnny Mize*	.297	1936–53	StLN	L	<u>6</u>	4/9	RB
12	Steve Garvey	.296	1969–87	LA	R	2	1	SR
13	Orlando Cepeda	.296	1958–74	SF	R	2	<u>4</u>	RB
14	Bob Watson	.295	1966–84	Hou	R	3		SB
15	Keith Hernandez	.293	1974–90	StLN	L	3		SS

Notes: See Guide to the Tables in the beginning of the chapter.

Players are "tied" if their averages agree to 4 decimal places.

First Basemen

Dan Brouthers, the top hitting first baseman, carried a big bat *and* a big suitcase (Table 7.4). He is the only top 100 hitter who doesn't qualify for any team. His 5 batting titles were won for 4 different teams. Brouthers played in Boston for three years from 1889 to 1891, but in three different leagues (NL, PL, and AA). All told, he played for 11 different teams in 19 years.

The next three hitters — George Sisler, Lou Gehrig, and Don Mattingly — all suffered physical maladies that affected their game. Sisler developed double vision, Gehrig contracted amyotropic lateral sclerosis, otherwise known as either ALS or Lou Gehrig's disease, and Mattingly developed chronic back problems.

Let's look at these three hitters before and after their injuries (Table 7.5).

Table 7.5   The Effect of Injury on Three Top Hitting First Basemen

	Before Injury			After Injury		
Player	*Years*	*AB*	*BA*	*Years*	*AB*	*BA*
George Sisler	1915–22	4155	.332	1924–30	4112	.284
Lou Gehrig	1923–37	7397	.312	1938–39	604	.266
Don Mattingly	1982–89	4022	.324	1990–95	2981	.286

Gehrig retired on May 2, 1939, after medical exams revealed problems (later diagnosed as amyotrophic lateral sclerosis at the Mayo Clinic on June 21), ending his string of playing in 2,130 consecutive games. Gehrig only managed 4 singles in 28 at bats in 1939. I included 1938 in his "after injury" period as well since his batting average was over 50 points lower than his previous two years and his slugging average was down over 100 points, probably associated with his disease. David Stephan, in a personal correspondence, contends that Gehrig's disease began to affect his performance on August 14, 1937.

There are other "hard luck" stories among the top hitting first basemen. Cap Anson hit .352 over 5 seasons in the National Association before the "official" beginning of major league baseball in 1876. Before 1898, the teams played many fewer games than they do now. Thus, Cap Anson did not get his 8000th at bat until he turned 43. Through age 36, Anson batted .3127. Johnny Mize spent three years in the military service during World War II. He hit .311 before the service and .277 after. Finally, Bill Terry had his career cut short because of a knee injury.

Gehrig, Foxx, and Mize were major home run hitters, with at least 3 titles and 9 top 5 finishes. The seven hitters with batting titles, other than Mattingly and Hernandez, are in the Hall of Fame.

There have been two golden ages for first basemen. The first was from 1930 to 1942, when Terry ('30), Gehrig ('32), Foxx ('35), McCormick ('42), and Mize ('42) were in mid-career. The second was from 1979 to 1989 when Garvey ('79), Cooper ('81), Hernandez ('82), Murray ('86), and Mattingly ('89) were in mid-career.

Second Basemen

When it comes to hitting for average, there are definitely a "Big 4" among second basemen (Table 7.6). Rod Carew, Rogers Hornsby, and

Table 7.6   Top Hitting Second Basemen

	Player	BA	Years	Team	H	BA Top 5	HR Top 5	Trend
1	*Rod Carew*	.332	1967–85	Min	L	7/12		SR
2	*Rogers Hornsby*	.330	1915–37	StLN	R	7/12	11	SR
3	*Nap Lajoie*	.322	1896–1916	Cle	R	4/7	<u>3</u>	SR
4	*Eddie Collins*	.310	1906–30	ChiA	L	<u>11</u>		RB
5	*Charlie Gehringer*	.292	1924–42	Det	L	<u>5</u>		RS
6	Johnny Ray	.291	1981–90	Pit	B	1		RR
7	*Billy Herman*	.290	1931–47	ChiN	R	2		SR
8	*Nellie Fox*	.289	1947–65	ChiA	L	5		SR
9	Larry Doyle	.288	1907–20	NYN	L	<u>4</u>	4	BR
10	Glenn Beckert	.286	1965–75	ChiN	R	1		SR

Note: See Guide to the Tables in the beginning of the chapter.

Nap Lajoie are all top 10 hitters, while Eddie Collins is a solid .310 hitter. A near 20-point gap separates them from the remaining top hitting second basemen. Three of these top hitters played during the early decades of the century.

Most of the second basemen lack the home run clout seen among the outfielders and first basemen. Hornsby stands alone as a major home run hitter. Several others had modest power, though. Lajoie and Doyle also had top 5 home run finishes and Gehringer hit 184 homers during his career.

In 1997, Nellie Fox was elected to the Hall of Fame. Consequently, of the top 10 hitting second basemen, those with 7500 or more at bats are in the Hall of Fame (leaving out Ray [5188 AB], Doyle [6509 AB], and Beckert [5208 AB]).

Interestingly, four of the ten second basemen played for Chicago teams.

Shortstops

Honus Wagner completely dominates the list of shortstops, having won 8 batting titles and finishing 28 points higher than his closest competitor — Arky Vaughan (Table 7.7). Arky Vaughan was the last of four "qualifying" shortstops who batted left-handed.

Table 7.7   Top Hitting Shortstops

	Player	BA	Years	Team	H	BA Top 5	HR Top 5	Trend
1	*Honus Wagner*	.326	1897–1917	Pit	R	8/13	4	SS
2	*Arky Vaughan*	.298	1932–48	Pit	L	4̲		RR
3	*Luke Appling*	.297	1930–50	ChiA	R	3		SS
4	Robin Yount	.292	1974–93	MilA	R	2		SS
5	Alan Trammell	.291	1977–96	Det	R	4		SS
6	*Lou Boudreau*	.288	1938–52	Cle	R	2̲		SR
7	*George Davis*	.287	1890–1909	NYN	B	1	1	SR
8	Al Dark	.285	1946–60	NYN	R	1		RB
9	Maury Wills	.285	1959–72	LA	B			RB
10	Jack Glassock	.284	1879–95	—	R	2̲		SR

Note: See Guide to the Tables in the beginning of the chapter.

Remarkably, four of the shortstops surged throughout their career (having an SS trend)—Wagner, Appling, Yount, and Trammell. Perhaps this occurred because shortstops need to hone their fielding skills in order to make the major leagues. Once they have established themselves, they can improve their hitting—and four of the top five hitters did!

Of the top 7 hitting shortstops, the ones eligible for the Hall of Fame are in. Yount and Trammell, who have retired within the last 5 years, appear to be likely inductees as well.

There was a cluster of top hitting shortstops that were in mid-career around World War II—Arky Vaughan (1938), Luke Appling (1940), and Lou Boudreau (1944).

Third Basemen

The past quarter century has been the golden age for third base hitters (Table 7.8). George Brett and Bill Madlock both began their careers in 1973. In 1987, Bill Madlock became the best hitting third baseman, breaking a 30-year reign held by George Kell. Two years later, George Brett topped Madlock, only to be surpassed in 7 years by Wade Boggs. Recent stars Carney Lansford and Kevin Seitzer also claimed top 10 spots.

Table 7.8 Top Hitting Third Basemen

	Player	BA	Years	Team	H	BA Top 5	HR Top 5	Trend
1	Wade Boggs	.324	1982–	Bos	L	5/11		SB
2	George Brett	.307	1973–93	KC	L	3/5		SB
3	Bill Madlock	.302	1973–87	Pit	R	3/6		BB
4	*George Kell*	.299	1943–57	Det	R	7		SR
5	Carney Lansford	.295	1978–92	Oak	R	2		SR
6	*Frank Baker*	.294	1908–22	PhiA	L	3	4/8	RR
7	Kevin Seitzer	.291	1986–97	KC	R			BR
8	Stan Hack	.289	1932–47	ChiN	L	3		SR
9	*Brooks Robinson*	.288	1955–77	Bal	R	2		SR
10	Denny Lyons	.287	1885–97	Phia	R	2	3	RB

Note: See Guide to the Tables in the beginning of the chapter.

A surprising member of the third base contingent is Brooks Robinson. It is widely acknowledged that Robinson was a great fielder, but his unadjusted lifetime batting average is an unimpressive .267. Robinson however, played in the American League throughout the 1960s (when batting averages had slumped to their lowest level), played in a poor hitter's park (Baltimore), and dropped substantially past his 8000th at bat. Robinson had an adjusted batting average of .288, good enough for 9th place. Equally surprising, Pie Traynor, thought by many to be an outstanding hitting third baseman, fails to make the list.

Catchers

The top hitting catchers are relatively recent players (Table 7.9). None of the catchers began play until 1925, when the sport was already half a century old. Hall-of-Famer Buck Ewing, a .283 hitter, played other positions as well and did not qualify as a catcher. Johnny Kling, the best hitting early catcher, narrowly missed the top 10. Only one catcher has won a batting championship—Ernie Lombardi—even though *Total Baseball* (1989) does not count his second "official" title in 1942 because he had only 309 AB.

Thurmon Munson, who died in a plane crash in 1979, holds the highest BA for a catcher in the only position (excluding DH) without

Table 7.9 Top Hitting Catchers

	Player	BA	Years	Team	H	BA Top 5	HR Top 5	Trend
1	Thurmon Munson	.299	1969–79	NYA	R	1		RR
2	*Ernie Lombardi*	.295	1931–47	Cin	R	1̲	1	SR
3	*Bill Dickey*	.292	1928–46	NYA	L			RR
4	Manny Sanguillen	.290	1967–80	Pit	R	2		BR
5	*Mickey Cochrane*	.289	1925–37	PhiA	L	2		SR
6	Smokey Burgess	.288	1949–67	Pit	L			RR
7	Elston Howard	.282	1955–68	NYA	R	1	1	SB
8	*Yogi Berra*	.281	1946–65	NYA	L		5	RB
9	Ted Simmons	.281	1968–88	StLN	B	2		RB
10	Spud Davis	.279	1928–45	PhiN	R			BR

Note: See Guide to the Tables in the beginning of the chapter.

any .300 hitters. If Mike Piazza continues his stellar hitting, however, he will smash Munson's mark.

Interestingly, 4 of the catchers in this list are New York Yankees: Bill Dickey was the starting catcher from 1929 to 1943, Yogi Berra from 1949 to 1959, Elston Howard from 1960 to 1966, and Thurman Munson from 1970 to 1979. Thus, for 43 years in a 51-year stretch, the Yankees were led by a top hitting catcher.

The 1930s was the golden age for catchers, with four — Lombardi, Dickey, Cochrane, and Spud Davis — placing in the top 10.

Utility Players

Like catchers, good-hitting utility players are of more recent vintage (Table 7.10). King Kelly, Hardy Richardson, Buck Ewing, and Harry Stovey set the early standard for utility players. Three of them have since been supplanted by hitters who started half a century later, leaving Kelly as the only remaining nineteenth-century player.

The apex for utility players was from 1948 to 1958, when 5 of the top hitters (Robinson, Kuenn, Pesky, Goodman, and Runnels) were in their prime. The last three each played at least 5 years for the Boston Red Sox.

Three of the players really demonstrated their versatility by having

Table 7.10 Top Hitting Utility Players

	Player	BA	Years	Team	H	BA Top 5	HR Top 5	Trend
1	Paul Molitor	.307	1978–	MilA	R	6		RS
2	*Jackie Robinson*	.304	1947–56	Bkn	R	<u>4</u>		SB
3	Pedro Guerrero	.302	1978–92	LA	R	3	3	SB
4	Harvey Kuenn	.297	1952–66	Det	R	<u>6</u>		RR
5	Dick Allen	.296	1963–77	PhiN	R	3	4	BB
6	Johnny Pesky	.294	1942–54	Bos	L	3		BB
7	Joe Torre	.292	1960–77	MilN	R	<u>3</u>	1	BR
8	*King Kelly*	.291	1878–93	ChiN	R	6	1	SR
9	Pete Runnels	.290	1951–64	Was	L	4		SS
10	Billy Goodman	.290	1947–62	BosA	L	2		RR

Note: See Guide to the Tables in the beginning of the chapter.

played at least 300 games in each of 3 positions (Joe Torre — 903 C, 787 1B, 515 3B; Pete Runnels — 644 1B, 642 2B, 463 SS; Billy Goodman — 624 2B, 406 1B, 330 3B).

Only two top-hitting utility players — Jackie Robinson and King Kelly — are in the Hall of Fame. One reason for this is that utility players tend to have fewer at bats than most Hall of Famers. Only 5 players in the list exceeded 6000 AB.

Designated Hitters

It has been 25 years since the American League began their "experiment" with designated hitters batting in place of pitchers (Table 7.11).

Table 7.11 Top Hitting Designated Hitters

	Player	BA	Years	Team	H	BA Top 5	HR Top 5	Trend
1	Harold Baines	.288	1980–	ChiA	L			SR
2	Hal McRae	.286	1968–87	KC	R	1		SR
3	Don Baylor	.266	1970–88	Cal	R		2	BB

Note: See Guide to the Tables in the beginning of the chapter.

It looks like the DH is here to stay. It was often a "second career" for older players with wobbly knees or other defensive weaknesses or for players with nagging injuries. For the most part, it continues that way today. Through the 1997 season, only four players "qualify" by having played 1000 games at DH: Harold Baines, Don Baylor, Hal McRae, and Paul Molitor (Chili Davis is five games shy).

Given Molitor's versatility in the infield in the early part of his career, I have placed him as a "utility player." Baines qualifies both as an outfielder and a DH, but has played more as a DH.

No Position

Six of the top 100 hitters did not qualify at any position (Table 7.12). Browning, Carty, Polonia, and Stephenson primarily played in the outfield, Chance was predominantly a first baseman, and Zimmerman mainly played third base. Pete Browning won four batting titles in the American Association and finished five other times among the top 5.

Table 7.12 Top Hitters Who Did Not Qualify at a Position

	Player	BA	Years	Team	H	BA Top 5	HR Top 5	Trend
1	Pete Browning	.317	1882–94	Loua	R	4/9	2	BR
2	Riggs Stephenson	.300	1921–34	ChiN	R	2		RR
3	*Frank Chance*	.298	1898–1914	ChiN	R	2		BB
4	H. Zimmerman	.298	1907–19	ChiN	R	2̲	1̲	RR
5	Rico Carty	.297	1963–79	Atl	R	3̲		RB
6	Luis Polonia	.2945	1987–96	Cal	L			BR

Note: See Guide to the Tables in the beginning of the chapter.

Stan Musial

Best Single-Season
Batting Averages

8

Now that we have adjusted batting averages for era of play and the ballpark effect, the list of top single-season averages is completely different. This is true for both individual player and team averages. We will look at both in this chapter.

Best Individual Single-Seasons

The standard against which all modern batting averages have been compared is Ted Williams's unadjusted .406 average in 1941. Going into the final day, Williams's average stood at .3996, which rounds to .400. Rather than sit out the final day and assure himself of becoming the first player in a decade to hit at least .400, Williams played both games of a double-header, going 6-for-8. These final day heroics vaulted him from eighth to second place on the top adjusted single-season averages, with a .377 average.

In recent years Rod Carew, George Brett, and Tony Gwynn have each made runs at .400. All of these years rank among the 10 best of all time — Carew placed seventh in 1977, Brett finished third in 1980, and Gwynn topped the list with his 1994 season.

Gwynn's great year was abruptly cut short by a player strike. Gwynn played in 110 of 117 Padres games in 1994, hitting an adjusted .378. Gwynn's winning margin as best single-season average ever was razor thin — half a hit better than Williams's 1941 season and one hit better than Brett's 1980 and Hornsby's 1924 seasons.

Gwynn only had 419 at bats in 1994 — which may have helped him in fashioning the best season ever. Dozens of players hit above .400 for the first several weeks of a baseball season. Only rarely do players today average .400 through May. Notice that in 4 of the top 5 seasons, the hitter had fewer than 460 at bats. Roger Hornsby holds the highest single-season average for a player with at least 500 at bats, with his .376 adjusted average in 1924. Rod Carew sets the standard for players with 600 or more at bats, with his .372 average in 1977.

Table 8.1 shows the 50 best single-season batting averages. The top 11 lifetime hitters dominate the single-season list as well. Tony Gwynn has six top years. Ty Cobb has five top years, including 4 consecutive years from 1909 to 1912. Gwynn's years are ranked 1, 10, 11, 18, 26, and 39, while Cobb's years are ranked 15, 16, 31, 42, and 43. Once

Table 8.1 Top 50 Adjusted Batting Averages

	Year	Player	Team	League	AB	BA
1	1994	Tony Gwynn	SD	NL	419	.378
2	1941	Ted Williams	Bos	AL	456	.377
3	1980	George Brett	KC	AL	449	.376
4	1924	Rogers Hornsby	StL	NL	536	.376
5	1957	Ted Williams	Bos	AL	420	.373
6	1901	Nap Lajoie	Phi	AL	543	.372
7	1977	Rod Carew	Min	AL	616	.372
8	1961	Norm Cash	Det	AL	535	.369
9	1887	Tip O'Neill	StL	AA	517	.368
10	1997	Tony Gwynn	SD	NL	592	.367
11	1987	Tony Gwynn	SD	NL	589	.365
12	1910	Nap Lajoie	Cle	AL	592	.365
13	1922	George Sisler	StL	AL	586	.364
14	1916	Tris Speaker	Cle	AL	546	.364
15	1910	Ty Cobb	Det	AL	508	.363
16	1909	Ty Cobb	Det	AL	573	.362
17	1997	Mike Piazza	LA	NL	556	.362
18	1995	Tony Gwynn	SD	NL	535	.361
19	1908	Honus Wagner	Pit	NL	568	.360
20	1928	Rogers Hornsby	StL	NL	486	.360
21	1948	Stan Musial	StL	NL	611	.360
22	1904	Nap Lajoie	Cle	AL	553	.359
23	1985	Willie McGee	StL	NL	612	.359
24	1957	Mickey Mantle	NY	AL	474	.359
25	1988	Wade Boggs	Bos	AL	584	.358
26	1984	Tony Gwynn	SD	NL	606	.358
27	1974	Ralph Garr	Atl	NL	606	.357
28	1974	Rod Carew	Min	AL	599	.357
29	1994	Jeff Bagwell	Hou	NL	400	.356
30	1985	Wade Boggs	Bos	AL	580	.356
31	1917	Ty Cobb	Det	AL	588	.356
32	1946	Stan Musial	StL	NL	624	.356
33	1993	John Olerud	Tor	AL	551	.356
34	1975	Rod Carew	Min	AL	535	.356

(continued)

Table 8.1   Top 50 Adjusted Batting Averages (continued)

	Year	Player	Team	League	AB	BA
35	1886	King Kelly	Chi	NL	451	.355
36	1931	Al Simmons	Phi	AL	513	.354
37	1906	George Stone	StL	AL	581	.354
38	1912	Heinie Zimmerman	Chi	NL	557	.354
39	1989	Tony Gwynn	SD	NL	604	.354
40	1939	Joe DiMaggio	NY	AL	462	.353
41	1988	Kirby Puckett	Min	AL	635	.353
42	1912	Ty Cobb	Det	AL	553	.353
43	1911	Ty Cobb	Det	AL	591	.353
44	1989	Will Clark	SF	NL	588	.353
45	1986	Don Mattingly	NY	AL	677	.352
46	1987	Paul Molitor	Mil	AL	465	.352
47	1905	Cy Seymour	Cin	NL	581	.351
48	1947	Harry Walker	StL-Phi	NL	513	.351
49	1920	George Sisler	StL	AL	631	.350
50	1909	Honus Wagner	Pit	NL	495	.350

again, Gwynn edges out Cobb, this time in both number of top years and in having lower ranks. Besides Gwynn and Cobb the other top 11 hitters (except for Joe Jackson) contribute 1–3 years each. Altogether the top 11 hitters account for 28 of the top 50 averages.

Seven players with top single-season averages failed to win the batting title that year. Leading the group is Ty Cobb, who "officially" won the 1910 batting title but finished second to Nap Lajoie after his hit and at bat totals have been corrected. The remaining 6 times have occurred since 1985. Tony Gwynn kept Will Clark ('89), Jeff Bagwell ('94), and Mike Piazza ('97) from claiming batting titles, Wade Boggs was involved in close batting races with high averages three years in a row, 1986–88. In all three years, Boggs was the "official" champion. However, in 1986 and 1987, Don Mattingly and Paul Molitor had higher adjusted batting averages, respectively, which placed in the top 50. Finally in 1988, Wade Boggs hit an adjusted .358, over shadowing Kirby Puckett's .353 mark.

Best Team Single-Season Batting Averages

The two best hitting teams in the twentieth-century National League to date are the 1908 New York Giants and the 1976 Cincinnati Reds. The Giants, under the diminutive, dictatorial manager John McGraw, often called "Little Napoléon," were trying to reclaim the NL pennant from the Chicago Cubs.

The 1908 Giants were party to perhaps the most controversial game in baseball history. The game — which is unfortunately known as "Merkle's boner" — took place on September 23d between the Giants and the Cubs. Nineteen-year-old rookie Fred Merkle was filling in for first baseman Fred Tenney, who was ill with a lumbago attack. A classic baseball situation ensued — the Giants had Fred Merkle on first and Moose McCormick on third with two outs in the bottom of the ninth of a 1–1 game. Al Bridwell singled to center, scoring McCormick. Giants fans rushed onto the field in jubilation and, as was common practice, Merkle failed to touch second base, taking off instead for a clubhouse door in centerfield to escape the fans. Johnny Evers yelled for Solly Hofman to throw him the ball at second. The ball sailed over Evers's head. Giant first base coach Joe McGinnity wrestled Cub shortstop Joe Tinker for it before throwing it toward short. A Giant fan picked the ball up. Rube Kroh, a Cub pitcher, who was not in the game, demanded it from the fan — punching him out when he wouldn't release it. Kroh, now with the ball, worked his way to second and handed the ball to Evers. Umpire Hank O'Day called Merkle out, disallowed the run, and in his report used darkness as the rationale for calling the game a tie. The Giants appealed for the win since, in spite of a clearly stated rule, Merkle's action was the common practice. The Cubs appealed for a Giant forfeit, since the fans had mobbed the field, preventing further play that day. As fate would have it, both appeals were denied and the Giants and Cubs finished the season with equal records. The tie game was rescheduled for October 8, where "Three-Finger" Brown came on in relief to beat Christy Mathewson for a 4–2 Cubs victory and their third straight NL pennant.

In *Greatest Teams*, Tim Crothers ranks the Cincinnati Reds of 1970–76 — known as the "Big Red Machine" — the second best team in baseball history to the New York Yankees dynasty (whose most glorious years ranged from 1923 to 1964). The Reds lost the 1970 World Series to the Baltimore Orioles and the 1972 World Series to the Oakland A's, both of whom are also among Crothers's nine best baseball teams. The 1976 Reds were defending World Champions, having beaten the Boston Red Sox in an exciting 7-game series in 1975.

Let's compare the 1908 Giants and 1976 Reds position by position (Table 8.2).

Both teams were led by great hitting right fielders — Mike Donlin for the Giants, Ken Griffey Sr. for the Reds — with strong side support from second base — Larry Doyle (Giants), Joe Morgan (Reds). Pete Rose hit .323 as a third baseman for Cincinnati, clearly outmatching Giant Art Devlin. However, Reds catcher Johnny Bench suffered through the worst hitting year of his career and was strongly outhit by Giant Roger Bresnahan.

Ultimately, it was the pitchers that pushed the Giants past the Reds. Giants' pitchers hit .206 compared to only .144 for Reds' pitchers. This difference amounted to more than 20 additional hits for the Giants, who topped the Reds by less than 2 hits overall, batting .2807 compared to .2804. (Note: Table 8.2 is presented for illustration only; the formal comparison is based on the team fully-adjusted batting averages.)

Table 8.2   Lineups of Two Best Hitting National League Teams

| | 1908 New York Giants | | 1976 Cincinnati Reds | |
POS	Name	BA	Name	BA
1B	Fred Tenney	.270	Tony Perez	.260
2B	Larry Doyle	.318	Joe Morgan	.320
SS	Al Bridwell	.297	Dave Concepcion	.281
3B	Art Devlin	.267	Pete Rose	.323
RF	Mike Donlin	.342	Ken Griffey Sr.	.336
CF	Cy Seymour	.281	Cesar Geronimo	.307
LF	Spike Shannon	.240	George Foster	.306
	Moose McCormick	.312		
C	Roger Bresnahan	.295	Johnny Bench	.234
	Substitutes	.235	Substitutes	.262
	Pitchers	.206	Pitchers	.144

Note: Fully adjusted batting averages are given. Interestingly, the adjusted averages for the 1976 Reds equal the unadjusted averages.

Table 8.3 Lineups of Two Best Hitting American League Teams

POS	Chicago White Sox 1919		Boston Red Sox 1950	
	Name	BA	*Name*	BA
1B	Chick Gandil	.297	Walt Dropo	.297
2B	Eddie Collins	.302	Bobby Doerr	.270
SS	Swede Risberg	.253	Vern Stephens	.271
3B	Buck Weaver	.285	Johnny Pesky	.288
RF	Nemo Leibold	.289	Al Zarilla	.300
CF	Happy Felsh	.268	Dom DiMaggio	.303
LF	Joe Jackson	.328	Ted Williams	.293
			Billy Goodman	.327
C	Ray Schalk	.273	Birdie Tebbetts	.286
			Matt Batts	.252
	Substitutes	.279	Substitutes	.259
	Pitchers	.167	Pitchers	.187

The American League battle for best hitting team narrows down to the 1919 Chicago White Sox against the 1950 Boston Red Sox. Yes, this is the infamous White Sox team — often called the "Black Sox" — who were accused of throwing the World Series, resulting in the expulsion of Joe Jackson and 7 other Chicago players. The 1950 Red Sox, with Hall of Fame superstar Ted Williams, were trying to recover from a final day loss to the Yankees that cost them the 1949 AL pennant, as described in the book *Summer of '49* by David Halberstam. Table 8.3 lists the teams by position.

Ted Williams broke his elbow and hit for his lowest average until he turned 40. Utility player Billy Goodman filled in more than adequately, however, capturing the 1950 batting title. Joe Jackson hit equally well for Chicago. Boston's Dom DiMaggio topped Happy Felsh by 35 points in centerfield, but Chicago's Eddie Collins returned the favor, besting Bobby Doerr in a match-up of Hall of Fame second basemen. The substitutes and pitchers hit to a draw. The remaining edge of Stephens over Risberg proved decisive, with Boston and Chicago batting .2781 and .2777 overall, respectively.

The top 25 hitting NL teams in the twentieth century are shown in Table 8.4. The 1908 Giants proved that they were no fluke by placing their 1911 squad on the list also. Likewise, the 1976 Reds are

Table 8.4   Top Hitting National League Teams

	Team	Year	BA	Win Pct		Top 3 Hitters	
1	New York	1908	.281	.636	Donlin	**Doyle**	Bridwell
2	*Cincinnati*	1976	.280	.630	**Griffey**	**Rose**	Morgan
3	*Chicago*	1906	.278	.763	Steinfeldt	**Chance**	Kling
4	Brooklyn	1901	.278	.581	**Keeler**	Sheckard	Daly
5	*Pittsburgh*	1902	.277	.741	**Beaumont**	**Wagner**	**Clarke**
6	Cincinnati	1968	.277	.512	Rose	**A. Johnson**	May
7	*San Fran.*	1962	.276	.624	F. Alou	**Cepeda**	**Mays**
8	Pittsburgh	1928	.276	.559	**P. Waner**	Traynor	L. Waner
9	*Pittsburgh*	1909	.275	.724	**Wagner**	**Clarke**	Miller
10	Cincinnati	1918	.274	.531	**Roush**	Groh	Chase
11	*Cincinnati*	1994	.274	.579	Morris	Mitchell	Boone
12	St. Louis	1963	.274	.574	Groat	White	Flood
13	San Fran.	1963	.273	.543	**Cepeda**	**Mays**	**Kuenn**
14	San Fran.	1993	.273	.636	Bonds	Thompson	McGee
15	*Boston*	1948	.273	.595	**Holmes**	Dark	Stanky
16	*Pittsburgh*	1972	.273	.619	Davalillo	**Oliver**	**Clemente**
17	*Brooklyn*	1953	.273	.682	**Furillo**	Snider	**J. Robinson**
18	Houston	1995	.273	.528	D. Bell	Magadan	Biggio
19	Cincinnati	1969	.272	.549	**Rose**	**A. Johnson**	Tolan
20	*Pittsburgh*	1927	.272	.610	**P. Waner**	L. Waner	Traynor
21	Cincinnati	1938	.272	.547	**Lombardi**	**McCormick**	Berger
22	*Chicago*	1910	.272	.675	Hofman	Schulte	**Chance**
23	*Pittsburgh*	1960	.272	.617	Groat	**Clemente**	**Burgess**
24	*New York*	1911	.272	.647	Meyers	**Doyle**	Snodgrass
25	*Chicago*	1937	.272	.604	Hartnett	**Bi Herman**	Demaree

Notes: Names in bold represent top 100 hitters or top 10 hitters at position.

Teams in italics won their league's pennant.

joined by their 1968 and 1969 teams that led to the "Big Red Machine" of 1970–76.

The Pittsburgh Pirates had 6 top hitting teams, clustered in 3 pairs and led by Hall of Famers. In the first decade of the twentieth century — in 1902 and 1909 — Pirate teams, led by shortstop Honus Wagner, were 2 of only 4 National League teams since 1900 to win more than 70% of their games. The 1927–28 Pirate teams also rank among the best ever. The Pirates were led by three Hall of Famers: the Waner brothers, Paul and Lloyd — otherwise known as "Big Poison" and "Little Poison" — and Pie Traynor. Finally, Roberto Clemente anchored two playoff-bound Pirate teams — in 1960 and 1972. The latter came just months before his tragic death.

The Chicago Cubs, along with the Pirates, were at the apex of the National League in the first decade of the twentieth century. The double play combination of "Tinker to Evers to Chance" was immortalized in a lamenting poem by sportswriter Franklin P. Adams, which appeared in the 1910 New York *Evening Mail*:

> These are the saddest of possible words:
> Tinker to Evers to Chance.
> Trio of bear Cubs and fleeter than birds,
> Tinker to Evers to Chance.
> Ruthlessly pricking our gonfalon bubble,
> Making a Giant hit into a double,
> Words that are weighty with nothing but trouble,
> Tinker to Evers to Chance.

Although the Cubs teams of 1906–10 were only tied for having the third most total double plays (491), they were indisputably among the all-time best teams. During those 5 years, the Cubs won 4 NL pennants and 2 World Series titles. Their combined winning percentage was .693, which included the other two NL teams (besides the Pirates) that won over 70% of their games. The 1906 and 1910 teams made the list of greatest hitting teams, while the 1908 team, which beat the 1908 Giants for the NL pennant, just missed.

The 1962–63 San Francisco Giants are also prominent on the list of top hitting teams. This should be no surprise, since these teams included Willie Mays, Orlando Cepeda, Harvey Kuenn, Felipe Alou, and Willie McCovey.

The top 25 hitting AL teams are given in Table 8.5. Unlike the National League, the top two American League teams enjoyed but a single season in the limelight. In 1920, the Chicago White Sox were embroiled in controversy and before the season ended, five of the starting nonpitchers from the 1919 team were banned from major league baseball for life. As for the Red Sox, Williams left for military duty in Korea in 1952. When he returned full-time in 1954, most of his 1950 teammates had either retired or been traded.

The New York Yankees, baseball's dynasty, dominate the list of top

Table 8.5   Top Hitting American League Teams

	Team	Year	BA	Win Pct.	Top 3 Hitters		
1	Boston	1950	.278	.610	**Goodman**	D. DiMaggio	Zarilla
2	*Chicago*	1919	.278	.629	**J. Jackson**	**E. Collins**	Leibold
3	St. Louis	1922	.278	.604	**Sisler**	K. Williams	Tobin
4	Cleveland	1906	.277	.582	**Lajoie**	Congalton	**Flick**
5	*Baltimore*	1971	.277	.639	Rettenmund	Buford	D. Johnson
6	*Baltimore*	1969	.277	.673	**F. Robinson**	Powell	Buford
7	Oakland	1968	.277	.506	Cater	Campaneris	Monday
8	*New York*	1947	.276	.630	**J. DiMaggio**	McQuinn	Henrich
9	*Baltimore*	1966	.275	.606	**F. Robinson**	Snyder	Powell
10	St. Louis	1920	.275	.497	**Sisler**	Jacobson	Tobin
11	*Cleveland*	1995	.275	.694	**Murray**	Belle	Baerga
12	Detroit	1908	.274	.588	**Cobb**	**Crawford**	McIntyre
13	*New York*	1927	.274	.714	**Gehrig**	**Ruth**	Combs
14	Cleveland	1986	.274	.519	Tabler	J. Franco	Carter
15	New York	1930	.273	.558	**Gehrig**	**Ruth**	Combs
16	*New York*	1977	.273	.617	Rivers	**Munson**	Chambliss
17	Philadelphia	1927	.273	.591	**Simmons**	Cobb	**Cochrane**
18	*Minnesota*	1969	.273	.599	**Carew**	Reese	**Oliva**
19	*Detroit*	1909	.273	.645	**Cobb**	**Crawford**	Bush
20	*New York*	1942	.273	.669	Gordon	**J. DiMaggio**	**Dickey**
21	Boston	1909	.272	.583	Lord	**Speaker**	Gessler
22	New York	1931	.272	.614	**Ruth**	Gehrig	**Dickey**
23	*Cleveland*	1948	.272	.626	**Boudreau**	Mitchell	Doby
24	*New York*	1976	.272	.610	Rivers	**Munson**	Chambliss
25	New York	1948	.272	.610	**J. DiMaggio**	Lindell	Henrich
	New York	1994	.272	.619	O'Neill	**Boggs**	**Polonia**

Notes: Names in bold represent top 100 hitters or top 10 hitters at position.

Teams in italics won their league's pennant.

hitting AL teams with nine teams represented, although their best hit-ting team — the 1947 Yankees — only ranks 8th.

The 1927 Yankees are frequently considered to be the greatest team of all time and their lineup was referred to as "Murderers' Row." This team, however, only ranks 13th for batting average. Hall of Famers Lou Gehrig (.332), Babe Ruth (.317), and Earle Combs (.317) all hit well, as did Bob Meusel (.300). However, shortstop Mark Koenig

(.254), third baseman Joe Dugan (.239), and catchers Pat Collins (.245) and Johnny Grabowski (.247) all had lackluster years, lowering the team's ranking. Notably, the 1927 Philadelphia Athletics, led by Hall of Famers Al Simmons, Ty Cobb, and Mickey Cochrane, sported a top hitting team of their own.

After adding Hall of Fame catcher Bill Dickey to their lineup, the Yankees returned to the top 25 in 1930–31. Even so, the Philadelphia Athletics won the AL pennant both years.

The Yankee Clipper, Joe DiMaggio, spearheaded three top hitting squads in 1942 and 1947–48. The 1948 team lost out to the equally good hitting Cleveland team, led by Hall of Fame hitters Lou Boudreau and Larry Doby.

The Yankees had back-to-back top hitting teams in 1976–77, led by Mickey Rivers, Thurmon Munson, and Chris Chambliss. The 1976 team lost the World Series to the Big Red Machine.

Early in his career—in 1908 and 1909—Cobb was part of two outstanding Detroit Tiger teams, with Sam Crawford adding the strongest second bat. The Tigers won pennants both years but ran into the 1908 Chicago and 1909 Pittsburgh buzzsaws—whom we have just discussed—in the two World Series that followed. The Tigers lost both series, as they had in 1907. Though only 22 years old in 1909, Cobb never made it back to the World Series.

In 1920 and 1922, George Sisler won batting crowns and, with the outfield trio of Baby Doll Jacobson, Jack Tobin, and Ken Williams, put two St. Louis Browns teams in the top 10. Sisler missed the 1923 season with sinus problems, which led to double vision. Sisler never won a batting title again and the Browns never again had a top hitting team.

The Browns moved to Baltimore in 1954 and became known as the Orioles. The 1966–71 Orioles rate as the 8th best baseball team, according to Tim Crothers in *Greatest Teams*. Led by outfielders Frank Robinson and Don Buford, third baseman Brooks Robinson, and first baseman Boog Powell, Baltimore placed 3 of its teams among the top 9 AL teams—in 1966, 1969, and 1971. All of these teams played in the World Series, but only the 1966 team won. (The Orioles also won the 1970 World Series over the first Big Red Machine team.)

Wade Boggs

The Ballparks 9

Have you ever wondered why the best pitchers of the last quarter of a century seem to play for the Baltimore Orioles, Houston Astros, Los Angeles Dodgers, New York Mets, or Oakland A's? (The recent Atlanta Braves are an exception.) Or why the best hitters come from the Boston Red Sox, Chicago Cubs, Cincinnati Reds, Colorado Rockies, Minnesota Twins, Pittsburgh Pirates, or St. Louis Cardinals? (Tony Gwynn is an exception.) The answer is — ballpark effects.

The Boston Red Sox are known for their great hitters — Ted Williams, Carl Yastrzemski, and Wade Boggs among them. Well . . . Fenway Park has been a solid hitter's park since 1934. Between 1934 and 1997, 21 batting titles have been won by Boston stars. By contrast, only one Boston pitcher has led the league in yielding the lowest batting average — and he did it twice. Yes, Red Sox fans, it's the pitcher that got away — Roger Clemens.

Ballparks give rise to the character of the team. There are standard dimensions for basketball courts, hockey rinks, and football fields. There is no standard size, however, for baseball fields. In this chapter, we will relive the batting average eras of the twentieth-century major league baseball teams, which are affected by the altitude, size, and other attributes of the ballparks.

Hitter's Park, Pitcher's Park

Hitting and pitching are opposing forces in the game of baseball. Players in good hitting parks lead the league in batting more easily than players from poor hitting parks — often called pitcher's parks. (Note: Often the term *hitter's park* refers to a park where either home run hitting or run scoring is high. Throughout this book, it will refer to parks where batting averages are high.) Meanwhile, pitchers in hitter's parks find it more difficult to limit opposing batters to a low batting average. This average is called *opposing batting average*, or OBA, for short.

Let's contrast two parks, a strong hitter's park — Fenway Park in Boston — with a strong pitcher's park — Oakland-Alameda County Coliseum. Since 1934, when a major renovation was made to Fenway, 21 individual and 20 team batting championships have been won in Boston. Since the Athletics moved to Oakland in 1968, no player has won a batting title and the team has won only once. On the other hand, only 2 individual titles and one team titles have been won in in OBA 64 years (1934–97) by Red Sox pitchers, while 3 individual and 8 team OBA titles have been garnered by Oakland players in 30 years (1968–97).

Think of the Boston Red Sox from 1934 to 1997 and great hitters come to mind — Ted Williams, Wade Boggs, Carl Yastrzemski, Jimmie Foxx, Johnny Pesky, Jim Rice, Billy Goodman, and Pete Runnels. The main standout pitchers are Lefty Grove and Roger Clemens.

The Oakland A's are known for their outstanding pitching. The World Series champions of the early 1970s had Catfish Hunter, Vida Blue, Blue Moon Odom, and Rollie Fingers. From 1970 to 1975 the A's pitchers won four of the six American League OBA titles. From 1988 to 1990, the team won three straight AL pennants and one World Series. Pitchers Dave Stewart, Bob Welch, and Dennis Eckersley led the staff to two more OBA titles. During neither stretch of champion teams did the hitters win either an individual or a team batting title.

An average hitter in an average AL ballpark would hit .255 after standardizing to the league average. (To have a consistent way of identifying hitter's parks and pitcher's parks over time for the purposes of the tables which follow, we do not use the DH adjustment for average after 1972.) An average hitter in Boston from 1950 to 1997 would hit .262, the ballpark effect batting average, while an average hitter in Oakland from 1968 to 1992 would hit .247 — a 15-point difference. A player from Boston receives a 7-point boost (the ballpark effect) to his average (.262–.255), while a Oakland player's average is hurt by 8 points (.247–.255). These averages combine the player's home and away batting averages. The batting average of an average hitter when playing *in* Boston is even greater, while *in* Oakland it is even lower.

In this chapter, ballpark effect batting averages are presented for each team for each ballpark era. The statistical details of the era determination are described below.

As you peruse the tables throughout this chapter, notice how the percentage of batting titles and opposing titles depends on the ballpark BA. Overall, from 1901 to 1997, there have been $97 \times 2 = 194$ individual batting titles in the two leagues combined. There have been 1866 total team-years for the 28 franchises. Thus, about 10% ($194/1866 \times 100$) of the team-years have produced championships. Table 9.1 shows how this varies based on the ballpark batting average.

More than a quarter of the team-years in ballparks with batting

Table 9.1 Percentage of Years Resulting in Championships
by Ballpark Batting Average

Ballpark BA	Team-Years	PL BA	Team BA	PL OBA	Team OBA
.261 +	258	26	27	3	4
.258–.260	232	19	16	5	4
.251–.257	1082	7	7	12	11
.250 –	294	3	2	15	19

averages of .261 or more have resulted in BA titles, compared to 3–4% of the OBA titles. By contrast, for ballparks with averages of at most .250, only 2–3% of the team-years led to batting titles but 15–19% led to opposing batting titles.

The BA and OBA titles — obtained from *Total Baseball* — are based on unadjusted averages. Thus, Table 9.1 gives us some additional assurance that the ballpark batting averages determined in chapter 5 are reasonably accurate, since what the players did at the ballparks fits our estimates of the ballpark effects.

Individual Team Ballpark Eras

The ballpark effect batting averages of the major league teams were determined from the methods described in chapter 5 and are provided in Appendix IV. For the original 16 franchises of the twentieth century, 8 to 11 different ballpark effects were determined over each team's history. New effects were obtained either at league change years or whenever the teams moved into a new park or had a major stadium renovation. Sometimes the ballpark effects changed dramatically, sometimes very little.

While the detailed values given in Appendix IV were used to identify the alltime best hitters, to simplify the presentation here, a regression method called backward elimination was applied to combine ballpark eras when the averages changed very little. Consequently, not all ballparks are mentioned in the text. An excellent account of the ballparks (and a principal source for my ballpark analysis) is given by Philip Lowry in *Green Cathedrals*.

Backward Elimination in Regression

Backward elimination methods are used to drop variables from a regression model that do not have great impact on how well the model fits the data. Statistics called *F-tests* are computed for each variable. The variable with the highest (least significant) *p*-value is eliminated. This process is repeated until all *p*-values are less than the *significance level-to-stay* selected. The remaining variables are part of the final model.

In the backward eliminations performed for the tables in this chapter, the variables are the ballpark eras from 1901 to 1982 (see Appendix IV for a delineation of the eras for a given park). The significance level-to-stay used was 0.20. Successive eras where batting averages changed less than 4 points tended to get combined. Different methods were used in chapter 5 to determine the ballpark effect batting averages for 1983–92 and 1993–97. I combined these two averages if the change was less than 4 points and then combined them with the last era before 1983 if that difference was less than 4 points.

Guide to the Ballpark Tables in This Chapter

The table format used in this chapter is the same for all teams. For each era, the average team winning percentage and the ballpark effect batting average are given. The numbers of player and team batting titles during the era are given under **PL BA** and **Team BA**. The lowest "opposing batting average" (OBA), that is the lowest batting average given up by a pitcher, is provided for players and teams under **PL OBA** and **Team OBA**. Finally, the number of years in the era is given.

Numbers in **bold** represent ballpark eras for which the number of championships is at least twice the expected number. (The expected number is obtained by dividing the number of years for the era by the average number of teams in the league. For example, in the era 1934–49 in Fenway Park, the expected number of championships is $16 \div 8$

= 2.) Numbers underlined represent ballpark eras for which the number of championships is at most half of the expected number.

Let's visit the ballparks!

American League Teams

Boston Red Sox

Fenway Park, built in 1912, favored the pitcher until a major remodeling occurred in 1934. The center field wall was moved from 468 ft. to 389 ft. and the deepest corner just to the right of center was moved in from 593 ft. to 420 ft. The left field wall — replaced and the height raised from 25 ft. to 37 ft. — became affectionately known as the "Green Monster."

These changes converted Fenway to a hitter's park — the best one in the American League since 1938 (Table 9.2), except for Metropolitan Stadium in Minnesota from 1970 to 1982. Before 1934, no Red Sox player had won a batting title. Since 1934, they have attained one-third of all the individual titles. The batting champions with number of titles are: Ted Williams (7); Wade Boggs (5); Carl Yastrzemski (3); Pete Runnells (2); Jimmie Foxx (1); Billy Goodman (1); Fred Lynn (1); and Carney Lansford (1).

Chicago White Sox

From 1901 to 1909, the White Sox played in the poorest hitting field in major league history — South Side Park (Table 9.3). In 1906, the

Table 9.2   Red Sox Ballpark Eras

Years	Win Pct	Bat Avg	PL BA	Team BA	PL OBA	Team OBA	No. Years
1901–11	.523	.257	0	1	1	3	11
1912–33	.458	.249	0	0	3	2	22
1934–49	.547	.259	5	7	0	0	16
1950–97	.519	.262	16	13	2	1	48
Total	.510	.258	21	21	6	6	97

Note: See Guide to the Ballpark Tables on p. 189.

THE FINDINGS

White Sox won the pennant with a mean-adjusted BA of .232, the lowest BA in the league. This weak hitting effort earned the club the immortal sobriquet of "The Hitless Wonders."

From 1910 to 1990, the club played at Comiskey Park. Initially a strong pitcher's park, Comiskey became a neutral park in 1920 and remained so since, except for a 13-year stretch from 1970 to 1982, when it favored the hitter. White Sox pitchers won 4 consecutive team OBA titles from 1964 to 1967 and added two individual titles for the most productive stretch in franchise history.

The new Comiskey Park — which opened in 1991 — is similar to the old Comiskey Park in batting effect. In 1997, Frank Thomas became the first White Sox player in 54 years to win the batting crown.

Table 9.3   White Sox Ballpark Eras

Years	Win Pct	Bat Avg	Pl BA	Team BA	Pl OBA	Team OBA	No. Years
1901–9	.563	.241	0	0	0	1	9
1910–19	.535	.249	0	1	1	1	10
1920–69	.493	.253	2	4	5	7	50
1970–82	.475	.259	0	0	0	0	13
1983–97	.513	.254	1	0	0	2	15
Total	.504	.253	3	5	6	11	97

Note: See Guide to the Ballpark Tables on p. 189.

Cleveland Indians

Cleveland's first two ballparks — League Park I (1901–10) and League Park II (1911–32) — were strong hitter's parks (Table 9.4). Between 1932 and 1946 Cleveland played its home games in both League Park II (where 59% of the games were played) and Municipal Stadium, before moving into the latter stadium completely in 1947. Since 1932, Cleveland has been an average batting city, even with the new Jacobs Field, which opened in 1995.

Cleveland's heyday for individual batting titles was from 1903 to 1916. During that time Nap Lajoie "won" three titles, including the controversial 1910 title, and Tris Speaker added an undisputed batting title in 1916.

Table 9.4   Indians Ballpark Eras

Years	Win Pct	Bat Avg	PL BA	Team BA	PL OBA	Team OBA	No. Years
1901–19	.511	.260	5	4	5	0	19
1920–31	.513	.264	1	1	1	0	12
1932–97	.510	.255	1	6	13	7	66
Total	.511	.257	7	11	19	7	97

Note: See Guide to the Ballpark Tables on p. 189.

Cleveland has had three periods with great pitchers — winning 5 of 7 individual titles from 1938 to 1944, 4 individual and 6 team titles in 12 years from 1948 to 1959, and adding 3 of 4 individual titles from 1965 to 1968.

Detroit Tigers

Detroit's first two ballparks — Bennett Park (1901–11) and Navin Field (1912–37) — were hitter's parks (Table 9.5). Outfielders Ty Cobb and Sam Crawford spearheaded three consecutive team batting championships for the pennant-winning Tigers (1907–9). Bobby Veach and Harry Heilmann joined the Tiger outfield, giving them three more team titles (1915–17). The team titles were fitting sideshows to Cobb's personal accomplishment of an unparalleled 10 championships in 13 years (1907–19). In all, the first 37 years of Tiger baseball yielded 28 combined batting championships, but only one OBA title.

The Tigers home ballparks have all been on the same land. When Navin Field was constructed in 1912 the baseball diamond was turned

Table 9.5   Tigers Ballpark Eras

Years	Win Pct	Bat Avg	PL BA	Team BA	PL OBA	Team OBA	No. Years
1901–37	.517	.261	16	12	1	1	37
1938–49	.541	.252	1	2	4	1	12
1950–60	.478	.261	2	1	0	0	11
1961–97	.513	.252	1	1	2	5	37
Total	.514	.256	20	16	7	7	97

Note: See Guide to the Ballpark Tables on p. 189.

(Bennett Park's home plate area was changed into right field). The seating capacity was greatly expanded in 1938 and the ballpark was renamed Briggs Stadium. In 1961, it was renamed Tiger Stadium. Since 1938, the stadium has favored the pitcher, except during the 1950s. The pitchers won 5 consecutive team titles from 1980 to 1985 but no individual or team batting titles have been won since 1961.

New York Yankees

After moving from Baltimore, the New York Highlanders settled into a hitter's park—Hilltop Park (1903–12) (Table 9.6). From 1913 to 1922 they played in pitcher-friendly Polo Grounds, winning 4 consecutive team OBA championships from 1919 to 1922.

Yankee Stadium—the house that Ruth built—has vacillated from being a neutral park to favoring the pitcher. Between 1932 and 1943, the Yankees won 10 of 12 team OBA titles and followed it up by winning 6 of 9 more between 1955 and 1963. During that entire time, 1932–63, 9 different pitchers won a total of 13 of the 32 individual pitching titles.

On the other hand, batting titles have proved elusive. Paul O'Neill's title in 1994 was the first since Mantle won in 1956 and the team titles in 1993–94 were the first since 1962.

Table 9.6   Yankees Ballpark Eras

Years	Win Pct	Bat Avg	PL BA	Team BA	PL OBA	Team OBA	No. Years
1901–2	.437	.269	0	1	0	0	2
1903–12	.493	.259	0	0	1	0	10
1913–22	.520	.248	0	0	0	4	10
1923–34	.608	.255	2	4	4	4	12
1935–49	.621	.250	3	1	6	10	15
1950–97	.561	.254	3	8	7	9	48
Total	.562	.254	8	14	18	27	97

Note: See Guide to the Ballpark Tables on p. 189.

Philadelphia - Kansas City - Oakland Athletics

The Athletics (Table 9.7) are the only American League team to have played in three cities for any appreciable time (the Baltimore Orioles played in St. Louis and in Milwaukee for one year).

Table 9.7   Athletics Ballpark Eras

Years	Win Pct	Bat Avg	PL BA	Team BA	PL OBA	Team OBA	No. Years
1901–8	.557	.256	1	1	2	2	8
1909–19	.489	.263	1	5	1	3	11
1920–34	.534	.252	4	2	2	4	15
1935–54	.399	.256	2	0	0	1	20
1955–67	.404	.260	0	0	0	0	13
1968–92	.526	.247	0	1	3	8	25
1993–97	.443	.253	0	0	0	0	5
Total	.479	.254	8	9	8	18	97

Note: See Guide to the Ballpark Tables on p. 189.

The ballclub began in Philadelphia at Columbia Park (1901–8) and Shibe Park (1909–54). Initially, Shibe was a strong hitter's park. The Athletics had outstanding teams in 1910–14, winning 5 consecutive team batting championships and four pennants. Interestingly, from 1909 to 1911 they had 3 team pitching titles as well. Between 1920 and 1934, Shibe favored the pitcher. The pitchers won 4 of 6 team titles between 1926 and 1931. Al Simmons and Jimmie Foxx, however, split the four individual batting titles from 1930 to 1933.

From 1955 to 1967, the team played poorly in Municipal Stadium in Kansas City — producing no titles in the hitter's park.

Since 1968 the team has played at Oakland-Alameda County Coliseum in Oakland — a strong pitcher's park. There have been 11 combined pitching titles compared to a lone team batting title.

St. Louis Browns – Baltimore Orioles

This franchise has produced the fewest team championships of any of the original AL franchises — 23. While in St. Louis (1902–53), the Browns played in Sportman's Park (Table 9.8). George Sisler won two individual batting titles in 1920 and 1922, and the team won both years too. Their pitcher, Dixie Davis, won the 1922 OBA title. After Sisler developed double vision, however, and the Browns never again won any titles.

In 1954, the team moved to Memorial Stadium in Baltimore. In spite of the fact that Memorial Stadium was a strong pitcher's park, only 8 total pitching championships took place there in 38 years. Frank

Table 9.8   Browns-Orioles Ballpark Eras

Years	Win Pct	Bat Avg	PL BA	Team BA	PL OBA	Team OBA	No. Years
1901–19	.427	.252	1	0	2	2	19
1920–53	.435	.255	2	2	1	0	34
1954–60	.459	.247	0	0	2	0	7
1961–69	.565	.253	1	1	1	2	9
1970–82	.589	.248	0	1	0	2	13
1983–97	.503	.253	0	0	1	2	15
Total	.479	.253	4	4	7	8	97

Note: See Guide to the Ballpark Tables on p. 189.

Robinson won the only batting title as an Oriole. Since 1992 the Orioles have played at Camden Yards, which has been a neutral park so far.

Washington Senators – Minnesota Twins

This franchise has witnessed two heydays — one for the pitcher, one for the hitter (Table 9.9). During Walter Johnson's prime, 1912–15, the team won four consecutive OBA titles, with Johnson taking individual honors twice. He led a second charge late in his career, leading himself and the team to two more titles in 1924–25 — and two AL pennants plus one World Series title.

Table 9.9   Senators-Twins Ballpark Eras

Years	Win Pct	Bat Avg	PL BA	Team BA	PL OBA	Team OBA	No. Years
1901–10	.374	.254	1	0	0	0	10
1911–19	.514	.248	0	0	3	4	9
1920–49	.496	.256	3	2	4	4	30
1950–60	.421	.251	1	0	0	0	11
1961–69	.542	.259	3	3	0	0	9
1970–92	.492	.262	8	6	0	0	23
1993–97	.439	.256	0	0	0	0	5
Total	.477	.256	16	11	7	8	97

Note: See Guide to the Ballpark Tables on p. 189.

The Senators moved to Metropolitan Stadium in Minnesota in 1961, changing their name to the "Twins." Minnesota's two ballparks (the Twins moved into the Metrodome in 1982) have favored the hitter until very recently. Between 1964 and 1978, Minnesota — led by Rod Carew and Tony Oliva — won 10 individual and 6 team batting titles. There have been no pitching titles in Minnesota.

California Angels (1961 Expansion)

The Angels played in Wrigley Field in Los Angeles in 1961 and Dodger Stadium from 1962 to 1965, before settling in Anaheim Stadium (now Edison International Field) in 1966. Edison International is favorable to pitchers (Table 9.10). Nolan Ryan won 5 individual championships and Andy Messersmith added 2 more during an 11-year stretch from 1969–79. In 1970, Alex Johnson eked out the only batting title ever attained by the Angels.

Table 9.10   Angels Ballpark Eras

Years	Win Pct	Bat Avg	PL BA	Team BA	PL OBA	Team OBA	No. Years
1961–97	.482	.252	1	0	7	1	37

Note: See Guide to the Ballpark Tables on p. 189.

Washington Senators II - Texas Rangers (1961 Expansion)

When the *original* Washington Senators moved to Minnesota in 1961, a *new* Washington Senators franchise was established (Table 9.11). Eleven years later, *they* moved to Texas as the "Rangers." While Arlington Stadium (1972–93) was a neutral park, the Rangers have won more than their share of individual OBA titles, led by Nolan Ryan's 3. In 1994, Texas moved into the Ballpark at Arlington.

Table 9.11   Senators II–Rangers Ballpark Eras

Years	Win Pct	Bat Avg	PL BA	Team BA	PL OBA	Team OBA	No. Years
1961–71	.418	.250	0	0	0	0	11
1972–97	.481	.257	1	1	5	1	26
Total	.462	.255	1	1	5	1	37

Note: See Guide to the Ballpark Tables on p. 189.

THE FINDINGS

Kansas City Royals (1969 Expansion)

The Kansas City Royals played in Municipal Stadium, the recently vacated home of the Kansas City Athletics, from 1969 to 1972. Royals Stadium, which opened in 1973, is a hitter's ballpark (Table 9.12). Hitters have been responsible for seven of the eight total championships, with George Brett contributing 3 of the 4 individual batting championships.

Table 9.12   Royals Ballpark Eras

Years	Win Pct	Bat Avg	PL BA	Team BA	PL OBA	Team OBA	No. Years
1969–97	.512	.259	4	3	0	1	29

Note: See Guide to the Ballpark Tales on p. 189.

Milwaukee Brewers (1969 Expansion)

This expansion club lasted only one year in Seattle before coming to County Stadium in Milwaukee, the same park used by the NL Milwaukee Braves from 1953 to 1965 (Table 9.13). The park has recently begun to favor the hitter. During the 29 years in Milwaukee, only two team titles and no individual titles have been captured.

Table 9.13   Brewers Ballpark Eras

Years	Win Pct	Bat Avg	PL BA	Team BA	PL OBA	Team OBA	No. Years
1969–92	.486	.253	0	1	0	1	24
1993–97	.463	.259	0	0	0	0	5
Total	.482	.254	0	1	0	1	29

Note: See Guide to the Ballpark Tables on p. 189.

Seattle Mariners (1977 Expansion)

Since joining the American League as an expansion team in 1977, the Mariners have played in the Kingdome. An average hitter's park, the Kingdome has been the home of many recent individual championships — 3 batting titles and 4 pitching titles (all won by Randy Johnson) since 1992 (table 9.14).

Table 9.14   Mariners Ballpark Eras

Years	Win Pct	Bat Avg	PL BA	Team BA	PL OBA	Team OBA	No. Years
1977–97	.447	.254	3	0	4	0	21

Note: See Guide to the Ballpark Tables on p. 189.

Toronto Blue Jays (1977 Expansion)

The Blue Jays played in Exhibition Stadium from 1977 until they moved into the Skydome in 1989 (Table 9.15). From 1984 to 1987, Dave Stieb and Jimmy Key won 3 individual OBA titles.

Table 9.15   Blue Jays Ballpark Eras

Years	Win Pct	Bat Avg	PL BA	Team BA	PL OBA	Team OBA	No. Years
1977–82	.379	.250	0	0	0	0	6
1983–97	.533	.255	1	1	3	1	15
Total	.489	.253	1	1	3	1	21

Note: See Guide to the Ballpark Tables on p. 189.

National League Teams

Boston - Milwaukee - Atlanta Braves

Boston played at South End Grounds from 1876 to 1914 (Table 9.16). In 1915, they moved to Braves Field, where the team remained until they moved to Milwaukee in 1953. In Milwaukee (1953–65), the Braves played in County Stadium. In 1966 they moved south to At-lanta-Fulton County Stadium. In 1997, the team moved into Turner Field.

The Boston parks both favored the pitcher, although the team played poorly there and only combined for 3 batting titles (player and team) and 2 pitching titles. County Stadium favored the hitter and Hank Aaron won a pair of titles and led the team to 2 titles.

Four eras can be seen for Atlanta-Fulton County Stadium. For 18 years, during two stretches (1966–73 and 1983–92), the park favored the hitters. The park has been neutral since 1993, but the pitching staff has won team titles all five years.

Table 9.16   Braves Ballpark Eras

Years	Win Pct	Bat Avg	PL BA	Team BA	PL OBA	Team OBA	No. Years
1901–37	.423	.248	1	0	0	1	37
1938–52	.472	.251	0	2	0	1	15
1953–65	.563	.260	2	2	1	2	13
1966–73	.497	.262	1	1	0	0	8
1974–82	.459	.248	1	0	1	0	9
1983–92	.464	.262	1	1	0	1	10
1993–97	.616	.256	0	0	2	5	5
Total	.473	.253	6	6	4	10	97

Note: See Guide to the Ballpark Tables on p. 189.

Brooklyn–Los Angeles Dodgers

The Brooklyn Dodgers played in Washington Park from 1898 to 1912 before moving into Ebbets Field (Table 9.17). The first seven years at Ebbets favored the hitters, but from 1920 to 1957 the pitcher enjoyed a slight advantage, which is also reflected in the championships in the table below.

Since moving to Los Angeles, the Dodgers have continued to play in pitcher's parks (Memorial Coliseum from 1958 to 1961 and Dodger Stadium since 1962). The Los Angeles ballclubs have won 20 pitching championships—in sharp contrast to the 2 batting championships, won by Tommy Davis in 1962–63.

Sandy Koufax won 7 of 8 OBA titles for the Dodgers from 1958 to 1965, while the team won 8 of 12 OBA titles from 1955 to 1966. The

Table 9.17   Dodgers Ballpark Eras

Years	Win Pct	Bat Avg	PL BA	Team BA	PL OBA	Team OBA	No. Years
1901–12	.427	.250	0	1	1	1	12
1913–20	.509	.260	3	2	1	1	8
1921–57	.538	.254	5	5	10	10	37
1958–69	.541	.249	2	0	7	5	12
1970–92	.540	.255	0	0	2	6	23
1993–97	.530	.248	0	0	0	0	5
Total	.522	.253	10	8	21	23	97

Note: See Guide to the Ballpark Tables on p. 189.

Dodgers added 4 consecutive team and individual OBA titles from 1972 to 1975. The Dodger franchise has had 44 individual and team OBA titles — the most of any NL franchise.

Chicago Cubs

West Side Grounds, home to the Cubs from 1893 to 1915, was a strong pitcher's park (Table 9.18). From 1901 to 1915 the powerful Cubs won 17 of the 30 possible pitching championships but only 2 batting championships. The championships came in spurts — 8 consecutive individual titles from 1903 to 1910 and 7 team titles from 1905 to 1911. Both of them have been unmatched by any other team (although the Atlanta Braves currently have 5 straight team titles).

In 1916, the team moved into Wrigley Field (known as Cubs Park from 1916 to 1925) — now one of the venerable old major league parks still in use. Initially a neutral ballpark, Wrigley Field now favors the hitter. Since all games at Wrigley were played during the day until very recently and players bat better in the day, this may account for some of the shift.

From 1972 to 1980, the Cubs won 4 individual batting titles. By contrast, there has not been a Cubs pitching title since 1952, in spite of star pitchers like Fergie Jenkins and Greg Maddux.

Table 9.18   Cubs Ballpark Eras

Years	Win Pct	Bat Avg	PL BA	Team BA	PL OBA	Team OBA	No. Years
1901–15	.594	.250	1	1	8	9	15
1916–69	.498	.254	2	4	7	7	54
1970–97	.476	.258	4	3	0	0	28
Total	.507	.254	7	8	15	16	97

Note: See Guide to the Ballpark Tables on p. 189.

Cincinnati Reds

Cincinnati has played in four different parks since 1900: League Park in 1901, Palace of the Fans from 1902 to 1911, Crosley Field (also known as Redland Park) from 1912 to 1970, and Riverfront Stadium (now Cinergy Field) since 1970 (Table 9.19).

Crosley Field underwent several changes in ballpark effect over its history. In 1921, left field was shortened by 40 ft. while the distance to

Table 9.19 Reds Ballpark Eras

Years	Win Pct	Bat Avg	PL BA	Team BA	PL OBA	Team OBA	No. Years
1901–20	.484	.260	4	3	1	2	20
1921–49	.483	.250	1	1	8	4	29
1950–61	.488	.257	0	1	1	0	12
1962–69	.541	.263	2	2	0	0	8
1970–97	.540	.256	1	4	3	0	28
Total	.505	.256	8	11	13	6	97

Note: See Guide to the Ballpark Tables on p. 189.

right field was lengthened by 24 ft., coinciding with its shift from a hitter's to a pitcher's park. From 1938 to 1940, the Reds won all 3 individual and team pitching championships. In 1938, Johnny Vander Meer pitched back-to-back no hitters, one in Cincinnati and one in the first night game ever at Ebbets Field in Brooklyn. The Reds have not won a team OBA title since 1940.

In the 1950s and 1960s, Crosley Field once again favored the hitter. Pete Rose helped to retire the park with back-to-back batting titles in 1968–69.

New York–San Francisco Giants

The New York Giants played in the Polo Grounds from 1901 to 1957, although a concrete stadium replaced a wooden one that burned down in 1911 (Table 9.20). Most of the team championships came during the first third of the century. The Giants won 7 team batting titles from 1904 to 1913 and 4 from 1919 to 1924. The pitchers won 4 individual and 2 team OBA championships from 1912 to 1917 and 3 individual

Table 9.20 Giants Ballpark Eras

Years	Win Pct	Bat Avg	PL BA	Team BA	PL OBA	Team OBA	No. Years
1901–49	.558	.256	2	12	8	8	49
1950–57	.533	.251	1	0	2	3	8
1958–93	.513	.251	0	2	2	3	40
Total	.537	.254	3	14	12	14	97

Note: See Guide to the Ballpark Tables on p. 189.

and 3 team championships from 1931 to 1934. During the last 8 years in New York (1950–57), the Polo Grounds favored the pitcher.

When the team moved to San Francisco in 1958, the Giants' home ballpark continued to favor the pitcher. No individual batting titles and only 2 team titles have been won in San Francisco.

Philadelphia Phillies

Philadelphia has both the lowest numbers of batting and pitching championships of any of the 8 principal NL franchises (Table 9.21). The Phillies also have the lowest winning percentage of any of the teams. The Phillies played in the Baker Bowl from 1895 to 1937. During its last 17 years (1921–37), the Baker Bowl was one of the all-time best hitter's parks. However, only Lefty O'Doul and Chuck Klein won batting titles. The ballclub finished last 8 times and next to last 6 times during those 18 hapless years.

In 1938, the Phillies joined the AL Athletics in Shibe Park. From 1938 to 1954 (when the Athletics went to Kansas City), Shibe Park was a slightly underaverage hitting park in the NL (.253) and a slightly better than average park in the AL (.256). In 1971, the Phillies moved to Veterans Stadium, also known as "The Vet."

Table 9.21   Phillies Ballpark Eras

Years	Win Pct	Bat Avg	PL BA	Team BA	PL OBA	Team OBA	No. Years
1901–20	.492	.254	1	0	3	1	20
1921–37	.383	.264	2	2	0	0	17
1938–70	.441	.253	3	0	1	1	33
1971–97	.495	.256	1	3	1	0	27
Total	.456	.256	7	5	5	2	97

Note: See Guide to the Ballpark Tables on p. 189.

Pittsburgh Pirates

Pittsburgh has been a mecca for batting champions (Table 9.22). With the home ballpark being favorable to the hitter in 72 of 97 years, 41 individual and team batting titles have been amassed—two less than the total achieved by the St. Louis Cardinals. Besides these two clubs, the greatest NL total is 19.

Table 9.22　Pirates Ballpark Eras

Years	Win Pct	Bat Avg	PL BA	Team BA	PL OBA	Team OBA	No. Years
1901–8	.634	.258	6	2	0	0	8
1909–20	.516	.252	2	1	0	1	12
1921–61	.501	.259	7	9	3	3	41
1962–69	.524	.269	4	3	0	0	8
1970–82	.552	.262	2	3	0	0	13
1983–97	.484	.255	1	1	0	0	15
Total	.520	.258	22	19	3	4	97

Note: See Guide to the Ballpark Tables on p. 189.

The individual championships came in clusters: 8 in 10 years from 1902 to 1911 (led by Honus Wagner's 7), 5 in 11 years from 1926 to 1936 (led by Paul Waner's 4), 6 in 8 years from 1960 to 1967 (led by Clemente's 4), and 3 in 7 years from 1977 to 1983. The Pirates also claimed 8 of 15 batting titles during 1960 to 1974.

On the other hand, the Pirates have only obtained 7 pitching championships this century (with the last one being in 1935), tying them for last with the Phillies among the original NL franchises.

The Pirates have played in three different parks — Exposition Park from 1891 to 1909, Forbes Field from 1909 to 1970 and Three Rivers Stadium since July 16, 1970.

St. Louis

Along with Pittsburgh, St. Louis fans have been treated to a large number of batting championships — 43 altogether (Table 9.23). Rogers Hornsby and Stan Musial, both of whom won 7 championships, dominate the list of individual batting champions. Led by Stan Musial and aided by one of the best hitting ballparks from 1938 to 1965, the team won 4 of 5 championships from 1942 to 1946 and 5 of 9 championships from 1949 to 1957.

Three of their five team OBA titles came during the war years, 1942–64, when the Cardinals won 68% of their games and claimed 2 World Series.

St. Louis played in Robison Field from 1893–1919, Sportman's Park #3 (renamed Busch Stadium in 1954) from 1920 to 1965 (which

Table 9.23   Cardinals Ballpark Eras

Years	Win Pct	Bat Avg	PL BA	Team BA	PL OBA	Team OBA	No. Years
1901–37	.482	.256	9	3	0	1	37
1938–82	.543	.262	11	16	4	4	45
1983–97	.507	.254	2	2	1	0	15
Total	.514	.259	22	21	5	5	97

Note: See Guide to the Ballpark Tables on p. 189.

they shared with the St. Louis Browns from 1920 to 1953), and Busch Stadium II since 1966.

Houston Astros (1962 Expansion)

Colt Stadium, used between 1962 and 1964, was one of the hardest stadiums ever for hits (Table 9.24). In 1965, the team moved into the Astrodome. A slight pitcher's park, 18 pitching championships — but no batting championships — have been won at the Astrodome. Seven of the 11 individual and all 7 team pitcher championships were won between 1977 and 1987, led by J. R. Richard and Nolan Ryan.

Table 9.24   Astros Ballpark Eras

Years	Win Pct	Bat Avg	PL BA	Team BA	PL OBA	Team OBA	No. Years
1962–64	.403	.241	0	0	0	0	3
1965–97	.497	.252	0	0	11	7	33
Total	.489	.251	0	0	11	7	36

Note: See Guide to the Ballpark Tables on p. 189.

New York Mets (1962 Expansion)

The Mets played in the Polo Grounds in 1962 and 1963 and have played in Shea Stadium since 1964 (Table 9.25). Shea Stadium is decidedly a pitcher's park. From 1968 to 1971, the Mets won 4 consecutive team opposing batting average championships. Sid Fernandez and Dwight Gooden captured 4 of the 7 individual OBA titles between 1984 and 1990.

Table 9.25   Mets Ballpark Eras

Years	Win Pct	Bat Avg	PL BA	Team BA	PL OBA	Team OBA	No. Years
1962–82	.429	.248	0	0	2	5	21
1983–97	.518	.252	0	2	4	2	15
Total	.466	.249	0	2	6	7	36

Note: See Guide to the Ballpark Tables on p. 189.

Montreal Expos (1969 Expansion)

Montreal has played their home games in two stadiums: Parc Jarry from 1969 to 1976 and Olympic Stadium since 1977. While Parc Jarry was a pitcher's park no championships were garnered there. Olympic Stadium is a neutral park.

Table 9.26   Expos Ballpark Eras

Years	Win Pct	Bat Avg	PL BA	Team BA	PL OBA	Team OBA	No. Years
1969–82	.472	.250	1	0	0	0	14
1983–97	.518	.254	1	0	1	2	15
Total	.496	.252	2	0	1	2	29

Note: See Guide to the Ballpark Tables on p. 189.

San Diego Padres (1969 Expansion)

The Padres have played in Jack Murphy (now Qualcomm) Stadium since the franchise began in 1969 (Table 9.27). Tony Gwynn won 4 batting championships in the 1980s and 4 more in the 1990s, from 1994 to 1997.

Table 9.27   Padres Ballpark Eras

Years	Win Pct	Bat Avg	PL BA	Team BA	PL OBA	Team OBA	No. Years
1969–97	.451	.251	9	0	0	1	29

Note: See Guide to the Ballpark Tables on p. 189.

Colorado Rockies (1993 Expansion)

Coors Field is the best hitter's ballpark of all time by a mile. Since the team began to play there in 1995 (moving from Mile High Stadium), the team has won all 3 team batting titles (Table 9.28). Meanwhile, the individual title was a three-man chase — between Tony Gwynn of the Padres, Mike Piazza of the Dodgers, and *somebody* from the Rockies. The somebodies were: Dante Bichette (1995), Ellis Burks (1996), and Larry Walker (1997).

Table 9.28   Rockies Ballpark Eras

Years	Win Pct	Bat Avg	PL BA	Team BA	PL OBA	Team OBA	No. Years
1993–94	.434	.273	1	0	0	0	2
1995–97	.520	.282	0	3	0	0	3
Total	.485	.278	1	3	0	0	5

Note: See Guide to the Ballpark Tables on p. 189.

Florida Marlins (1993 Expansion)

Pro Player Stadium, home to the Florida Marlins, is a neutral ballpark (Table 9.29). In 1996, the franchise picked up its first and only title, an OBA title by Al Leiter.

Table 9.29   Marlins Ballpark Eras

Years	Win Pct	Bat Avg	PL BA	Team BA	PL OBA	Team OBA	No. Years
1993–97	.474	.255	0	0	1	0	5

Note: See Guide to the Ballpark Tables on p. 189.

Best and Worst Hitter's Parks

Table 9.30 shows the best park eras in baseball history. Coors Field, with its .282 batting average, is 11 points higher than the top one in the list, Lake Front Park in Chicago, from the first decade of baseball. Coors is not included in the list because a 5 or more year era is needed for inclusion.

Table 9.30   Best Places for Batting Average

BA	Team	League	No. Years	Win Years	Pct.	Key Players
.271	Chi	NL	1878–84	6	.619	Anson, Kelly
.269	NY	NL	1883–88	6	.452	—
.269	Pit	NL	1962–69	8	.524	Matty Alou, Clemente
.268	Bal	NL	1892–99	8	.594	Keeler
.265	Lou	AA	1882–91	10	.482	Browning
.264	Phi	NL	1921–37	17	.384	—
.264	Cle	AL	1920–31	12	.513	Speaker
.263	Phi	AL	1909–19	11	.489	F. Baker, E. Collins
.263	Cin	NL	1962–69	8	.541	F. Robinson, Rose
.262	Phi	NL	1887–1900	14	.542	Hamilton, Delahanty, Lajoie, S. Thompson
.262	Pit	NL	1970–82	13	.552	Madlock, Oliver, Sanguillen
.262	StL	NL	1938–82	45	.543	Hernandez, McGee, Mize, Musial, Slaughter, T. Simmons, Torre
.262	Bos	AL	1950–97	48	.519	Boggs, Goodman, Greenwell, T. Williams, Yastrzemski
.262	Min	AL	1970–92	23	.492	Carew, Oliva, Puckett
.262	Atl	NL	1983–92	10	.464	—
.262	Atl	NL	1966–73	8	.497	Aaron, Carty
.261	Det	AL	1901–37	37	.517	Cobb, Crawford, Gehringer, Heilmann
.260	Det	AL	1950–60	11	.478	Kaline, Kuenn
.260	Buf	NL	1879–83	5	.499	—
.260	Chi	NL	1983–92	10	.491	Grace
.260	Bkn	NL	1913–20	8	.509	Wheat
.260	KC	AL	1955–67	13	.404	—
.260	Cin	NL	1901–20	20	.484	Roush, Seymour
.260	Mil	NL	1953–65	13	.563	Aaron, Torre
.260	Cle	AL	1901–19	19	.511	Flick, J. Jackson, Lajoie, Speaker
.260	Phi	AA	1883–91	9	.529	Lyons

Notes: Minimum period of era = 5 years.

Win Pct = winning percentage of team during period.

Key Players = Top 100 hitters or top 10 at position with at least 2000 AB during period.

Table 9.31   Worst Places for Batting Average

BA	Team	League	No. of Years	Win Years	Pct	Key Players
.240	Chi	AL	1901–9	9	.563	G. Davis
.245	Bal	AA	1882–91	10	.435	—
.245	Cle	NL	1879–84	6	.452	—
.247	Oak	AL	1968–92	25	.526	Henderson, Lansford
.247	Bal	AL	1954–60	7	.459	—
.248	Bos	NL	1901–37	37	.423	—
.248	Bal	AL	1970–82	13	.589	Murray, B. Robinson
.248	NY	NL	1962–82	21	.429	—
.248	Lou	NL	1893–99	7	.370	F. Clarke
.248	NY	AL	1913–22	10	.520	F. Baker
.248	Cin	NL	1890–1900	11	.524	—
.248	Was	AL	1911–19	9	.514	—
.248	Atl	NL	1974–82	9	.459	—
.248	LA	NL	1993–97	5	.530	Mondesi, Piazza
.249	Bos	AL	1912–33	22	.458	Speaker
.249	SD	NL	1969–82	14	.413	—
.249	Mon	NL	1969–76	14	.430	—
.249	Chi	AL	1910–19	10	.535	E. Collins, J. Jackson
.249	Pro	NL	1878–85	8	.609	—
.250	Chi	NL	1901–15	15	.594	Chance
.250	LA	NL	1958–69	12	.541	T. Davis, Wills
.250	Bkn	NL	1901–12	12	.427	—
.250	Cin	NL	1921–49	29	.483	Daubert, Lombardi, F. McCormick, Roush
.250	NY	AL	1935–49	15	.621	Dickey, J. DiMaggio, Gehrig
.250	Tor	AL	1977–82	6	.379	—
.250	Bkn	AA	1884–89	6	.528	—
.250	Was	AL	1961–71	11	.418	—
.250	Mon	NL	1969–82	14	.472	—

Notes: Minimum period of era = 5 years.

Win Pct = winning percentage of team during period.

Key Players = Top 100 hitters or top 10 at position with at least 2000 AB during period.

The best hitter's park this century, besides those in Denver, is Forbes Field from 1962 to 1969. Forbes had been a favorable park for the hitter since 1921, but for some reason it seemed to jump 10 points in the 1960s. It *is* possible that the Pirates just had unusually great hitters then and that the regression model overestimated the ballpark effect. It would be very interesting to get the home and away stats for Forbes for these years. Crosley Field also appeared to be particularly favorable to the hitter from1962 to 1969.

Boston's Fenway Park, Sportsman's Park, and Busch Stadium in St. Louis, and Bennett Park and Navin Field in Detroit had great hitter's parks for at least a third of a century.

The Philadelphia ballparks where Billy Hamilton, Ed Delahanty, and Sam Thompson played in the 1890s and Cleveland ballparks (1901–19) which were home to three of the top 11 hitters — Joe Jackson, Nap Lajoie, and Tris Speaker — also stand out.

The toughest parks for hitters this century have been South Side Park in Chicago, where the "Hitless Wonders" played, and Oakland-Alameda County Coliseum (Table 9.31).

It is interesting that there are many fewer top hitters listed for the tough hitting parks than for the good hitting parks. After all, the top hitting list should have adjusted out the ballpark effect. Once again the question seems to arise: "Does the ballpark make the hitter?"

Ballpark-Adjusted Batting Champions

Of the four adjustments used in this book, only the ballpark adjustment affects the relative ordering of batting averages within a single season. This gives rise to some interesting consequences. Sometimes the "official" batting champion for the league was not the best hitter for the year. This last occurred in 1993, where Mile High Stadium in Colorado lifted Andres Galarraga over Tony Gwynn — .370 to .358. After adjusting for the tremendous boost that the Colorado stadium gave Galarraga, Gwynn was really better by 16 points — .350 to .334.

Due to ballpark effects, players who were not the best hitter "officially" won 40 batting championships. This occurred 20 times in the American League, 15 times in the National League, and 5 times before 1901. Complete lists of these instances are given in Table 9.32.

From the table we see that Boggs, Heilmann, Oliva, Runnels, and

Table 9.32   Batting Title Changes after Ballpark Adjustment

Year	"Official" Champ	Team	Adj. BA	Adjusted Champ	Team	Adj. BA
National League						
1911	Wagner	Pit	.330	D. Miller	Bos	.332
1914	Daubert	Bkn	.329	Becker	Phi	.333
1919	Roush	Cin	.313	Hornsby	StL	.315
1929	O'Doul	Phi	.330	Babe Herman	Bkn	.331
1931	Hafey	StL	.316	Terry	NY	.320
1939	Mize	StL	.318	F. McCormick	Cin	.319
1945	Cavaretta	Chi	.341	Holmes	Bos	.344
1951	Musial	StL	.337	Ashburn	Phi	.340
1960	Groat	Pit	.321	Mays	SF	.326
1964	Clemente	Pit	.322	Carty	Mil	.324
1965	Clemente	Pit	.317	Mays	SF	.326
1967	Clemente	Pit	.343	Gonzalez	Phi	.348
1969	Rose	Cin	.336	Jones	NY	.349
1976	Madlock	Chi	.3359	Griffey Sr.	Cin	.3363
1993	Galarraga	Col	.334	Gwynn	SD	.350
American League						
1921	Heilmann	Det	.328	Ruth	NY	.330
1925	Heilmann	Det	.330	A. Simmons	Phi	.335
1926	Manush	Det	.329	Ruth	NY	.331
1929	Fonseca	Cle	.315	A. Simmons	Phi	.325
1935	Myer	Was	.315	Vosmik	Cle	.319
1938	Foxx	Bos	.3119	Heath	Cle	.312
1960	Runnels	Bos	.313	A. Smith	Chi	.316
1962	Runnels	Bos	.321	Mantle	NY	.330
1963	Yastrzemski	Bos	.325	Kaline	Det	.329
1964	Oliva	Min	.334	B. Robinson	Bal	.336
1968	Yastrzemski	Bos	.322	Cater	Oak	.332
1971	Oliva	Min	.335	Murcer	NY	.345
1972	Carew	Min	.327	Rudi	Oak	.337
1979	Lynn	Bos	.318	Downing	Cal	.323
1981	Lansford	Bos	.337	R. Henderson	Oak	.341
1982	W. Wilson	KC	.322	Yount	Mil	.330

(continued)

THE FINDINGS

Table 9.32   Batting Title Changes after Ballpark
              Adjustment (continued)

Year	"Official" Champ	Team	Adj. BA	Adjusted Champ	Team	Adj. BA
American League						
1986	Boggs	Bos	.345	Mattingly	NY	.352
1987	Boggs	Bos	.347	Molitor	Mil	.352
1989	Puckett	Min	.333	Lansford	Oak	.345
1990	Brett	KC	.332	R. Henderson	Oak	.339
Pre-1901						
1884*	K. Kelly	Chi	.319	Sutton	Bos	.324
1899*	Delahanty	Phi	.344	Burkett	StL	.348
1886**	Hecker	Lou	.323	Orr	NY	.342
1890**	Wolf	Lou	.329	S. Johnson	Clm	.330
1890†	Browning	Cle	.313	Orr	Bkn	.333

Notes:

* National League

** American Association

† Player's League

Yastrzemski, who played at hitter-friendly ballparks, each "lose" two batting crowns after the park adjustment, while Roberto Clemente "loses" three. Three of the seven players played at Fenway Park in Boston. All but Pete Runnels had other official batting titles that remained on top after the ballpark adjustment.

Where there are losers, there are also winners. Five players pick up two park-adjusted batting titles each.

Dave Orr, who is not a top 100 hitter only because he did not have 4000 career at bats, claims two adjusted titles in 1886 in the American Association and in 1890 in the Player's League. Although *Total Baseball, Fifth Edition* now considers pitcher-utility player Guy Hecker to be the unadjusted 1886 champion, their first edition and *The Baseball Encyclopedia* identify Pete Browning as the champion. Browning was also the "official" winner of the 1890 Player's League batting title. In both seasons, Browning was at hitter's parks while Orr played in pitcher's parks. Orr's lifetime fully-adjusted average of .329

would place him in 5th place, just ahead of Ted Williams and 7 places ahead of Pete Browning.

In the 1920s, four batting titles move into new hands. Al Simmons adds 2 adjusted batting championships to his 2 official ones while Ruth's total jumps from 1 to 3.

Willie Mays — with a single official title — picks up two park-adjusted batting titles. These superior performances were masked because Mays played at Candlestick Park in San Francisco. Rickey Henderson, just across the bay in Oakland, also wins two park-adjusted batting titles.

Carney Lansford is both a winner and a loser. In 1983, he moved from the best AL hitter's park — Fenway — to the worst hitter's park — Oakland-Alameda County Coliseum. Lansford's 1981 title should have been awarded to Henderson, while in 1989 he was really the best hitter, not Kirby Puckett of the Minnesota Twins.

In the National League, 3 of 5 titles between 1931 and 1951 were "lost" by St. Louis ballplayers, and Pittsburgh Pirates players lost 4 of the 5 that changed hands during the 1960s. In the American League, three of the first four championships were "lost" by Detroit ballplayers. Since 1938, all championships were lost by players at Boston (10), Minnesota (4), or Kansas City (2). Between 1935 and 1954 all three winners played for Cleveland.

No Bay area player has yet won an "official" batting title. However, Mays won 2 adjusted batting titles for San Francisco in the 1960s and 4 different Oakland players have won adjusted titles.

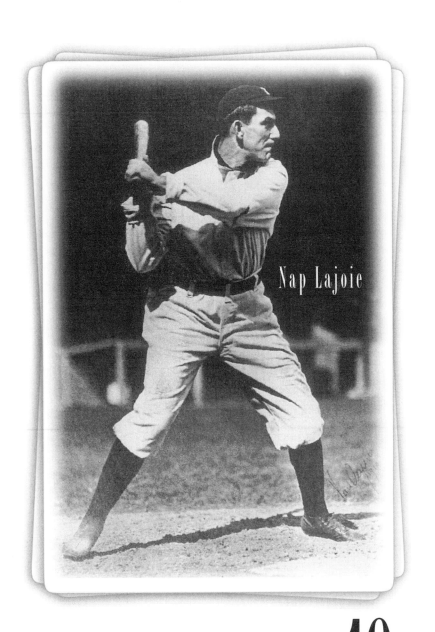

Nap Lajoie

On Base Percentage 10

After buying his first-inning hot dog, John sat in his box seat, rejoining his friend Steve. Smith, the leadoff hitter was on first base.

"How'd he get on?" John asked.

"Does it matter?" Steve shot back.

So . . . does it matter?

There are quite a number of ways to get on first, such as getting hit by a pitch, beating out a dropped third strike catcher's interference, or pinch running for someone who is on first already. The four most common ways are getting on via a hit, a walk, an error, or a fielder's choice. The two that depend most on the hitter's ability are a hit or a walk. These will be combined into a statistic called the "on base percentage."

Baseball games are won by runs, not hits — although hits do help to get runs. But so do walks. The *on base percentage* (OBP) gives hits and walks equal weight. The OBP is obtained by dividing hits (H) plus walks (BB) plus hit-by-pitch by at bats (AB) plus walks plus hit-by-pitch plus sacrifice flies. (The standard abbreviation for walks is "BB," for "base on balls.") Unfortunately, hit-by-pitch and sacrifice fly data are not readily available in the encyclopedias. Thus, a simplified version of on base percentage, defined as

$$OBP = (H + BB)/(AB + BB), \quad \text{Formula 1}$$

will be used in this book.

Defining the "walk" or "bases on balls" average (BBA) as

$$BBA = BB/(AB + BB),$$

the on base percentage can also be calculated as

$$OBP = BBA + (1 - BBA) \times BA, \quad \text{Formula 2}$$

as the technical note shows.

Formula 2 for OBP is quite useful since it shows how OBP can be obtained from the batting average (BA) and the walk average (BBA). It also makes a lot of sense, as mentioned in the Technical Note.

The same basic methods used to identify the best hitters earlier need to be used in order to obtain an *adjusted* walk average. Though

TECHNICAL NOTE

Equivalence of On Base Percentage Formulae

The algebra below shows that the two formulae for on base percentage are equal.

$$OBP = (H + BB) / (AB + BB) \qquad \text{Formula 1}$$
$$= H / (AB + BB) + BB / (AB + BB)$$

since the numerator can be split into two terms

$$= H / (AB + BB) + BBA$$

since $BBA = BB / (AB + BB)$

$$= (AB / AB) \times H / (AB + BB) + BBA$$

since we are multiplying by AB/AB $= 1$

$$= (H / AB) \times (AB / (AB + BB)) + BBA$$

since the order of multiplication can be changed

$$= BA \times (AB / (AB + BB)) + BBA$$

since $BA = H/AB$

$$= BA \times (1 - BBA) + BBA$$

since $1 = (AB + BB) / (AB + BB)$

$$= BBA + (1 - BBA) \times BA \qquad \text{Formula 2}$$

The OBP is the probability of getting a walk (BBA) plus the probability of getting a hit (obtained by multiplying the probability of getting a hit on the "condition" of not getting a walk (BA) by the probability of the "condition" of not getting a walk (1 - BBA).

home and away ballpark data from recent years (1982–97) demonstrate that there is a ballpark effect on walks (see Table 5.3), multiple regression analysis similar to that done in chapter 5 did not yield reliable estimates for use in the years before 1982. Thus, no ballpark adjustment has been applied to the walk average.

The walk averages of players with 200 or more at bats does not have a normal bell-shaped distribution. However, the square roots of the walk averages does have a normal distribution. (Interestingly, this is often the case for things being counted — walks in this case.) Thus, both the mean and standard deviation adjustments are applied to the

Fully Adjusted Base on Balls Average

The fully adjusted base on balls average is:

$$FABBA = [BBMN + .058/BBSD \times (BBA \times SBB/LBBA - BBMN)]^2,$$

where .058 is the chosen standardized standard deviation of the square root of player walk averages and the other factors are as defined below. LBBA, the league base on balls average for the year being studied, is given in Appendix V. SBB, the chosen standardized base on balls average, is .087 for years without the DH and .090 for years with the DH. BBMN and BBSD are the 5-year moving averages for the mean and standard deviation of the square root of individual walk averages after the league base on balls adjustment has been applied for players with at least 200 at bats for the year (also in Appendix V).

The longevity adjustment is also applied in order to obtain the career FABBA. No ballpark adjustment is applied, however, because reliable estimates of the ballpark effects are not yet available.

square root of the walk averages. When that is done, the resulting average is squared to get the adjusted walk average. This procedure is shown in the technical note above.

The 100 Best Walkers

Using the fully adjusted base on balls average formula, the list of players with the 100 best adjusted walk averages can be compiled. This list is given in Table 10.1.

Surprisingly, Max Bishop, who played second base from 1924 to 1935 for the Philadelphia Athletics and Boston Red Sox, tops the list. Bishop walked almost 20% of the time! Bishop was not a particularly

Table 10.1   List of *Adjusted* Top 100 Walk Averages

Rank	Player	Team	BB Avg
1	Max Bishop	PhiA	.196
2	Babe Ruth	NYA	.192
3	Ted Williams	BosA	.191
4	Roy Thomas	PhiN	.187
5	Gene Tenace	OakA	.185
6	John McGraw	BalN	.185
7	Topsy Hartsel	PhiA	.184
8	Eddie Stanky	BknN	.178
9	Roy Cullenbine	DetA	.172
10	Mel Ott	NYN	.171
11	Mickey Mantle	NYA	.171
12	Billy Hamilton	PhiN	.167
13	Joe Morgan	CinN	.167
14	Ferris Fain	PhiA	.166
15	Miller Huggins	CinN	.165
16	Eddie Yost	WasA	.164
17	Rickey Henderson	OakA	.163
18	Dolph Camilli	PhiN	.162
19	Harmon Killebrew	MinA	.160
20	Jack Clark	SFN	.160
21	Charlie Keller	NYA	.159
22	Eddie Mathews	MilN	.157
23	Jim Wynn	HouN	.156
24	Earl Torgeson	BosN	.153
25	Mike Hargrove	TexA	.153
	Mike Schmidt	PhiN	.153
27	Lu Blue	DetA	.153
	Cupid Childs	CleN	.153
29	Roger Bresnahan	NYN	.153
30	Ralph Kiner	PitN	.151
	Dwayne Murphy	OakA	.151
32	Lou Gehrig	NYA	.151
33	Elbie Fletcher	BosN	.151
34	Ken Singleton	BalA	.151
			(continued)

Table 10.1 List of *Adjusted* Top 100 Walk Averages *(continued)*

Rank	Player	Team	BB Avg
35	George Grantham	PitN	.150
36	Jason Thompson	PitN	.150
37	Darrell Evans	SFN	.149
38	George Gore	ChiN	.149
39	Hack Wilson	ChiN	.148
40	John Kruk	PhiN	.148
41	Augie Galan	ChiN	.147
42	Ned Williamson	ChiN	.146
43	Donie Bush	DetA	.146
44	Jack Clements	PhiN	.146
	Harlond Clift	StLN	.146
46	Willie McCovey	SFN	.145
47	Johnny Briggs	PhiN	.145
48	Jimmie Foxx	PhiA	.144
	Andy Thornton	CleA	.144
50	John Mayberry	KCA	.143
	Darrell Porter	KCA	.143
52	Elmer Valo	PhiA	.143
53	Eddie Joost	PhiA	.143
	Jimmy Sheckard	ChiN	.143
55	Billy North	OakA	.141
56	Carl Yastrzemski	BosA	.141
57	Bobby Grich	CalA	.141
58	Paul Radford	—	.139
59	Arky Vaughan	PitN	.139
60	Toby Harrah	TexA	.139
61	Willie Randolph	NYA	.138
62	Stan Hack	ChiN	.138
63	Wade Boggs	BosA	.138
64	Mickey Cochrane	PhiA	.137
65	Wally Schang	—	.137
66	Rogers Hornsby	StLN	.137
67	Lee Mazzilli	NYN	.136

(continued)

Table 10.1 List of *Adjusted* Top 100 Walk Averages *(continued)*

Rank	Player	Team	BB Avg
68	Dwight Evans	BosA	.136
69	Ross Youngs	NYN	.136
70	Norm Siebern	KCA	.136
71	Bob Allison	MinA	.136
	Brian Downing	CalA	.136
73	Jack Graney	CleA	.135
74	Jim Gilliam	BknN	.134
75	Ron Fairly	LAN	.134
76	Norm Cash	DetA	.134
77	Jeff Burroughs	TexA	.133
78	Dick Allen	PhiN	.132
79	Boog Powell	BalA	.131
80	Roger Connor	NYN	.131
81	Eddie Collins	PhiA	.131
82	Don Mincher	MinA	.130
83	Burt Shotton	StLA	.130
84	Hank Greenberg	DetA	.129
85	Dummy Hoy	—	.129
86	Frank Chance	ChiN	.129
	Gene Woodling	NYA	.129
88	Ron Santo	ChiN	.129
89	Sal Bando	OakA	.128
90	Keith Hernandez	StLN	.128
91	Rick Monday	ChiN	.128
92	Tim Raines	MonN	.127
93	Heinie Groh	CinN	.127
94	Dan Brouthers	—	.126
95	Dave Bancroft	PhiN	.126
	Frank Robinson	CinN	.126
97	Rocky Colavito	CleA	.126
98	Lou Whitaker	DetA	.126
99	Bob Johnson	PhiA	.125
100	Brett Butler	LAN	.125

(continued)

Table 10.1   List of *Adjusted* Top 100 Walk Averages *(continued)*

Rank	Player	Team	BB Avg
	Len Dykstra	PhiN	.125
	Rick Ferrell	WasA	.125
	Jackie Robinson	BknN	.125
	Elmer Smith	PitN	.125

Note: Players are "tied" if their averages agree to 4 decimal places.

good hitter, having an adjusted batting average of .248. He was not a home run hitter, hitting less than 1 per 100 at bats. Consequently, pitchers would surely not have wanted to pitch around him in order to face Al Simmons, Mickey Cochrane, or Jimmie Foxx instead. In order to walk so frequently, then, Bishop must have had an eagle eye at the plate, refusing to swing at bad pitches. The example of Max Bishop suggests that *any* major league baseball player can walk a lot if he made a serious effort. Why should a player want to?

Max Bishop scored as often per plate appearance (time at the plate, whether registered as an at bat or not) as his Hall of Fame team-mates did. However, he only drove in one-half to one-third as many runs as the Hall of Famers. There was probably no more upsetting thing to an opposing pitcher than to walk Bishop only to see Simmons or Foxx stride to the plate!

After Bishop come Ruth and Williams. OK, now we're talking baseball's greatest players! A bunch of unlikely names, however, follow them — Roy Thomas, Gene Tenace, John McGraw, Topsy Hartsel, Eddie Stanky, and Roy Cullenbine. This gives more support to the viewpoint that almost any ballplayer can walk if he makes an effort to add it to his offensive repertoire.

Very few players rank among the top 100 on *both* batting average and walk average lists — only nineteen. A single player is in the top 10 for both lists — Ted Williams. Babe Ruth ranks among the top 25 of both lists, while Lou Gehrig, Billy Hamilton, and Mickey Mantle are in the top 50 of both lists. The remaining players are Dick Allen, Wade Boggs, Dan Brouthers, Frank Chance, Eddie Collins, Jimmie Foxx, Rickey Henderson, Keith Hernandez, Rogers Hornsby, Tim Raines, Frank Robinson, Carl Yastrzemski, and Ross Youngs.

The 100 Best Players for On Base Percentage

Many fans are fixated on batting average as a measure of player ability. This could be expected since the newspapers show batting average lists more often than any other. For years, Sunday newspapers have presented extended lists of players sorted by batting average. Consequently, fans have a good appreciation for batting average differences. For example, a .270 hitter is recognized as a decent hitter, while a .310 hitter is considered to be a star. The difference in batting average between these two players is a whopping 40 points. However, differences in walk averages can be *extraordinary*. For example, Joe Morgan beat Kirby Puckett by 109 walk points (.167 to .058), easily overcoming Puckett's 38-point edge in adjusted batting average (.313 to .275), which gave Morgan an overall 40-point edge in on base percentage!

How is it that players' walk averages differ so much? Serious baseball researchers frequently argue that neither players nor managers widely recognize the value of a walk. However, since Williams and Ruth rank second and third on the adjusted walk list, that should tell us something!

The on base percentage statistic really allows the cream to begin to rise to the top, with Ted Williams (#1), and Babe Ruth (#2), heading the list. Sluggers Mickey Mantle (#4), Rogers Hornsby (#5), and Lou Gehrig (#9), also place among the top 10 as do stolen base experts Billy Hamilton (#3) and Rickey Henderson (#10). Wade Boggs, who places 61st best for walk average and 7th for OBP, almost always watches the first pitch, as George Will notes in *Men At Work*. Walk experts John McGraw (#6), and Roy Thomas (#8), complete the top 10.

The top hitters tend to have decent walk averages. All but two of the top 11 hitters had walk averages better than the average player. The two exceptions are Tony Gwynn and Nap Lajoie. Tony Gwynn's walk average is only .080, dropping him to 32nd place on the OBP list, while Nap Lajoie, with an anemic .067 walk average, fails to place in the OBP top 100. Notably, Max Bishop, in spite of his lowly .248 batting average, holds an OBP better than 4 of the top 11 hitters — Gwynn, Joe Jackson, Lajoie, and Honus Wagner.

Table 10.2   *Adjusted* List of 100 Best Players for On Base Percentage

Rank	Player	Team	OBP	Bat Avg	BB Avg
1	Ted Williams	BosA	.455	.327	.191
2	Babe Ruth	NYA	.444	.312	.192
3	Billy Hamilton	PhiN	.424	.308	.167
4	Mickey Mantle	NYA	.422	.303	.171
5	Rogers Hornsby	StLN	.422	.330	.137
6	John McGraw	BalN	.418	.286	.185
7	Wade Boggs	BosA	.417	.324	.138
8	Roy Thomas	PhiN	.415	.281	.187
9	Lou Gehrig	NYA	.413	.308	.151
10	Rickey Henderson	OakA	.411	.296	.163
11	Mel Ott	NYN	.409	.287	.171
12	Topsy Hartsel	PhiA	.409	.276	.184
13	Stan Musial	StLN	.408	.325	.124
14	Ty Cobb	DetA	.406	.340	.100
15	Tris Speaker	CleA	.405	.322	.122
16	John Kruk	PhiN	.404	.301	.148
17	Ferris Fain	PhiA	.402	.283	.166
18	Eddie Collins	PhiA	.400	.310	.131
	Dan Brouthers	—	.400	.313	.126
20	Jimmie Foxx	PhiA	.398	.298	.144
21	Mike Hargrove	TexA	.398	.289	.153
22	Roy Cullenbine	DetA	.398	.273	.172
23	Ken Singleton	BalA	.397	.291	.151
24	Charlie Keller	NYA	.397	.283	.159
25	Rod Carew	MinA	.397	.332	.098
26	Arky Vaughan	PitN	.396	.298	.139
27	Joe Morgan	CinN	.396	.275	.167
28	Max Bishop	PhiA	.396	.248	.196
29	Joe Jackson	CleA	.395	.331	.096
30	Eddie Stanky	BknN	.395	.264	.178
31	Jesse Burkett	CleN	.394	.311	.122
32	Tony Gwynn	SDN	.394	.342	.080
33	Carl Yastrzemski	BosA	.394	.295	.141
34	Willie Mays	SFN	.394	.314	.117

(continued)

Table 10.2 *Adjusted* List of 100 Best Players for On Base Percentage
(*continued*)

Rank	Player	Team	OBP	Bat Avg	BB Avg
35	Honus Wagner	PitN	.394	.327	.100
36	Frank Robinson	CinN	.392	.304	.126
37	Jackie Robinson	BknN	.391	.304	.125
38	Ross Youngs	NYN	.391	.295	.136
39	George Gore	ChiN	.391	.284	.149
40	Richie Ashburn	PhiN	.390	.304	.124
41	Gene Tenace	OakA	.390	.251	.185
42	Cupid Childs	CleN	.390	.280	.153
43	Pete Browning	Loua	.389	.317	.105
44	Dick Allen	PhiN	.388	.296	.132
45	Frank Chance	ChiN	.388	.298	.129
46	Stan Hack	ChiN	.387	.289	.138
	Tim Raines	MonN	.387	.298	.127
48	Roger Bresnahan	NYN	.387	.277	.153
49	Miller Huggins	CinN	.387	.265	.165
	Mickey Cochrane	PhiA	.387	.289	.137
51	Paul Waner	PitN	.387	.307	.115
	Cap Anson	ChiN	.386	.305	.117
53	Jack Clark	SFN	.385	.269	.160
54	Roger Connor	NYN	.385	.292	.131
55	Hack Wilson	ChiN	.384	.277	.148
56	Keith Hernandez	StLN	.384	.293	.128
57	Hank Greenberg	DetA	.383	.291	.129
58	Augie Galan	ChiN	.382	.276	.147
59	Eddie Murray	BalA	.382	.299	.118
60	Willie McCovey	SFN	.382	.277	.145
61	Eddie Mathews	MilN	.381	.266	.157
62	Dolph Camilli	PhiN	.381	.261	.162
63	Ralph Kiner	PitN	.380	.270	.151
64	Brett Butler	LAN	.380	.292	.125
65	Al Kaline	DetA	.380	.307	.106
66	Elmer Flick	PhiN	.380	.294	.121
67	Harmon Killebrew	MinA	.380	.262	.160

Table 10.2 *Adjusted* List of 100 Best Players for On Base Percentage
(*continued*)

Rank	Player	Team	OBP	Bat Avg	BB Avg
68	Elmer Valo	PhiA	.380	.276	.143
69	Norm Cash	DetA	.379	.284	.134
70	George Grantham	PitN	.379	.270	.150
71	Riggs Stephenson	ChiN	.379	.300	.112
72	George Brett	KCA	.379	.307	.103
73	Johnny Mize	StLN	.378	.297	.116
74	Tip O'Neill	StLa	.378	.312	.097
75	Mike Schmidt	PhiN	.378	.266	.153
76	Willie Randolph	NYA	.378	.278	.138
	Duke Snider	BknN	.378	.292	.121
78	Bobby Grich	CalA	.376	.274	.141
79	Luke Appling	ChiA	.376	.297	.113
80	Jack Fournier	—	.376	.292	.119
81	Gene Woodling	NYA	.376	.284	.129
82	Denny Lyons	Phia	.375	.287	.124
83	Jimmy Sheckard	ChiN	.375	.271	.143
84	Earl Torgeson	BosN	.375	.262	.153
85	Elbie Fletcher	BosN	.375	.264	.151
86	Len Dykstra	PhiN	.375	.285	.125
	Pedro Guerrero	LAN	.374	.303	.103
88	Eddie Yost	WasA	.374	.251	.164
89	Pete Rose	CinN	.374	.306	.098
90	Ron Santo	ChiN	.373	.281	.129
91	Rusty Staub	—	.373	.288	.119
	Norm Siebern	KCA	.373	.275	.136
93	Hank Aaron	AtlN	.373	.308	.094
	Paul Molitor	MilA	.373	.307	.094
95	Jim Wynn	HouN	.373	.256	.156
	Joe Kelley	BalN	.372	.283	.125
97	Joe DiMaggio	NYA	.372	.311	.089
98	Rico Carty	AtlN	.372	.297	.107
99	Ed Delahanty	PhiN	.371	.303	.098
100	Elmer Smith	PitN	.371	.281	.125

Note: Players are "tied" if their averages agree to 4 decimal places.

Eight of the nineteen players who appear on both the batting average and walk average lists (and mentioned in the previous section) rank in the top 10 for on base percentage. The remaining two players in the top 10 — John McGraw and Roy Thomas — are outstanding walkers, not outstanding hitters.

Tris Speaker

The Hall of Fame 11

A favorite pastime of avid baseball fans is to suggest who should be enshrined in the Baseball Hall of Fame in Cooperstown, New York. A player whose cause is being championed is naturally compared to those already in the Hall, especially to players at the same position. However, some Hall of Fame selections seem to have been misguided. Bill James forcefully argues his opinions on many of these questionable choices in his book *Whatever Happened to the Hall of Fame?* (previously published as *The Politics of Glory*).

Bill James, Pete Palmer, John Thorn, and other recent baseball number crunchers have emphasized that the fundamental goal of a ballplayer is (or should be) to help his team win games and that *runs win games*. Thus, a player's primary goal should be to "produce" runs for his team, while limiting them for the opposition.

Years ago, when learning about multiple regression (used in chapter 5 to estimate the ballpark effects), I investigated which factors led to winning teams — batting average? Home runs? Stolen bases? Earned run average (ERA)? . . . The answer boiled down to just two factors — runs scored and ERA. Since ERA does not count runs scored due to fielding errors (about 10% of runs scored), the total number of runs allowed would have been a better choice, but was unavailable to me. In the regression equation, the multiplying numbers for runs scored and ERA were nearly equal and of opposite sign. Thus winning ballgames reduced down to a single term — run differential over the season! The more runs a team scores compared to its opponents, the more games they'll win. Why did I need statistics to figure that out? Perhaps it is useful in noting that there is no special value in home runs or stolen bases or any other hitting event other than their ability to produce runs.

One *big* question, then, is: How much do individual baseball events contribute to runs? In *The Hidden Game of Baseball*, John Thorn and Pete Palmer developed what eventually became known as the Total Player Rating (TPR for short) to answer this question. They broke down the contribution of non-pitchers into three components: Adjusted Batting Runs, Stolen Base Runs, and Fielding Runs. For most players, the impact of Stolen Base Runs is not that great. Fielding Runs represents the number of runs saved by superior play in the field, which is largely a result of making plays on balls due to range, which is strongly associated with "total chances" in the field.

Batting Runs is based on a computer simulation by Pete Palmer on the contribution of various batting events to runs at the team level. Their formula, in *Total Baseball, Fifth Edition* (p. 571) is:

Runs = .47 × (singles) + .78 × (doubles) + 1.09 × (triples) + 1.40 × (home runs) + .33 × (bases on balls and hit batsman) + .33 × (stolen bases) − .60 × (times caught stealing) − .25 × (outs) − .50 × (outs on base).

An adjusted Batting Runs formula is obtained by adjusting for the league average and the ballpark effect for runs.

From the formula, we see that singles *are* more valuable than walks, .47 to .33. One reason is that a single can drive home a run whereas a walk cannot, unless the bases are loaded. However, the question at the beginning of chapter 10 was more specific. I don't have a definitive answer to it, but it is my belief that that a leadoff single and a leadoff walk are equal in run production potential.

The "Batting Runs" component of TPR is highly related to On Base Plus Slugging (abbreviated OPS), which is defined as On Base Percentage plus Slugging Average. Slugging Average (SLG) is the average number of bases that a player hits himself per at bat. Thus, a single counts as one base, a double as two, a triple as three, and a home run as four. The On Base Percentage (OBP), as we saw in the last chapter, counts one for each hit and each walk divided by the number of at bats plus walks. Adding the counts for of OBP and SLG, together, we get 1 (= 1+ 0) for walks is 2 (= 1 + 1) for singles, 3 (= 1 + 2) for doubles, 4 (= 1 + 3) for triples, and 5 = (1 + 4) for home runs. The relative weighting (compared to walks) in the "Runs" formula above is 1.4 (= .47/.33) for singles, 2.4 (= .78/.33) for doubles, 3.3 (= 1.09/.33) for triples, and 4.2 (= 1.40/.33) for home runs. Thus, compared to "Runs," OPS undervalues walks. An approximation, closer to the "Runs" formula than OPS, is obtained by 1.4 × OBA + SLG, which gives relative weights compared to walks of 1.7 (= 2.4/1.4) for singles, 2.4 (= 3.4/1.4) for doubles, 3.1 (= 4.4/1.4) for triples, and 3.9 (= 5.4/1.4) for home runs. In any event, on base percentage has some relationship with run production, which has some relationship with who the best players are.

Guide to the Tables in This Chapter

For the six tables in this chapter, players are organized by their primary fielding position. Players are included according to the following criteria:

1. Members of the Hall of Fame.
2. Among the top N players eligible for the Hall of Fame at that position, according to the TPR, where N is the number of Hall of Famers at that position.
3. Players ineligible for HOF (for example, players who are retired for less than 5 years), whose TPR values are at least as high as the lowest TPR of those selected by criterion 2.

Column Headings in Tables

Player Symbols
> bold — not in Hall of Fame
> * — Hall of Fame (HOF) player with lower TPR than eligible non-HOF players in list
> † — not eligible for Hall of Fame

Adj OBP — Adjusted on base percentage, using FABBA from chapter 10.

Adj BA — Adjusted batting average, using FABA from chapter 5.

AB — Number of at bats (in thousands).

Yrs to Hall — Number of years from retirement to election into the Hall of Fame. Since the first year of Hall of Fame voting was 1936 and players must be retired at least 5 years to be eligible for election, the number of years until election since 1936 is used for all players who retired prior to 1931. Asterisks are used to denote these early players.

Top 5 — Number of times that the player finished in the top 5 for a season in the category given. An underlined number represents one championship, while a bold number represents 2 or more championships among the total. The source of the information is *Total Baseball, First Edition* for 1876–1988 and *Total Baseball, Fifth Edition* for 1989–96.

BA — Batting average

OBP — On base percentage

HR — Home runs

Field — Fielding runs

What to Look for in the Tables

The tables list Hall of Fame players and those rated as "best" by the Total Player Rating (TPR) side-by-side. TPR uses two adjustments very similar to those described in this book — mean- and ballpark-adjustments for runs. Their rating coincides reasonably well with adjusted OBP since players with high TPR cluster toward the top.

The table lists are organized by decreasing adjusted on base percentage. Since OBP is one of the key components of run production, we should expect that the "best" players by TPR standards will rank higher in the list. The Hall of Fame players with lower TPR ratings will tend to either be lower in the lists or have relatively few career at bats (since the Rating is a lifetime achievement award). It is also interesting to note that the Hall of Fame players not ranked among the TPR "best," were quite often selected more than 20 years after retirement (or possible selection for old-timers) — in contrast to the clear-cut Hall of Famers.

Recommended Changes in Hall of Fame Membership

Overall, according to the Total Player Rating formula for determining "true" Hall of Fame–caliber players, 38 of the 121 non-pitcher Hall of Famers would be "replaced." The replaced players have a combined adjusted on base percentage of .348 and adjusted batting average of .282, while the "superior" players have .362 and .280 averages, respectively. The "superior" players have 19 more top 5 HR finishes (58 to 39) and 22 more top 5 fielding finishes (71 to 49). So why were the players with lower averages chosen in the first place?

The Hall of Fame players have been selected by the Baseball Writer's Association of America (BBWAA) and three committees — the Old Timer's Committee (1939–49), the Veteran's Committee (1953–77), and the New Veteran's Committee (1978–present). Although the rules have changed over time, for many years the BBWAA has been charged to select players who have been retired for 5 to 20 years. Nineteenth-century players and those who have been retired more than 20 years are selected by the Committees.

The most clearcut selections get made by the BBWAA. Overall, 51/57 (89%) of their selections place among the best by the TPR

Table 11.1 Actual and Recommended Hall of Fame Outfielders

	Adj OBP	Adj BA	AB	Yrs to Hall	Top 5			
					BA	OBP	HR	Field
Ted Williams	.455	.327	7.7	6	12	12	9	
Babe Ruth	.444	.312	8.4	0	8̲	14	16	
Billy Hamilton	.424	.308	6.3	25*	7	11		
Mickey Mantle	.422	.303	8.1	6	8̲	12	9	
Roy Thomas	.415	.281	5.3	—	1	9		
R. Henderson†	.411	.296	8.9	—	3	10̲		2
Mel Ott	.409	.287	9.5	4		12	15	1
Stan Musial	.408	.325	11.0	6	16	16	4	
Ty Cobb	.406	.340	11.4	0*	16	16	6̲	1
Tris Speaker	.405	.322	10.2	1*	13̲	14	5̲	
Charlie Keller	.397	.283	3.8	—		5	4	
Joe Jackson†	.395	.331	5.0	—	7	7̲	3	
Jesse Burkett	.394	.310	8.4	10*	7	7̲	1	
Tony Gwynn†	.394	.342	8.2	—	13	5		
Carl Yastrzemski	.394	.295	12.0	6	5	7	3̲	
Willie Mays	.394	.314	10.9	6	7̲	10	10	2
Frank Robinson	.392	.304	10.0	6	9̲	11	10̲	1
Ross Youngs*	.391	.295	4.6	36*	3	5		
Richie Ashburn	.390	.304	8.4	33	4	6		9
Pete Browning	.388	.317	4.8	—	9	7		
Tim Raines†	.387	.298	8.2	—	3̲	6̲		
Paul Waner	.386	.307	9.5	7	8̲	9̲		1̲
Jack Clark	.385	.269	6.8	—		4̲		1
Hack Wilson*	.384	.277	4.8	45		3̲	6	
Ralph Kiner	.380	.270	5.2	20	2	3	8	
Brett Butler†	.380	.292	8.2	—	1	3̲		1
Al Kaline	.380	.306	10.1	6	7̲	7		3
Elmer Flick	.380	.294	5.6	27*	5̲	6	1	1
Duke Snider	.378	.292	7.2	16	4	4̲	4̲	
Len Dykstra†	.374	.285	4.6	—	1	2		1
Rusty Staub	.373	.288	9.7	—	1	4		
Hank Aaron	.373	.308	12.5	6	11	7	13	1
Jim Wynn	.372	.256	6.7	—		4	3	
Joe Kelley*	.372	.283	7.0	35*	2	2		

(continued)

Table 11.1   Actual and Recommended Hall of Fame Outfielders *(continued)*

	Adj OBP	Adj BA	AB	Yrs to Hall	Top 5			
					BA	OBP	HR	Field
Joe DiMaggio	.372	.311	6.8	4	4	3	10	
Ed Delahanty	.372	.303	7.5	9*	9	6	6	1
Harry Heilmann	.371	.302	7.8	20	8	7	4	
Reggie Jackson	.370	.282	9.9	6		3	8	
King Kelly	.370	.291	5.9	9*	5	4	1	
Billy Williams	.369	.299	9.3	11	3	1	5	
Fred Clarke	.369	.295	8.6	15*	2	2		
Larry Doby*	.368	.279	5.3	39	1	2	3	
Bob Johnson	.368	.278	6.9	—	2	3	4	2
Minnie Minoso	.368	.297	6.6	—	4	5		2
Dwight Evans†	.366	.267	7.8	—		2	2	
Sherry Magee	.366	.295	7.4	—	3	3	3	
Reggie Smith	.366	.288	7.0	—	1	3	2	
Rocky Colavito	.364	.273	6.5	—		2	6	
Enos Slaughter*	.364	.287	7.9	26	3	4	1	1
Fred Lynn	.364	.282	6.4	—	2	2		
Earle Combs*	.364	.292	5.7	32	1	1		
Max Carey	.363	.276	9.4	25*		3		6
Kiki Cuyler*	.361	.290	7.2	30	3	3		
Dave Winfield†	.361	.289	11.0	—	2	4	2	
Sam Crawford	.360	.300	9.6	21*	8	5	6	
Willie Keeler*	.360	.311	8.6	3*	10	3		
Earl Averill*	.359	.287	6.4	36	1	2	4	1
Jim O'Rourke*	.359	.292	7.4	9*	5	4	1	
Jose Cruz	.358	.286	7.9	—	2			
Harry Hooper*	.358	.272	8.8	46		1		
Zach Wheat	.357	.302	9.1	23*	6	3	2	
Chuck Klein	.356	.285	6.5	41	4	3	7	1
Hugh Duffy*	.355	.292	7.0	9*	3	2	3	
Tony Oliva	.355	.311	6.3	—	7	1		
Bobby Bonds	.355	.271	7.0	—			3	
Sam Thompson	.353	.300	6.0	38*	5		4	
Edd Roush*	.352	.302	7.4	31	7	3		
Kirby Puckett†	.352	.313	7.2		5			4

(continued)

Table 11.1 Actual and Recommended Hall of Fame Outfielders *(continued)*

	Adj OBP	Adj BA	AB	Yrs to Hall	Top 5			
					BA	OBP	HR	Field
Goose Goslin	.351	.286	8.7	31	2	2	4	
Willie Stargell	.351	.273	7.9	6		2	4	
Wally Berger	.350	.285	5.2	—			6	
Roberto Clemente	.350	.306	9.5	1	10	2		3
Al Simmons	.349	.306	8.8	10	7	1	7	
Chet Lemon	.348	.275	6.9	—				1
Jim Rice†	.348	.292	8.2	—	4		4	
Chick Hafey*	.347	.285	4.6	34	1	1	1	
Tommy McCarthy*	.346	.276	5.1	10*	1	1		1
Joe Medwick	.345	.305	7.6	23	7	1	3	
Cesar Cedeno	.344	.285	7.3	—	3	1	1	
Sam Rice*	.343	.293	9.3	29				3
Lou Brock*	.340	.290	10.3	6				
Heinie Manush*	.339	.296	7.7	25	6	2		
George Foster	.337	.275	7.0	—	1		4	
Dave Parker†	.336	.288	9.4	—	3	2	3	1
Lloyd Waner*	.329	.288	7.8	23	1			1
Andre Dawson†	.325	.283	9.9	—	2		4	4
Joe Carter†	.300	.257	8.0	—			3	
Average	.371	.294	7.8		4.1	4.2	3.0	0.7

Notes: See Guide to the Tables on p. 230.

Players not bolded = Hall of Famers (N = 55).

Players in bold = non-HOF players (with TPR ≥ 21.4).

* = Hall of Famers with TPR < 21.4 (N = 19).

† = not currently eligible for the Hall of Fame (N = 13).

rating. The committees have had lower rates of "best" player selections: Old Timer's Committee (11/16 — 69%), Veteran's Committee (13/30 — 43%), and New Veteran's Committee (8/18 — 44%). Thus exactly half (32/64) of the committee selections are among the best by TPR criteria.

A particularly heavy string of "questionable" choices occurred between 1962 and 1977 by the Veteran's Committee, when only 6/21 (29%) of the choices are among the best by the Total Player Rating. Of the 15 "questionable" choices, twelve played between 1922 and 1934

Table 11.2   Actual and Recommended Hall of Fame First Basemen

	Adj OBP	Adj BA	AB	Yrs to Hall	Top 5			
					BA	OBP	HR	Field
Lou Gehrig	.412	.308	8.0	0	9	11	12	
Dan Brouthers	.400	.313	6.7	9*	11	12	6	
Jimmie Foxx	.398	.298	8.1	6	7	10	12	
Dick Allen	.388	.296	6.3	—	3	3	4	
Frank Chance*	.388	.298	4.3	10*		2		
Cap Anson	.386	.305	9.1	3*	10	11	4	1
Roger Connor	.385	.292	7.8	40*	6	10	6	
Keith Hernandez†	.384	.293	7.4	—	3	7		1
Hank Greenberg	.383	.291	5.2	9	2	3	6	
Eddie Murray†	.382	.299	11.3	—	4	5	3	
Willie McCovey	.382	.276	8.2	10	1	5	7	
Harmon Killebrew	.380	.262	8.1	9	1	4	11	
Norm Cash	.379	.284	6.7	—	1	2	4	
Johnny Mize	.378	.297	6.4	28	6	6	9	
Jack Fournier	.376	.292	5.2	—	4	5	5	
Bill Terry	.369	.307	6.4	18	7	3	2	1
George Sisler	.347	.309	8.3	9	7	4	2	1
Jim Bottomley*	.344	.276	7.5	37	2	1	4	
Jake Beckley	.338	.290	9.5	35*	3	1	1	
George Kelly*	.319	.266	6.0	41			4	1
Average	**.376**	**.293**	**7.3**		**4.4**	**5.2**	**5.0**	**0.2**

Notes: See Guide to the Tables on p. 230.

Players not bolded = Hall of Famers (N = 15).

Players in bold = non-HOF players (with TPR ≥ 22.7).

* = Hall of Famers with TPR < 22.7 (N = 3).

† = not currently eligible for the Hall of Fame (N = 2).

and nine are among the top 100 *unadjusted* hitters. In the 1960s and 1970s, hitting for average was at a low ebb. The .300 + career batting averages of the 1920s and 1930s players selected for the Hall must have made them seem better. The league batting averages were at all-time twentieth-century highs during these years, however, contributing to the "apparent" superiority of the "questionable" Hall of Famers. Once batting averages are adjusted, these players do not stand out as much.

Table 11.3   Actual and Recommended Hall of Fame Second Basemen

	Adj OBP	Adj BA	AB	Yrs to Hall	Top 5			
					BA	OBP	HR	Field
Rogers Hornsby	.422	.330	8.2	5	12	11	11	1
Eddie Collins	.400	.310	9.9	3	11	15		4
Rod Carew	.397	.332	9.3	6	12	7		1
Joe Morgan	.396	.275	9.3	6	2	8	1	
Jackie Robinson	.391	.304	4.9	6	4	5		3
Cupid Childs	.390	.280	5.6	—	1	2		2
Bobby Grich	.376	.274	6.9	—			1	5
Johnny Evers*	.368	.278	6.1	10*	2	4		3
C. Gehringer	.366	.292	8.9	7	5	4		1
Nap Lajoie	.365	.322	9.6	1*	7	7	3	8
Billy Herman	.358	.290	7.7	28	2	1		7
Tony Lazerri*	.351	.266	6.3	52	1	1	3	
Bid McPhee	.351	.266	8.3	—				9
Frankie Frisch	.347	.286	9.1	10	2			5
Ryne Sandberg†	.342	.281	8.4	—	1		2	2
Bobby Doerr	.338	.273	7.1	35	2	1	1	7
Nellie Fox*	.336	.289	9.2	32	5	1		2
Red Schoendienst*	.321	.276	8.5	26	1			5
Bill Mazeroski	.294	.252	7.8	—				10
Average	.364	.288	7.9		3.7	3.5	1.2	4.0

Notes: See Guide to the Tables on p. 230.

Players not bolded = Hall of Famers (N = 14).

Players in bold = non-HOF players (with TPR ≥ 30.0).

* = Hall of Famers with TPR < 30.0 (N = 4).

† = not currently eligible for the Hall of Fame (N = 1).

Instead, it is the players of the 1960s and 1970s that have been primarily overlooked in Hall of Fame selections. If baseball writers and the New Veteran's Committee can come to terms with the importance of considering adjusted averages, many of the 1960s and 70s players can proudly take their places beside Hall of Fame counterparts whose raw numbers look so much better.

Table 11.4   Actual and Recommended Hall of Fame Shortstops

	Adj OBP	Adj BA	AB	Yrs to Hall	Top 5			
					BA	OBP	HR	Field
Arky Vaughan	.396	.298	6.6	37	4̲	5		1
Honus Wagner	.394	.326	10.4	0*	13	9	4	2
Luke Appling	.376	.297	8.9	14	3	6̲		4̲
Lou Boudreau	.362	.288	6.0	18	2̲	3		6̲
Alan Trammell†	.359	.291	8.3	—	4	1		
Joe Cronin	.358	.275	7.6	11		1		2
Pee Wee Reese*	.357	.265	8.1	26				2̲
George Davis	.356	.287	9.0	61*	1		1	5
Dave Bancroft	.356	.263	7.2	44		1		6
Bill Dahlen	.351	.265	9.0	—			2	10̲
Cal Ripken†	.351	.281	9.8	—	1		1	1̲
Jim Fregosi	.350	.279	6.5	—				
Joe Sewell	.348	.272	7.1	44		1		3
Robin Yount†	.347	.292	11.0	—	2			2
Bobby Wallace	.341	.267	8.6	16*			1	5
Jack Glassock	.340	.284	7.0	—	2̲	1		6
Ozzie Smith†	.339	.262	9.4	—				9
Ernie Banks	.337	.279	9.4	6			7	
Dick Bartell	.334	.260	7.6	—				4
Hugh Jennings	.329	.276	4.9	9*	1	3		4
Phil Rizzuto*	.332	.270	5.8	38				4
Joe Tinker	.319	.269	6.4	10*			1	4
Rabbit Maranville*	.318	.250	10.1	18*				8̲
Monte Ward*	.317	.266	7.6	28*	1		1	2
Travis Jackson	.315	.262	6.1	46				3
Luis Aparicio*	.312	.267	10.2	11	1			5̲
Art Fletcher	.300	.270	5.5	—				5
Average	**.344**	**.276**	**7.9**		1.3	1.1	0.9	4.0

Notes: See Guide to the Tables on p. 230.

Players not bolded = Hall of Famers (N = 18).

Players in bold = non-HOF players (with TPR ≥ 20.6).

* = Hall of Famers with TPR < 20.6 (N = 5).

† = not currently eligible for the Hall of Fame (N = 4).

Table 11.5   Actual and Recommended Hall of Fame Third Basemen

	Adj OBP	Adj BA	AB	Yrs to Hall	Top 5 BA	OBP	HR	Field
Wade Boggs†	.417	.324	8.5	—	11	9		2
Stan Hack	.387	.289	7.3	—	<u>3</u>	6		2
Eddie Mathews	.381	.266	8.5	10		<u>7</u>	8	
George Brett†	.379	.307	10.3	—	5	<u>4</u>		
Mike Schmidt	.378	.266	8.4	6	1	7	12	8
Ron Santo	.373	.281	8.1	—		4	2	<u>5</u>
Paul Molitor†	.373	.307	10.3	—	6			
Heinie Groh	.371	.280	6.1	—	3	4		
Darrell Evans	.365	.253	8.7	—		3	<u>2</u>	2
George Kell*	.349	.299	6.7	26	7	2		1
Frank Baker*	.348	.294	6.0	19*	3	2	8	1
Buddy Bell	.343	.282	9.0	—	1			4
Brooks Robinson*	.338	.288	10.7	6	2			5
Pie Traynor*	.332	.283	7.6	11	1			1
Jimmy Collins	.331	.277	6.8	9*	1		<u>1</u>	1
Fred Lindstrom*	.327	.280	5.6	40	2			1
Average	.362	.286	8.0		2.9	3.0	2.0	2.0

Notes: See Guide to the Tables on p. 230.

Players not bolded = Hall of Famers (N = 8).

Players in bold = non-HOF players (with TPR ≥ 22.9).

* = Hall of Famers with TPR < 22.9 (N = 5).

† = not currently eligible for the Hall of Fame (N = 3).

Table 11.6 Actual and Recommended Hall of Fame Catchers

	Adj OBP	Adj BA	AB	Yrs to Hall	Top 5			
					BA	OBP	HR	Field
Roger Bresnahan	.387	.277	4.5	9*	1	3		
Mickey Cochrane	.387	.289	5.2	10	2	4		
Wally Schang	.366	.266	5.3	—				
Gabby Hartnett	.357	.273	6.4	14			3	1
Bill Dickey	.355	.292	6.3	8		1		
Rick Ferrell*	.352	.260	6.0	37			1	
Roy Campanella	.350	.271	4.2	12	2		2	
Ernie Lombardi	.348	.295	5.9	39	1		1	
Ted Simmons	.346	.281	8.7	—	2	1	2	1
Johnny Bench	.346	.266	7.7	6			4	
Buck Ewing	.344	.283	5.4	3*	2		1	1
Carlton Fisk†	.338	.271	8.8	—	1		1	2
Gary Carter†	.336	.265	8.0	—			3	5
Yogi Berra	.334	.281	7.6	7			5	1
Ray Schalk*	.329	.249	5.3	19				1
Average	**.351**	**.274**	**6.3**		0.7	0.6	1.5	0.8

Notes: See Guide to the Tables on p. 230.

Players not bolded = Hall of Famers (N = 11).

Players in bold = non-HOF players (with TPR ≥ 16.8).

* = Hall of Famers with TPR < 16.8 (N = 2).

† = not currently eligible for the Hall of Fame (N = 2).

Pete Browning

Where Would the Current Stars Rank? 12

The list of adjusted top 100 hitters given as Table 6.1 goes through the 1997 season. Recall that players ultimately qualify for the list by having one of the 100 best adjusted batting averages with at least 4000 career at bats. Due to the longevity adjustment, at bats beyond the 8000th are not considered in the average, for the relatively few players that attain that many. Thus, the only active players presented in Table 6.1 are those who have already had 8000 at bats. Consequently, five active players are listed there: Tony Gwynn (1), Wade Boggs (9), Paul Molitor (29), Tim Raines (66), and Rickey Henderson (98). Because they all attained their 8000th at bats prior to 1998, their 1998 batting averages (which were all below their career averages), do not affect their rankings. Gwynn's .318 adjusted batting average in 1998, while down from his performance of recent years, still ranks as the 4th best single-season average ever for 38-year-old players (see Table 2.1).

Julio Franco ended his career after the 1997 season, although his impending retirement was unclear at the time. Since he had fewer than 8000 career at bats, he was not included in Table 6.1. With his retirement, however, Franco claims 65th place with a .298 average, knocking Hugh Duffy off the list.

Mike Piazza and Frank Thomas lead a cast of younger active players, many of whom will eventually earn spots in the top 100. In fact, if he maintains his current average, Piazza will place sixth behind Ted Williams and ahead of Honus Wagner. Meanwhile, Frank Thomas, with his sub-par 1998 season, lost 8 batting points putting him on target for 12th place, just ahead of Pete Browning. Seventeen other players are locking in on their ranking in the top 100 lineup, as Table 12.1 shows. Among them is Ken Griffey Jr. If Griffey retired tomorrow, he would not make the traditional top 100 given in chapter 1, but would place 67th on the adjusted list, joining his father, Ken Griffey Sr., who ranks 85th.

Current players have achieved or are on target for "top hitter" status for most of the fielding positions. Tony Gwynn, Wade Boggs, and Paul Molitor have already secured their spots as the best hitting outfielder, third baseman, and utility player of all time, respectively, since all have had 8000 at bats. Mike Piazza, Frank Thomas, and Edgar Martinez are vying to become the best hitting catcher, first baseman, and designated hitter, respectively. With only the top spots at second base and shortstop not recently claimed or under attack, we modern fans have certainly seen some of baseball's best hitters. Table 12.2 lists

Table 12.1 Current Top 100 "Rank" of Active Players

Active Player	Team	Adj. BA	AB	Overall Rank	Player Ahead of
Mike Piazza	NYN	.330	3119	6	T. Williams
Frank Thomas	ChiA	.318	4406	12	Browning
Edgar Martinez	Sea	.315	4374	13	Mays
Alex Rodriguez	Sea	.306	2070	34	Rose
Jeff Bagwell	Hou	.304	3657	41	Delahanty
Mark Grace	ChiN	.303	6053	42	Mantle
Will Clark	Tex	.303	6495	43	Guerrero
Kenny Lofton	Cle	.302	3914	45	Clemente
Roberto Alomar	Bal	.300	6048	52	Stephenson
Hal Morris	KC	.299	3727	62	Bi. Williams
Rusty Greer	Tex	.298	2435	65	Vaughan
Ken Griffey Jr.	Sea	.298	5226	66	Chance
John Olerud	NYN	.297	4185	72	Kuenn
Willie McGee	StL	.297	7378	73	Mize
Barry Larkin	Cin	.296	5708	75	Garvey
Shane Mack	KC	.294	2857	94	F. Baker
Manny Ramirez	Cle	.294	2509	95	Furillo
Raul Mondesi	LA	.294	2886	95	Furillo
Bernie Williams	NYA	.293	3678	99	Greenwell

Note: Players must have between 2000 and 7999 at bats.

the players whose averages currently rank among the top 10 at their positions (30 for outfielders).

There is a dearth of good hitting outfielders these days. Only Kenny Lofton is poised to take one of the 30 slots available. Lofton is currently the 28th best hitting outfielder and, more specifically, the 8th best hitting centerfielder.

Frank Thomas is on pace to become the best hitting first baseman ever. He needs to avoid the jinxes that struck George Sisler and Don Mattingly at similar points in their careers in order to maintain his perch. Thomas also needs to get more playing time as a first baseman. In 1998, Thomas, primarily a designated hitter in 1998, played only 14 games as a first baseman. He needs 146 more games at first base to qualify at that position.

Along with Thomas, four other active players—Jeff Bagwell, Mark

Table 12.2   Current Position "Rank" of Active Players

Active Player	Team	Adj. BA	AB	POS	Rank at POS	Player Ahead of
Kenny Lofton	Cle	.302	3914	OF	28	Clemente
Frank Thomas	ChiA	.318	4406	1B	1	Brouthers
Mark Grace	ChiN	.303	6053	1B	7	Murray
Jeff Bagwell	Hou	.304	4197	1B	7	Murray
Will Clark	Tex	.303	6495	1B	7	Murray
Hal Morris	KC	.299	3727	1B	10	Foxx
Roberto Alomar	Bal	.300	6048	2B	5	Gehringer
Craig Biggio	Hou	.293	5750	2B	5	Gehringer
Chuck Knoblauch	NYA	.291	4542	2B	6	Ray
Carlos Baerga	NYN	.288	4670	2B	10	Beckert
Alex Rodriguez	Sea	.306	2070	SS	2	Vaughan
Barry Larkin	Cin	.296	5708	SS	4	Yount
Tony Fernandez	Tor	.285	7303	SS	9	Wills
Dave Magadan	Oak	.293	3651	3B	7	Seitzer
Mike Piazza	NYN	.330	3119	C	1	Munson
Ivan Rodriguez	Tex	.286	3843	C	7	Howard
Bip Roberts	Oak	.292	4147	UT	8	Kelly
Edgar Martinez	Sea	.315	4374	DH	1	Baines

Note: Players must have between 2000 and 7999 at bats.

Grace, Will Clark, and Hal Morris — are engaged in an all-out siege for the first baseman ranks. Each one of them fell off his early pace and needs to stabilize or improve upon his recent hitting in order to place high on the list. Grace peaked at .310 in 1989, Clark at .313 in 1990, Morris at .319 in 1991, and Bagwell at .310 in 1994. (Note: all averages given throughout this chapter are fully adjusted averages.) Grace's career average had slipped to .297 by 1991, but he has averaged .310 over the past four seasons, pulling his average back to .303. Bagwell (.297), Clark (.292), and Morris (.288), on the other hand, have all averaged under .300 for the past four years.

Roberto Alomar, Craig Biggio, Chuck Knoblauch, and Carlos Baerga are all vying for second baseman slots. Alomar, at .300, is hitting 7 points better than Biggio, 9 points better than Knoblauch. These averages leave them all well short of the "Big Four" (Carew, Hornsby, Lajoie, and Collins) but have them hovering above or around Charlie Gehringer's 5th place mark of .292. Baerga — whose average has dropped 13 points since 1995 — needs to recover his hitting form in order to avoid slipping out of the list in 1999.

Dave Magadan, if he continues to play third base, could take 7th place from Kevin Seitzer. Magadan had great success early in his career, hitting .312 in 1349 at bats through 1990. Since then his average slipped 20 points to .292 by 1994, but it has been stable since then.

Piazza is redefining the word "catcher." Catchers aren't supposed to hit like Piazza. Piazza is currently hitting 31 points better than Thurmon Munson's mark. His biggest threat is probably playing enough games at catcher to qualify at the position. As noted in the first chapter, catchers have shorter careers than other position players. To avoid a short career, Piazza may be groomed for another position. If they do that too soon, though, there goes the best hitting catcher ranking!

In 1997, Slaught went 0-for-20 with San Diego, dropping him from 7th to 10th in the list of best catchers. This drastic decline in ranking caused by poor hitting during 0.5% of Slaught's career at bats shows how unforgiving these top hitter lists can be. By retiring, Slaught secured his position, displacing Spud Davis. Ivan "Pudge" Rodriguez, with a fine 1998 season, picked his career average up to .286, to place him currently 7th.

Barry Larkin has struggled with injuries the past several seasons. Still, he is looking to secure a middle rank in the shortstop list. Meanwhile, Alex Rodriguez, with just over 2000 career at bats, has his sights fixed on second place on the shortstop list.

Julio Franco, who retired after the 1997 season, assumes 5th in the list of top hitting utility players, dropping Billy Goodman from the list. Bip Roberts, whose average has dipped in recent years, would also rank among the top 10 utility players.

Edgar Martinez may be setting a new standard for designated hitters. He became the first DH to win a batting title in 1995. For his career, Martinez is hitting 27 points better than the top DH mark established by Harold Baines. At age 35, Martinez has played in 643 games at DH. He needs three more years as DH in order to qualify for the list.

Current Ranking for On Base Percentage

The same five active players presented earlier who, having had 8000 career at bats, have clinched top 100 positions for batting average, also make the top 100 list for adjusted on base percentage (see Table 10.2). They are: Wade Boggs (7), Rickey Henderson (10), Tony Gwynn (31), Tim Raines (47), and Paul Molitor (94).

Table 12.3 shows the 21 players with 2000–7999 at bats who, by maintaining their current adjusted on base percentages, would place among the top 100. Three of the players—Frank Thomas, Edgar Martinez, and Barry Bonds—are vying for top 10 rankings. Thomas, in

Table 12.3   Current Top 100 "Rank" of Active Players for On Base Percentage

Active Player	Team	Adj. OBP	AB	Overall Rank	Player Ahead of
Frank Thomas	ChiA	.438	4406	3	Hamilton
Edgar Martinez	Sea	.414	4374	9	Gehrig
Barry Bonds	SF	.412	6621	10	R. Henderson
Jeff Bagwell	Hou	.407	3657	14	Cobb
Dave Magadan	Oak	.399	3651	20	Foxx
Jim Thome	Cle	.395	2583	30	Stanky
Mike Piazza	NYN	.393	3119	36	F. Robinson
John Olerud	NYN	.393	4185	36	F. Robinson
Mark McGwire	StL	.389	5131	43	Browning
Gary Sheffield	LA	.384	4096	55	H. Wilson
Tim Salmon	Ana	.383	3130	57	Greenberg
Mark Grace	ChiN	.383	6053	58	Galan
Will Clark	Tex	.382	6495	60	McCovey
Fred McGriff	TB	.379	6257	71	Stephenson
Rusty Greer	Tex	.378	2435	78	Grich
Manny Ramirez	Cle	.377	2509	78	Grich
Tony Phillips	NYN	.375	7211	86	Dykstra
Chipper Jones	Atl	.374	2323	88	Yost
David Justice	Cle	.374	3893	88	Yost
Ken Griffey Jr.	Sea	.374	5226	90	Santo
Bernie Williams	NYA	.373	3678	93	Aaron

Note: Players must have between 2000 and 7999 at bats.

spite of lowering his career OBP by 9 points in 1998, would still place third behind Ted Williams and Babe Ruth. Eleven of the players on the OBP list were shown in Table 12.1 as being on target for securing a "top 100 hitter" spot. The remaining ten players, bolstered by exceptional walk averages (the other component of OBP), are: Barry Bonds, Chipper Jones, David Justice, Dave Magadan, Fred McGriff, Mark McGwire, Tony Phillips, Tim Salmon, Gary Sheffield, and Jim Thome.

McGwire, besides smashing the single-season record for home runs with 70 in 1998, set a National League record for the most walks with 162, surpassing the old mark of 151 held by Barry Bonds. His 1998 season catapulted McGwire's OBP target rank from 65th to 43d place. Prior to 1993, McGwire's walk average was an outstanding .145. From 1993–98, however, his walk average has been a fabulous .196! Based on his performance in recent years, McGwire will likely further improve his positioning of the OBP list in the coming years.

AFTERWORD Post-Game Wrap-Up

In this book I have tried to identify the best 100 hitters in the history of major league baseball. The book is split into two major parts—the method and the findings—so the wrap-up will be as well.

The Method

The method presented in this book to compare hitters across baseball history and identify the top 100 hitters involves four adjustments:

1. Late-career declines (longevity adjustment)
2. Hitting feasts and famines (mean adjustment)
3. The talent pool (standard deviation adjustment)
4. Ballpark differences ("full" adjustment).

The list of top 100 hitters is surely not perfectly ordered. However, I believe that the adjustments proposed greatly help us to *level the playing field*. In stronger words, when considering each adjustment, the traditional approach, which is *not* to adjust, has serious shortcomings, while the adjustments made in this book are arguably appropriate.

Looking at the four adjustments, the ballpark effect appears to have the greatest error in it. This is because a regression analysis was used to *estimate* the ballpark effects up through 1982. The home and away data that was used from 1983 on should soon become available for earlier periods as well. Of particular interest are the Detroit and Philadelphia parks when Ty Cobb played in them (to re-compare his performance with Tony Gwynn's). Forbes Field in Pittsburgh from 1962 to 1969, assessed was by regression as the the best hitting park this century outside of Denver also holds special interest. If new data show that it was not as much a hitter's park, Clemente and Matty Alou would move up the list of top hitters. With home and away data, we could also look more precisely at how and when ballparks have changed over time.

The adjustment for the talent pool may also be refined further. Should the number of at bats for inclusion in the standard deviation calculation be different? Should it be adjusted for the average number of at bats of the players that are included that year? Should something other than a 5-year moving average be used to smooth the standard deviations over time? Will some random effects model analysis into the sources of variability yield better answers?

Other ways to adjust for late-career declines could be considered. Is it better to use a given age rather than a given number of at bats? If so, should a higher age be used for modern players, because of the advances in sports medicine?

The most widely used adjustment applied to batting averages is the one for the era of play, and sports magazines have discussed it for at least 30 years. Still, the 1997 *Sports Illustrated* article comparing hitters over time, described in chapter 3, demonstrates that there is not yet agreement on the basic method to use for mean-adjustment. The mean-adjustment method presented in this book has mathematical validity not found in several of the alternatives.

While I have used standard deviation to reflect the talent pool changes over baseball history, my approach still *assumes* that the best players are comparably good over time. My method can be viewed as obtaining a percentile ranking for each player for the era he played in and then combining all the percentile rankings into a single list. While I don't believe this approach works over all percentile rankings (the 10th percentile, for example), it appears to be suitable at the top end (the best 100 hitters place in the 88th percentile or better).

Other statistical approaches are also being applied to batting averages with the goal of finding the game's best hitters. These include random effects models and hierarchical models. They hold both promise and peril. The promise is that they may help to better identify the best hitters than the methods used in this book. This is particularly true of models that try to assess the improvement in play over time, even among the game's best players. The peril is that the adjustment method will be so difficult to understand that fans with a wealth of knowledge about baseball will not be able to look for the potential "devil in the details" which may lurk therein.

A hierarchical model, recently developed by Scott Berry, Shane

Ross, and Pat Larkey, shows much promise. They ranked hitters by "peak" performance, which occurs from ages 26–29. Their 9 best hitters are all among the top 11 presented in this book, with Cobb edging out Gwynn by 4 points for the top spot. (My method gives Cobb a 3-point edge over Gwynn for the ages 26–29.) Although their model allowed for improvement of players over time, players from the opening decades of the twentieth century ranked right up there with the recent hitters, similar to my results.

Overall, I am quite excited about this competition of models. I am optimistic that, as different models are developed, critiqued, and revised, the "true" lists will look increasingly similar. It remains an open question of whether a model, such as mine, that is within the understanding of fans who have taken a single course in statistics, will continue to provide the most accurate glimpse of baseball's best hitters.

The issues and methods applied in this book to baseball are also applicable to a host of other questions where data are used. For example, the quality of hospitals in a given state or region are often compared with a "report card." Some adjustment for the severity of the disease or condition (a "ballpark" effect) should be made before the numbers are placed side-by-side. When comparing the present to the past, some adjustment may also be necessary to reflect the changes brought on by a new epidemic (a "hitting famine"), a new cure (a hitting "feast"), or a gradual improvement in health care. In looking at the comparative performance of hospitals over time, some knowledge of the overall quality of hospitals from each era (the "talent pool") is useful. Similar remarks could be made when schools, universities, U.S. states, or businesses within an industry are compared.

The Findings

The message of this book is that today's hitters are among the best of all-time! The adjustment method in this book can be tweaked here or there and the final rankings will change somewhat. However, if you have agreed with the basic rationale behind each of the four adjustments and don't have some major additional adjustments to suggest, this message is secure.

In particular, for those of us who have had the privilege of watching Tony Gwynn hit, we have arguably seen the best hitter of all-time!

Those who have seen Rod Carew or Wade Boggs in action have seen hitters in the "same league" as Shoeless Joe Jackson and Honus Wagner. Those who are avid fans of Mike Piazza or Frank Thomas may be looking at the next elite hitters.

Knowing about ballpark effects should make following baseball much more enjoyable. When evaluating hitter and pitcher performance, I now think like a real estate agent . . . location, location, location.

Baseball is a game of numbers. Comparing players from different eras is also a major topic of stadium jabber and sports radio broadcasts. I am happy to be part of the ongoing dialogue about our great American pastime.

APPENDIX 1 Abbreviations and Glossary

Abbreviations

1B	first baseman
2B	second baseman or doubles, depending on context
3B	third baseman or triples, depending on context
AA	American Association
AB	at bats
AL	American League
BA	batting average
Both	a hitter who bats both left and right
C	catcher
DH	designated hitter
ERA	earned run average
FABA	fully adjusted batting average
FABBA	fully adjusted base on balls average
H	player batting handedness
HR	home runs
Left	a left-handed hitter
LHP	left-handed pitcher
MABA	mean-adjusted batting average
Mid-Yr.	year of a player's mid-career
MN	5-year moving average of mean batting average for a given year
NL	National League
None	a player who doesn't qualify at a position
OBA	opposing batting average, the batting average yielded by the pitcher
OBP	on base percentage
OF	outfielder
P	pitcher
Park	ballpark effect
PL	Player's League
R	runs scored
RBA	relative batting average

RBI	runs batted in
RHP	right-handed pitcher
Right	a right-handed hitter
SB	stolen bases
SD	standard deviation
SDABA	standard deviation–adjusted batting average
SS	shortstop
Top 5	among the top 5 players in the category
UN	Union Association
UT	utility player
Win Pct	winning percentage of team

Team Name Abbreviations

In many of the tables throughout the book the player's team is identified. This is sometimes done with a two- or three-letter abbreviation for the team and a one-letter add-on for the league. The team codes are:

Atl	Atlanta	**Min**	Minnesota
Bal	Baltimore	**Mon**	Montreal
Bkn	Brooklyn	**NY**	New York
Bos	Boston	**Phi**	Philadelphia
Buf	Buffalo	**Pit**	Pittsburgh
Cal	California	**Pro**	Providence
Chi	Chicago	**Ric**	Richmond
Cin	Cincinnati	**Roc**	Rochester
Cle	Cleveland	**SD**	San Diego
Clm	Columbus	**Sea**	Seattle
Col	Colorado	**SF**	San Francisco
Det	Detroit	**StL**	St. Louis
Fla	Florida	**Syr**	Syracuse
Har	Hartford	**Tex**	Texas
Hou	Houston	**Tol**	Toledo
Ind	Indianapolis	**Tor**	Toronto
KC	Kansas City	**Tro**	Troy
Lou	Louisville	**Was**	Washington
Mil	Milwaukee	**Wor**	Worcester

The league add-ons are:

A	American League	**N**	National League
a	American Association	**U**	Union Association

Glossary

ballpark difference home batting average — away batting average for both teams

ballpark effect the ballpark effect batting average — .255

ballpark effect batting average batting average of an "average hitter" playing for the team whose ballpark is being evaluated, standardized to .255

batting trend a two-letter summary of the trend of a batter's career. The first letter indicates the change in batting average from 2000 at bats to 4000 at bats, the second letter indicates the change in batting average from 4000 at bats to the end of the player's career or 8000 at bats for longtime players. Averages that go up at least 5 points are given an "S" for surging." Averages that go down at least 5 points are given a "B" because the batter is good "out of the *box*." Averages that change less than 5 points in either direction are given an "R" for being "solid as a *rock*."

fully adjusted batting average (FABA) the fourth and final adjustment, which incorporates the adjustments for longevity, mean, standard deviation, and ballpark effect. See the Technical Note on p. 125 for further details.

longevity adjustment the first adjustment applied, which only looks at the batting average for a player's first 8000 at bats for longtime players

longtime players players who have had at least 8000 at bats

mean-adjusted batting average (MABA) the second adjustment, which divides the player's batting average by the league batting average and multiplies by a standardized average. The standardized average used in this book is .255 for years without a designated hitter and .2635 for years with a designated hitter. See the Technical Note on p. 60 for further details.

mid-career the year in which the player reached half of his career at bat total

milestone-at-bat every 1000th at bat in a player's career

park factor the ballpark effect batting average ÷ .255

qualifying players players who have had 4000 at bats and are retired or who are longtime players

relative batting average the player's batting average divided by the league batting average. This book uses mean-adjusted batting averages instead of this average.

standard deviation–adjusted batting average (SDABA) the third adjustment applied, incorporating the standard deviation as well as the mean. See the Technical Note on p. 96 for further details.

APPENDIX II Right- vs. Left-Handed Hitting

Throughout baseball history, there have been more right-handed pitchers than left-handed pitchers (also called *southpaws*). Since hitters generally hit better against an opposite-handed pitcher, left-handed hitters enjoy an advantage. What is the size of this advantage?

Tables II.1 and II.2 show the 10 top left-handed and 10 top right-handed hitters with at least 3500 at bats with batting average data against left- and right-handed pitching for 1981–92. (The two sources used were *Bill James Baseball Abstract* for 1981–83 and *The Elias Baseball Analyst* for the other years.)

Table II.1 Batting Averages of Top Left-Handed Hitters, 1981–92

Player	AB	BA vs. LHP	BA vs. RHP	Pct LHP	BA	Adj BA	Diff.
Boggs	6213	.302	.354	31	.338	.328	10
Gwynn	5511	.310	.338	36	.328	.324	4
Mattingly	5352	.303	.318	36	.313	.311	2
Brett	5845	.276	.311	35	.299	.294	5
Hernandez	4337	.286	.304	38	.297	.295	2
Butler	5254	.291	.294	34	.293	.292	1
Baines	5893	.284	.296	29	.293	.290	3
Cooper	3757	.290	.292	34	.291	.291	0
Cruz	3561	.276	.295	36	.288	.285	3
Buckner	3778	.262	.292	29	.284	.277	7
Average	**4950**	**.288**	**.310**	**34**	**.302**	**.299**	**3.6**

Notes:

LHP = left-handed pitcher.

RHP = right-handed pitcher.

Pct LHP = percent of at bats against left-handed pitchers.

Adj BA = batting average if player faced 50% left-handers.

Diff = 1000 × (BA − Adj BA), difference in BA if player faced 50% left-handers.

Table II.2   Batting Averages of Top Right-Handed Hitters, 1981–92

Player	AB	BA vs. LHP	BA vs. RHP	Pct LHP	BA	Adj BA	Diff.
Puckett	5645	.340	.314	27	.321	.327	−6
Molitor	5909	.314	.301	29	.305	.307	−2
Guerrero	4932	.297	.305	28	.303	.301	2
J. Franco	5280	.322	.295	28	.302	.308	−6
Yount	6719	.296	.293	29	.294	.295	−1
Lansford	5433	.297	.292	29	.294	.295	−1
Sandberg	6064	.302	.287	28	.291	.295	−3
Jim Rice	4569	.304	.286	27	.291	.295	−4
Trammell	5560	.296	.283	34	.288	.290	−2
Winfield	6050	.296	.282	33	.286	.289	−2
Average	5616	.307	.294	29	.297	.300	−2.7

Notes:

LHP = left-handed pitcher.

RHP = right-handed pitcher.

Pct LHP = percent of at bats against left-handed pitchers.

Adj BA = batting average if player faced 50% left-handers.

Diff = 1000 × (BA − Adj BA), difference in BA if player faced 50% left-handers.

All of the twenty players except Pedro Guerrero hit better against opposite-handed pitchers. Left-handers hit an average of 22 points better against right-handed pitchers, while right-handers only hit 13 points better against southpaws. Since left-handers pitch roughly 30% of the innings, left-handed hitters enjoy a batting advantage.

Suppose that each hitter faces left-handers half of the time. Then, the batting averages of left-handed hitters would drop 3.6 points, while right-handed hitters' averages would rise 2.7 points—a 6.3-point shift.

We must be cautious in interpreting these data. Since they were obtained from the 1980s to the 1990s, it is unclear whether the 6.3-point shift applies to other eras as well. We saw in chapter 1 that, among qualifying players, left-handers hit 14 points better than right-handers (Fig. 1.3). Left-handers however, are more likely to play first base or in the outfield, the best hitting positions. The position-specific batting average differences (Fig. 1.7) tended to be in the 3–8-point range, which fits well with the 6.3-point differential found here.

APPENDIX III League Batting Averages

Table III.1 National League Batting Averages, and 5-Year Moving
Averages of Mean-Adjusted Batting Average Means and
Standard Deviations of Players with 200 or More At Bats

Year	NL Avg	w/o Ballpark Adjustment		with Ballpark Adjustment	
		Mean	SD	Mean	SD
1876	.2653	.2647	.0467	.2645	.0435
1877	.2711	.2646	.0458	.2645	.0433
1878	.2594	.2650	.0447	.2650	.0423
1879	.2555	.2651	.0432	.2649	.0418
1880	.2447	.2659	.0427	.2653	.0410
1881	.2600	.2655	.0407	.2647	.0392
1882	.2513	.2661	.0410	.2643	.0388
1883	.2623	.2668	.0429	.2643	.0404
1884	.2469	.2675	.0446	.2652	.0421
1885	.2415	.2664	.0441	.2643	.0417
1886	.2507	.2675	.0439	.2656	.0415
1887	.2688	.2674	.0417	.2668	.0398
1888	.2388	.2666	.0390	.2669	.0378
1889	.2643	.2661	.0355	.2662	.0347
1890	.2538	.2665	.0353	.2670	.0346
1891	.2524	.2656	.0347	.2662	.0341
1892	.2447	.2647	.0352	.2648	.0344
1893	.2797	.2644	.0354	.2640	.0342
1894	.3091	.2651	.0360	.2645	.0345
1895	.2963	.2648	.0360	.2639	.0344
1896	.2904	.2654	.0357	.2644	.0340
1897	.2918	.2662	.0354	.2652	.0340
1898	.2706	.2662	.0349	.2655	.0338
1899	.2823	.2658	.0347	.2651	.0338

(continued)

Table III.1 National League Batting Averages, and 5-Year Moving
Averages of Mean-Adjusted Batting Average Means and
Standard Deviations of Players with 200 or More At Bats
(continued)

Year	NL Avg	w/o Ballpark Adjustment		with Ballpark Adjustment	
		Mean	SD	Mean	SD
1900	.2792	.2659	.0343	.2652	.0335
1901	.2668	.2693	.0386	.2703	.0380
1902	.2586	.2686	.0376	.2695	.0369
1903	.2690	.2687	.0374	.2695	.0366
1904	.2493	.2680	.0361	.2685	.0354
1905	.2551	.2679	.0350	.2683	.0345
1906	.2445	.2679	.0349	.2684	.0345
1907	.2432	.2684	.0347	.2691	.0343
1908	.2390	.2680	.0334	.2689	.0332
1909	.2437	.2680	.0326	.2690	.0324
1910	.2557	.2677	.0320	.2691	.0320
1911	.2597	.2677	.0302	.2691	.0302
1912	.2725	.2678	.0294	.2690	.0294
1913	.2618	.2680	.0289	.2690	.0289
1914	.2510	.2683	.0285	.2690	.0283
1915	.2480	.2689	.0282	.2693	.0277
1916	.2467	.2691	.0298	.2694	.0293
1917	.2493	.2691	.0298	.2693	.0293
1918	.2541	.2689	.0303	.2690	.0296
1919	.2576	.2684	.0296	.2685	.0291
1920	.2696	.2678	.0298	.2681	.0292
1921	.2895	.2672	.0291	.2675	.0288
1922	.2922	.2663	.0296	.2666	.0293
1923	.2857	.2663	.0293	.2667	.0291
1924	.2829	.2661	.0297	.2665	.0295
1925	.2915	.2660	.0296	.2664	.0294
1926	.2798	.2669	.0298	.2673	.0297
1927	.2819	.2678	.0297	.2682	.0294
1928	.2811	.2676	.0305	.2679	.0302
1929	.2944	.2681	.0308	.2684	.0304

(continued)

Table III.1 National League Batting Averages, and 5-Year Moving
Averages of Mean-Adjusted Batting Average Means and
Standard Deviations of Players with 200 or More At Bats
(continued)

Year	NL Avg	w/o Ballpark Adjustment		with Ballpark Adjustment	
		Mean	SD	Mean	SD
1930	.3035	.2684	.0314	.2687	.0308
1931	.2767	.2680	.0314	.2683	.0304
1932	.2763	.2675	.0307	.2679	.0298
1933	.2663	.2674	.0301	.2677	.0293
1934	.2791	.2669	.0302	.2673	.0294
1935	.2772	.2665	.0311	.2668	.0304
1936	.2781	.2658	.0303	.2661	.0298
1937	.2717	.2659	.0302	.2660	.0298
1938	.2672	.2665	.0302	.2666	.0297
1939	.2721	.2668	.0300	.2668	.0295
1940	.2635	.2672	.0286	.2671	.0280
1941	.2583	.2677	.0298	.2676	.0290
1942	.2488	.2678	.0307	.2677	.0298
1943	.2576	.2677	.0303	.2676	.0295
1944	.2608	.2678	.0303	.2678	.0295
1945	.2649	.2682	.0298	.2682	.0292
1946	.2557	.2685	.0293	.2686	.0289
1947	.2654	.2686	.0289	.2687	.0286
1948	.2608	.2692	.0289	.2693	.0287
1949	.2624	.2698	.0285	.2699	.0285
1950	.2613	.2698	.0295	.2698	.0293
1951	.2596	.2700	.0294	.2697	.0293
1952	.2527	.2703	.0297	.2697	.0298
1953	.2660	.2696	.0301	.2687	.0302
1954	.2651	.2690	.0304	.2678	.0303
1955	.2587	.2691	.0298	.2677	.0295
1956	.2561	.2689	.0299	.2676	.0295
1957	.2601	.2690	.0295	.2677	.0289
1958	.2616	.2697	.0287	.2685	.0280
1959	.2603	.2700	.0286	.2691	.0280

(continued)

Table III.1 National League Batting Averages, and 5-Year Moving
Averages of Mean-Adjusted Batting Average Means and
Standard Deviations of Players with 200 or More At Bats
(continued)

Year	NL Avg	w/o Ballpark Adjustment		with Ballpark Adjustment	
		Mean	SD	Mean	SD
1960	.2548	.2701	.0288	.2695	.0283
1961	.2618	.2706	.0294	.2702	.0287
1962	.2607	.2703	.0301	.2702	.0293
1963	.2451	.2705	.0312	.2702	.0301
1964	.2538	.2706	.0310	.2701	.0297
1965	.2491	.2711	.0326	.2703	.0310
1966	.2564	.2708	.0322	.2696	.0305
1967	.2489	.2709	.0325	.2697	.0306
1968	.2431	.2706	.0326	.2697	.0310
1969	.2504	.2705	.0339	.2698	.0322
1970	.2580	.2700	.0335	.2695	.0317
1971	.2517	.2698	.0333	.2695	.0319
1972	.2485	.2694	.0323	.2693	.0312
1973	.2545	.2694	.0324	.2694	.0312
1974	.2553	.2693	.0319	.2696	.0309
1975	.2572	.2688	.0308	.2693	.0300
1976	.2549	.2688	.0298	.2695	.0290
1977	.2618	.2687	.0292	.2693	.0284
1978	.2541	.2678	.0283	.2684	.0275
1979	.2607	.2682	.0280	.2687	.0273
1980	.2593	.2681	.0270	.2686	.0264
1981	.2552	.2680	.0269	.2685	.0263
1982	.2578	.2682	.0278	.2685	.0276
1983	.2554	.2688	.0278	.2691	.0278
1984	.2555	.2680	.0272	.2682	.0275
1985	.2521	.2685	.0283	.2686	.0287
1986	.2532	.2687	.0281	.2688	.0286
1987	.2607	.2688	.0286	.2689	.0289
1988	.2483	.2691	.0285	.2691	.0287
1989	.2464	.2698	.0280	.2698	.0280

(continued)

Table III.1 National League Batting Averages, and 5-Year Moving
Averages of Mean-Adjusted Batting Average Means and
Standard Deviations of Players with 200 or More At Bats
(continued)

Year	NL Avg	w/o Ballpark Adjustment		with Ballpark Adjustment	
		Mean	SD	Mean	SD
1990	.2564	.2698	.0286	.2698	.0285
1991	.2503	.2696	.0291	.2697	.0291
1992	.2515	.2693	.0288	.2694	.0288
1993	.2636	.2692	.0294	.2692	.0295
1994	.2669	.2691	.0300	.2691	.0300
1995	.2633	.2688	.0293	.2687	.0292
1996	.2625	.2688	.0296	.2686	.0296
1997	.2629	.2693	.0291	.2689	.0288

Table III.2 American League Batting Averages, and 5-Year Moving
Averages of Mean-Adjusted Batting Average Means and
Standard Deviations of Players with 200 or More At Bats

Year	AL Avg	w/o Ballpark Adjustment		with Ballpark Adjustment	
		Mean	SD	Mean	SD
1901	.2769	.2657	.0350	.2650	.0345
1902	.2750	.2657	.0355	.2653	.0350
1903	.2552	.2659	.0355	.2656	.0350
1904	.2444	.2664	.0369	.2663	.0362
1905	.2408	.2671	.0360	.2672	.0353
1906	.2487	.2672	.0353	.2674	.0345
1907	.2476	.2680	.0361	.2678	.0351
1908	.2390	.2688	.0375	.2682	.0361
1909	.2438	.2690	.0381	.2683	.0367
1910	.2431	.2693	.0403	.2685	.0387
1911	.2731	.2701	.0419	.2694	.0402
1912	.2648	.2705	.0411	.2702	.0394
1913	.2558	.2704	.0402	.2707	.0389
1914	.2475	.2707	.0392	.2713	.0381

(continued)

Table III.2   American League Batting Averages, and 5-Year Moving
Averages of Mean-Adjusted Batting Average Means and
Standard Deviations of Players with 200 or More At Bats

(continued)

Year	AL Avg	w/o Ballpark Adjustment		with Ballpark Adjustment	
		Mean	SD	Mean	SD
1915	.2482	.2704	.0392	.2713	.0382
1916	.2485	.2701	.0382	.2711	.0377
1917	.2477	.2696	.0378	.2708	.0376
1918	.2535	.2689	.0378	.2701	.0376
1919	.2680	.2681	.0362	.2692	.0358
1920	.2835	.2675	.0344	.2685	.0340
1921	.2924	.2671	.0341	.2678	.0333
1922	.2848	.2667	.0329	.2670	.0319
1923	.2823	.2666	.0325	.2666	.0314
1924	.2897	.2667	.0330	.2665	.0321
1925	.2915	.2670	.0329	.2667	.0321
1926	.2814	.2669	.0323	.2666	.0318
1927	.2855	.2670	.0331	.2667	.0326
1928	.2809	.2673	.0328	.2670	.0323
1929	.2839	.2676	.0327	.2674	.0322
1930	.2877	.2674	.0318	.2675	.0315
1931	.2783	.2674	.0314	.2677	.0312
1932	.2767	.2677	.0308	.2680	.0307
1933	.2727	.2675	.0287	.2678	.0287
1934	.2788	.2674	.0282	.2675	.0284
1935	.2798	.2677	.0286	.2676	.0288
1936	.2893	.2680	.0279	.2678	.0279
1937	.2812	.2677	.0276	.2677	.0276
1938	.2808	.2676	.0293	.2678	.0293
1939	.2786	.2678	.0301	.2682	.0300
1940	.2714	.2678	.0299	.2683	.0298
1941	.2665	.2673	.0304	.2679	.0306
1942	.2571	.2674	.0307	.2679	.0308
1943	.2493	.2672	.0296	.2677	.0297

(continued)

Table III.2 American League Batting Averages, and 5-Year Moving
Averages of Mean-Adjusted Batting Average Means and
Standard Deviations of Players with 200 or More At Bats
(continued)

Year	AL Avg	w/o Ballpark Adjustment		with Ballpark Adjustment	
		Mean	SD	Mean	SD
1944	.2600	.2674	.0296	.2679	.0296
1945	.2555	.2668	.0304	.2674	.0306
1946	.2555	.2669	.0309	.2675	.0310
1947	.2557	.2670	.0305	.2677	.0307
1948	.2660	.2673	.0311	.2676	.0309
1949	.2630	.2670	.0300	.2669	.0298
1950	.2706	.2679	.0285	.2675	.0283
1951	.2621	.2682	.0276	.2674	.0273
1952	.2526	.2680	.0285	.2671	.0281
1953	.2625	.2684	.0288	.2676	.0286
1954	.2569	.2686	.0297	.2679	.0293
1955	.2583	.2684	.0307	.2678	.0304
1956	.2604	.2688	.0317	.2684	.0312
1957	.2549	.2692	.0314	.2687	.0308
1958	.2542	.2692	.0301	.2688	.0298
1959	.2531	.2693	.0294	.2690	.0297
1960	.2555	.2691	.0282	.2688	.0284
1961	.2557	.2686	.0269	.2683	.0272
1962	.2547	.2687	.0262	.2684	.0265
1963	.2474	.2686	.0269	.2683	.0270
1964	.2471	.2684	.0264	.2682	.0262
1965	.2420	.2686	.0274	.2684	.0270
1966	.2405	.2694	.0288	.2696	.0285
1967	.2356	.2697	.0292	.2701	.0290
1968	.2301	.2698	.0295	.2704	.0294
1969	.2460	.2699	.0303	.2706	.0301
1970	.2498	.2701	.0300	.2708	.0300
1971	.2469	.2697	.0294	.2700	.0294
1972	.2390	.2692	.0294	.2690	.0293
1973	.2594	.2698	.0299	.2693	.0296

(continued)

Table III.2   American League Batting Averages, and 5-Year Moving
Averages of Mean-Adjusted Batting Average Means and
Standard Deviations of Players with 200 or More At Bats
(continued)

Year	AL Avg	w/o Ballpark Adjustment		with Ballpark Adjustment	
		Mean	SD	Mean	SD
1974	.2583	.2697	.0304	.2690	.0298
1975	.2553	.2694	.0305	.2688	.0299
1976	.2560	.2694	.0300	.2689	.0292
1977	.2662	.2692	.0298	.2690	.0289
1978	.2611	.2686	.0295	.2686	.0287
1979	.2696	.2692	.0294	.2693	.0287
1980	.2691	.2691	.0287	.2693	.0280
1981	.2562	.2691	.0295	.2692	.0290
1982	.2641	.2692	.0300	.2693	.0297
1983	.2655	.2692	.0295	.2693	.0293
1984	.2636	.2686	.0294	.2687	.0291
1985	.2612	.2687	.0301	.2687	.0299
1986	.2615	.2689	.0306	.2689	.0302
1987	.2650	.2690	.0303	.2690	.0298
1988	.2593	.2689	.0302	.2689	.0297
1989	.2607	.2688	.0308	.2689	.0303
1990	.2591	.2689	.0298	.2689	.0295
1991	.2602	.2689	.0293	.2688	.0291
1992	.2593	.2691	.0296	.2691	.0296
1993	.2666	.2694	.0301	.2693	.0302
1994	.2726	.2694	.0293	.2692	.0294
1995	.2703	.2694	.0296	.2692	.0297
1996	.2772	.2694	.0295	.2692	.0295
1997	.2706	.2692	.0290	.2690	.0290

Table III.3 League Batting Averages, and 5-Year Moving Averages of Mean-Adjusted Batting Average Means and Standard Deviations of Players with 200 or More At Bats

Year	League	Avg	w/o Ballpark Adjustment		with Ballpark Adjustment	
			Mean	SD	Mean	SD
1882	AA	.2437	.2691	.0410	.2679	.0397
1883	AA	.2517	.2686	.0412	.2677	.0400
1884	AA	.2395	.2678	.0412	.2673	.0400
1885	AA	.2465	.2669	.0401	.2669	.0391
1886	AA	.2427	.2668	.0415	.2672	.0404
1887	AA	.2726	.2654	.0403	.2660	.0397
1888	AA	.2384	.2664	.0409	.2672	.0402
1889	AA	.2616	.2668	.0404	.2672	.0398
1890	AA	.2525	.2671	.0403	.2674	.0397
1891	AA	.2552	.2678	.0401	.2680	.0395
1884	UN	.2450	.2759	.0544	.2704	.0497
1890	PL	.2739	.2639	.0370	.2643	.0367
1914	FL	.2672	.2670	.0368	.2658	.0351
1915	FL	.2545	.2678	.0340	.2696	.0339

APPENDIX IV Ballpark Effect Batting Averages

		Table IV.1	Nineteenth-Century National League Ballpark Effect Batting Averages		
Team	Years	Park Avg	Team	Years	Park Avg
Bal	1892–99	.2682	KC	1886	.2505
Bos	1876–81	.2528	Lou	1876–77	.2500
	1882–93	.2590		1892	.2421
	1894–1900	.2574		1893–99	.2478
Bkn	1890	.2526	Mil	1878	.2647
	1891–97	.2526	NY	1876	.2380
	1898–1900	.2535		1883–88	2689
Buf	1879–83	.2604		1889–90	.2609
	1884–85	.2709		1891–1900	.2560
Chi	1876–77	.2842	Phi	1876	.2810
	1878–82	.2705		1883–86	.2470
	1883–84	.2715		1887–94	.2607
	1885–92	.2560		1895–1900	.2646
	1893–1900	.2521	Pit	1887–90	.2431
Cin	1876	.2528		1891–1900	.2548
	1877–79	.2604	Pro	1878–85	.2494
	1880	.2514	StL	1876–77	.2328
	1890–93	.2469		1885–86	.2486
	1894–1900	.2487		1892	.2452
Cle	1879–84	.2451		1893–1900	.2524
	1889–90	.2450	Syr	1879	.2415
	1891–99	.2553	Tro	1879	.2553
Det	1881–88	.2577		1880–81	.2535
Har	1876	.2427		1882	.2537
	1877	.2514	Was	1886–89	.2402
Ind	1878	.2401		1892–99	.2579
	1887–89	.2622	Wor	1880–82	.2514

Table IV.2 Union Association Ballpark Effect Batting
Averages — 1884

Team	Park Avg	Team	Park Avg
Bal	.2513	KC	.2289
Bos	.2428	Phi	.2693
Cin	.2707	StL	.2793
CP*	.2441	Was	.2528

*Chicago-Pittsburgh team.

Table IV.3 Player's League Ballpark Effect Batting
Averages — 1890

Team	Park Avg	Team	Park Avg
Bos	.2534	Cle	.2712
Bkn	.2520	NYC	.2592
Buf	.2593	Phi	.2575
Chi	.2422	Pit	.2448

Table IV.4 American Association Ballpark Effect Batting Averages

Team	Years	Park Avg	Team	Years	Park Avg
Bal	1882–91	.2450	Phi	1882	.2517
Bos	1891	.2600	Phi	1883–91	.2597
Bkn	1884–89	.2501	Pit	1882–84	.2557
Cin	1882–83	.2586	Pit	1885–86	.2476
Cin	1884–89	.2568	Ric	1884	.2520
Cin	1891	.2394	Roc	1890	.2413
Cle	1887–88	.2555	StL	1882–91	.2557
Clm	1883–84	.2501	Syr	1890	.2666
Clm	1889–91	.2503	Tol	1884	.2506
Ind	1884	.2654	Tol	1890	.2531
KC	1888	.2460	Was	1884	.2362
KC	1889	.2549	Was	1891	.2641
Lou	1882–91	.2654			
NY	1883–85	.2581			
NY	1886–87	.2435			

Table IV.5   American League Ballpark Effect Batting Averages

	Bos	Chi	Cle	Det	NY	Phi	StL	Was
1901	.2565	.2405	.2616	.2597	.2689	.2556	.2511	.2541
1902							.2532	
1903					.2592			
1904								.2537
1909						.2632	.2512	
1910		.2492	.2582					
1911								.2480
1912	.2509			.2634				
1913					.2478			
1920	.2475	.2528	.2637	.2601		.2523	.2564	.2540
1923					.2549			
1932			.2538					
1934	.2585							
1935		.2528			.2497	.2561	.2546	.2581
1938				.2524				
1947			.2529					
1950	.2611	.2549		.2605	.2554			.2526
1954							.2472	
1955						.2600		
1956								.2498
1961	.2630	.2529	.2547	.2529	.2521	.2602	.2534	.2593
1968						.2456		
1970	.2617	.2594	.2566	.2538			.2476	.2637
1974					.2596			
1976					.2514			
1982								.2599
1983	.2634	.2551	.2577	.2498	.2542	.2481	.2522	
1991		.2529						
1992							.2545	
1993	.2619			.2519	.2540	.2525		.2556
1994			.2542					

Notes: Blanks—ballpark effect batting average same as above.

NY—(Bal 1901–2, NY 1903–).

Phi—(Phi 1901–54, KC 1955–67, Oak 1968–).

StL—(Mil 1901, StL 1902–53, Bal 1954–).
Was—(Was 1901–60, Min 1961–).

Table IV.5   American League Ballpark Effect Batting Averages *(continued)*

	Cal	Tex	KC	Mil	Sea	Tor
1961	.2496	.2527	—	—	—	—
1962	.2533	.2499	—	—	—	—
1965	.2547		—	—	—	—
1966	.2521		—	—	—	—
1969			.2598	.2505	—	—
1970				.2540	—	—
1972		.2566			—	—
1973			.2612		—	—
1977					.2526	.2497
1983	.2519	.2571	.2561	.2528	.2558	.2553
1989						.2547
1993	.2536		.2587	.2590	.2525	
1994		.2579				

Notes: Blanks—ballpark effect batting average same as above.

— Franchise did not yet exist.

Cal—(LA 1961–65, Cal 1966–96, Ana 1997–).

Tex—(WasII 1961–71, Tex 1972–).

Mil—(Sea 1969, Mil 1970–).

Table IV.6   National League Ballpark Effect Batting Averages

	Bos	Bkn	Chi	Cin	NY	Phi	Pit	StL
1901	.2492	.2496	.2490	.2491	.2557	.2547	.2580	.2557
1902				.2617				
1903			.2500					
1909							.2517	.2547
1910						.2537		
1911					.2574			
1912				.2593				
1913		.2601						
1915	.2478							
1916			.2530					
1920								.2577
1921	.2460	.2523		.2512	.2543	.2637	.2584	
1938	.2512	.2552	.2556	.2476	.2572	.2536	.2579	.2615
1948		.2548						
1950			.2530	.2573	.2510	.2525	.2594	.2629
1953	.2600							
1958		.2492			.2533			
1960					.2507			
1962		.2496	.2533	.2632		.2514	.2686	
1966	.2619							.2623
1970		.2564	.2571	.2551	.2508		.2624	
1971						.2583		
1974	.2480							
1983	.2620	.2542	.2602	.2582	.2515	.2553	.2543	.2543
1993	.2563	.2480	.2558	.2538	.2491	.2544	.2551	.2542

Notes: Blanks — ballpark effect batting average same as above.

Bos — (Bos 1901–52, Mil 1953–65, Atl 1966–).

Bkn — (Bkn 1901–57, LA 1958–).
NY — (NY 1901–57, SF 1958–).

Table IV.6 National League Ballpark Effect Batting Averages *(continued)*

	Hou	NY	Mon	SD	Col	Fla
1962	.2410	.2471	—	—	—	—
1964		.2463	—	—	—	—
1965	.2533		—	—	—	—
1969			.2487	.2489	—	—
1970		.2483			—	—
1977			.2521		—	—
1983	.2520	.2518	.2532	.2530	—	—
1993	.2492	.2530	.2564	.2514	.2727	.2548
1995					.2815	

Notes: Blanks—ballpark effect batting average same as above.

NY — New York Mets.

— Franchise did not yet exist.

APPENDIX V League Base on Balls Averages

Table V.1 National League Base on Balls Averages with 5-Year Mean-Adjusted Means and Standard Deviations of Players with 200 or More At Bats

Year	Avg	Mean	SD
1876	.0167	.2691	.1021
1877	.0252	.2732	.1025
1878	.0267	.2761	.0982
1879	.0210	.2786	.0918
1880	.0305	.2841	.0892
1881	.0424	.2882	.0837
1882	.0388	.2892	.0779
1883	.0386	.2907	.0787
1884	.0557	.2913	.0796
1885	.0593	.2915	.0771
1886	.0698	.2921	.0795
1887	.0761	.2929	.0773
1888	.0559	.2935	.0714
1889	.0962	.2946	.0643
1890	.1004	.2950	.0626
1891	.0975	.2951	.0570
1892	.0967	.2947	.0565
1893	.1079	.2939	.0571
1894	.1016	.2935	.0594
1895	.0902	.2935	.0612
1896	.0873	.2937	.0618
1897	.0834	.2942	.0622
1898	.0813	.2939	.0640
1899	.0793	.2938	.0644

(continued)

Table V.1 National League Base on Balls Averages with 5-Year Mean-Adjusted Means and Standard Deviations of Players with 200 or More At Bats *(continued)*

Year	Avg	Mean	SD
1900	.0775	.2941	.0635
1901	.0689	.2938	.0676
1902	.0686	.2940	.0662
1903	.0817	.2943	.0657
1904	.0724	.2943	.0650
1905	.0778	.2960	.0636
1906	.0850	.2965	.0623
1907	.0807	.2964	.0620
1908	.0763	.2966	.0608
1909	.0879	.2970	.0577
1910	.0990	.2963	.0563
1911	.1041	.2964	.0577
1912	.0923	.2974	.0570
1913	.0854	.2970	.0585
1914	.0881	.2971	.0607
1915	.0799	.2953	.0613
1916	.0734	.2946	.0594
1917	.0738	.2938	.0596
1918	.0753	.2943	.0562
1919	.0701	.2938	.0552
1920	.0715	.2951	.0539
1921	.0686	.2963	.0537
1922	.0803	.2963	.0528
1923	.0808	.2966	.0541
1924	.0757	.2975	.0527
1925	.0807	.2970	.0532
1926	.0827	.2960	.0541
1927	.0806	.2962	.0545
1928	.0916	.2959	.0545
1929	.0921	.2952	.0544
1930	.0845	.2956	.0537
1931	.0815	.2966	.0525

(continued)

Table V.1 National League Base on Balls Averages
with 5-Year Mean-Adjusted Means and
Standard Deviations of Players with 200
or More At Bats *(continued)*

Year	Avg	Mean	SD
1932	.0719	.2964	.0534
1933	.0700	.2959	.0552
1934	.0755	.2956	.0583
1935	.0756	.2955	.0590
1936	.0807	.2955	.0608
1937	.0860	.2960	.0597
1938	.0872	.2967	.0588
1939	.0904	.2974	.0569
1940	.0879	.2984	.0562
1941	.0977	.2982	.0554
1942	.0976	.2975	.0556
1943	.0953	.2975	.0556
1944	.0928	.2974	.0556
1945	.0969	.2964	.0571
1946	.1045	.2959	.0568
1947	.1055	.2961	.0585
1948	.1042	.2960	.0580
1949	.1031	.2959	.0594
1950	.1069	.2962	.0589
1951	.1022	.2966	.0585
1952	.0990	.2967	.0562
1953	.0990	.2960	.0556
1954	.1050	.2956	.0542
1955	.1014	.2956	.0540
1956	.0952	.2958	.0534
1957	.0900	.2966	.0527
1958	.0965	.2967	.0528
1959	.0939	.2968	.0519
1960	.0934	.2963	.0512
1961	.0948	.2959	.0511
1962	.0949	.2951	.0525
1963	.0832	.2954	.0526
1964	.0794	.2954	.0550

(continued)

Table V.1 National League Base on Balls Averages with 5-Year Mean-Adjusted Means and Standard Deviations of Players with 200 or More At Bats *(continued)*

Year	Avg	Mean	SD
1965	.0854	.2954	.0565
1966	.0796	.2952	.0580
1967	.0850	.2952	.0581
1968	.0778	.2953	.0595
1969	.0973	.2947	.0591
1970	.1041	.2947	.0592
1971	.0919	.2945	.0612
1972	.0948	.2944	.0622
1973	.0977	.2938	.0614
1974	.1031	.2938	.0616
1975	.1018	.2941	.0614
1976	.0952	.2940	.0601
1977	.0973	.2936	.0600
1978	.0964	.2938	.0600
1979	.0936	.2935	.0593
1980	.0901	.2934	.0590
1981	.0941	.2941	.0580
1982	.0900	.2946	.0573
1983	.0978	.2947	.0566
1984	.0933	.2956	.0548
1985	.0968	.2958	.0545
1986	.0998	.2960	.0546
1987	.0992	.2964	.0539
1988	.0884	.2970	.0539
1989	.0950	.2973	.0550
1990	.0943	.2977	.0554
1991	.0957	.2973	.0553
1992	.0909	.2971	.0559
1993	.0917	.2959	.0568
1994	.0943	.2948	.0577
1995	.0966	.2938	.0581
1996	.0965	.2932	.0585
1997	.0998	.2922	.0590

Table V.2 American League Base on Balls Averages
with 5-Year Mean-Adjusted Means and
Standard Deviations of Players with 200
or More At Bats

Year	Avg	Mean	SD
1901	.0729	.2936	.0656
1902	.0741	.2932	.0665
1903	.0605	.2931	.0659
1904	.0629	.2937	.0659
1905	.0736	.2926	.0660
1906	.0693	.2933	.0650
1907	.0689	.2935	.0625
1908	.0691	.2949	.0597
1909	.0734	.2951	.0584
1910	.0830	.2954	.0580
1911	.0865	.2954	.0548
1912	.0928	.2952	.0544
1913	.0936	.2932	.0570
1914	.0962	.2934	.0558
1915	.1047	.2944	.0537
1916	.0995	.2944	.0557
1917	.0948	.2949	.0576
1918	.0957	.2955	.0570
1919	.0901	.2951	.0586
1920	.0909	.2948	.0601
1921	.0924	.2951	.0599
1922	.0897	.2960	.0590
1923	.0973	.2972	.0586
1924	.0978	.2972	.0593
1925	.1007	.2969	.0602
1926	.1013	.2967	.0603
1927	.0954	.2960	.0609
1928	.0909	.2953	.0619
1929	.0961	.2958	.0616
1930	.0927	.2961	.0612
1931	.0954	.2958	.0597
1932	.1012	.2964	.0580

(continued)

Table V.2 American League Base on Balls
Averages with 5-Year Mean-Adjusted
Means and Standard Deviations of
Players with 200 or More At Bats
(continued)

Year	Avg	Mean	SD
1933	.1023	.2966	.0558
1934	.1074	.2963	.0546
1935	.1057	.2963	.0522
1936	.1108	.2975	.0515
1937	.1102	.2972	.0515
1938	.1159	.2977	.0522
1939	.1093	.2977	.0529
1940	.1045	.2976	.0551
1941	.1100	.2971	.0561
1942	.1029	.2967	.0560
1943	.1025	.2965	.0559
1944	.0924	.2967	.0559
1945	.0996	.2968	.0554
1946	.1042	.2971	.0535
1947	.1130	.2973	.0532
1948	.1241	.2972	.0510
1949	.1350	.2970	.0485
1950	.1278	.2971	.0468
1951	.1154	.2960	.0480
1952	.1094	.2956	.0492
1953	.1055	.2965	.0510
1954	.1102	.2962	.0525
1955	.1126	.2956	.0544
1956	.1195	.2957	.0558
1957	.1026	.2962	.0552
1958	.0967	.2944	.0556
1959	.1003	.2955	.0556
1960	.1063	.2950	.0557
1961	.1075	.2949	.0545
1962	.1027	.2945	.0548
1963	.0915	.2951	.0534

(continued)

Table V.2   American League Base on Balls
Averages with 5-Year Mean-Adjusted
Means and Standard Deviations of
Players with 200 or More At Bats
(continued)

Year	Avg	Mean	SD
1964	.0947	.2943	.0538
1965	.0994	.2956	.0532
1966	.0911	.2961	.0545
1967	.0922	.2964	.0545
1968	.0909	.2963	.0565
1969	.1073	.2961	.0569
1970	.1037	.2961	.0565
1971	.1002	.2963	.0551
1972	.0930	.2963	.0552
1973	.1003	.2967	.0552
1974	.0929	.2967	.0552
1975	.1021	.2955	.0566
1976	.0933	.2949	.0574
1977	.0941	.2949	.0578
1978	.0954	.2941	.0594
1979	.0966	.2941	.0603
1980	.0927	.2948	.0602
1981	.0937	.2952	.0601
1982	.0942	.2951	.0604
1983	.0912	.2960	.0588
1984	.0920	.2961	.0582
1985	.0966	.2965	.0571
1986	.0991	.2967	.0573
1987	.1004	.2970	.0567
1988	.0934	.2967	.0568
1989	.0945	.2961	.0574
1990	.0994	.2948	.0587
1991	.0996	.2940	.0588
1992	.0999	.2937	.0592
1993	.1033	.2938	.0591
1994	.1076	.2945	.0582

(continued)

Table V.2   American League Base on Balls
Averages with 5-Year Mean-Adjusted
Means and Standard Deviations of
Players with 200 or More At Bats

(continued)

Year	Avg	Mean	SD
1995	.1089	.2949	.0581
1996	.1086	.2953	.0583
1997	.1018	.2951	.0579

Table V.3   Other League Base on Balls Averages with 5-Year
Mean-Adjusted Means and Standard Deviations of
Players with 200 or More At Bats

Year	League	Avg	Mean	SD
1882	AA	.0373	.2830	.0796
1883	AA	.0418	.2849	.0774
1884	AA	.0432	.2856	.0758
1885	AA	.0533	.2868	.0743
1886	AA	.0817	.2883	.0753
1887	AA	.0853	.2898	.0713
1888	AA	.0693	.2904	.0686
1889	AA	.0951	.2913	.0667
1890	AA	.1012	.2918	.0664
1891	AA	.1095	.2927	.0618
1884	UN	.0373	.2810	.0753
1890	PL	.1088	.2926	.0583
1914	FL	.0884	.2950	.0558
1915	FL	.0898		

REFERENCES

Aaron, Hank (with Lonnie Wheeler). *I Had a Hammer: The Hank Aaron Story*. New York, NY: HarperCollins, 1991.

Adams, Franklin P. "Tinker To Evers To Chance." *Evening Mail*. New York, 1910.

The Baseball Encyclopedia, Tenth Edition. New York, NY: Macmillan Books, 1996.

Baseball's Hall of Fame: Cooperstown: Where The Legends Live Forever. New York, NY: Arlington House, 1988.

Bennett, Jay, and John Flueck. "Did Shoeless Joe Jackson Throw The 1919 World Series?" *American Statistician*, 47:241–50, 1993.

Berry, Scott M., C. Shane Reese, and Pat Larkey. "A Bridge Model for Comparing Players in Different Eras in Sports," Technical Report, Department of Statistics, Texas A & M University, 1998 (to appear in the *Journal of the American Statistical Association*).

Clifton, Merritt. "Relative Baseball." *Samisdat*, 1976.

Crothers, Tim. *Greatest Teams: The Most Dominant Powerhouses In Sports*. New York, NY: Bishop Books, 1998.

Dewan, John, Don Zminda, and STATS, Inc. *STATS Baseball Scoreboard 1997*. Skokie, IL: STATS Publishing, 1997.

Gould, Stephen Jay. "Entropic Homogeneity Isn't Why No One Hits .400 Any More." *Discover*, August, 1986: 60–66.

——. *Full House: The Spread Of Excellence From Plato To Darwin*. New York, NY: Three Rivers Press, 1996.

Halberstam, David. *Summer of '49*. New York, NY: Avon Books, 1989.

James, Bill. *Bill James Baseball Abstract*. 1983.

——. *Whatever Happened to the Hall of Fame?: Baseball, Cooperstown, and the Politics of Glory*. New York, NY: Fireside, 1995.

Larkin, Ward. "Batting Average Comparisons." *Baseball Analyst*, October 1982, no. 3: 7–13.

Lowry, Philip. *Green Cathedrals: The Ultimate Celebration Of All 273 Major League And Negro League Ballparks*. Reading, MA: Addison-Wesley, 1992.

Miller, Ruppert, and David Siegmund. "Maximally Selected Chi-Square Statistics." *Biometrics* 38:1011–16, 1982.

Neft, David S., and Richard M. Cohen. *The Sports Encyclopedia: Baseball 1997*, Seventeenth Edition. New York: St. Martin's Griffin, 1997.

Palacios, Oscar (with Dan Ford, Ethan Cooperson, and Mat Olkin). *STATS Diamond Diagrams*. Skokie, IL: STATS Publishing, 1997.

Price, S. L. "Whatever Happened To The White Athlete?" *Sports Illustrated: Special Report*, December 8, 1997: 30–51.

Shoebotham, David. "Relative Batting Averages." *Baseball Research Journal*, 1976.

Siwoff, Seymour, Steve Hirdt, and Pete Hirdt. *The 1985 Elias Baseball Analyst*. New York, NY: Macmillan, 1985. See also *Elias Baseball Analyst* for the years 1986 through 1993. The 1989–93 editions have a fourth coauthor, Tom Hirdt; in 1991, Fireside became the new publisher.

Thorn, John, and Pete Palmer. *The Hidden Game of Baseball: A Revolutionary Approach To Baseball And Its Statistics*. Garden City, NY: Dolphin/Doubleday, 1985.

———, eds. *Total Baseball*. New York, NY: Warner Books, 1989.

Thorn, John, Pete Palmer, Michael Gershman, and David Pietrusza, eds. *Total Baseball*, Fifth Edition. New York, NY: Viking, 1997.

Verducci, Tom. "The Best Hitter Since Ted Williams." *Sports Illustrated*, July 28, 1997: 40–47.

Will, George F. *Men At Work: The Craft of Baseball*. New York, NY: Macmillan, 1990.

Williams, Pete. "Can Gwynn Bounce Back—From .353?" *Baseball Weekly*, March 5–11, 1997, no. 3:8–10.

Williams, Ted, and John Underwood. *My Turn At Bat: The Story of My Life*. New York, NY: Fireside, 1988.

World Almanac and Book of Facts, The. New York, NY: Pharos Books, 1993.

World Book Encyclopedia. Chicago, IL: World Book, Inc., 1994.

Wright, Marshall D. *Nineteenth Century Baseball: Year-By-Year Statistics For The Major League Teams, 1981 Through 1900*. Jefferson, NC: McFarland, 1996.

INDEX

Batting Average, (cont.)
single-season, 12, 33–37, 69–70, 83, 126, 140, 142, 153, 173–83, 209, 242
Standard Deviation–Adjusted (SDABA), 95–101, 110, 125, 127–28, 249
Batts, Matt, 179
Baylor, Don, 18, 20, 170–71
Beaumont, Ginger, 10, 138, 162–63, 180
Becker, Beals, 210
Beckert, Glenn, 166, 244
Beckley, Jake, 10, 50, 52, 235
Bell, Buddy, 238
Bell, Derek,180
Bell, George,18
Belle, Albert, 182
Bench, Johnny, 178, 239
Bennett, Jay, 146
Bennett Park, 191–92, 209
Berger, Wally, 180, 234
Berra, Yogi, 169, 239
"best" hitters,
adjusted list, 136–40
adjusted top 11, 140–56
by position, 157–71
definition of, 5, 27
traditional list, 7–10, 25–27, 30, 43, 140–41
Bichette, Dante, 206
Biggio, Craig, 180, 244–45
Bill James Baseball Abstract, The (James), 104, 121
Bishop, Max, 216–17, 220–22
Blue, Lu, 217
Blue, Vida, 187
Boggs, Wade, 6, 8, 35–37, 100–101, 106, 109–10, 137, 141–42, 145, 148, 151–52, 167–68, 175–76, 182, 186–87, 190, 207, 209, 211, 218, 220–22, 238, 242, 246, 252, 257
Bolling, Frank, 81
Bonds, Barry, 180, 246–47
Bonds, Bobby, 233
Boone, Bret,180
Boston Braves, 112, 117, 140, 180, 198–99
Boston Red Sox, 104–6, 109, 116, 119, 123–24, 140, 149, 169, 178–79, 181–82, 186–87, 190, 211–12, 216

Bottomley, Jim, 10, 53, 235
Boudreau, Lou, 149, 167, 182–83, 237
Bradley, George, 46
Braves Field, 198
Bresnahan, Roger, 178, 217, 223, 239
Brett, George, 18, 35, 37, 42, 47, 56, 59, 70–71, 81, 89, 137, 167–68, 174–75, 197, 211, 224, 238, 257
Bridwell, Al, 177–78, 180
Briggs, Johnny, 218
Briggs Stadium, 116, 193
Brock, Lou, 130, 234
Brooklyn Dodgers, 117, 140, 180, 199
Brouthers, Dan, 8, 36, 43, 50, 52, 64, 69, 100–101, 137, 141, 148, 164, 219, 220, 222, 235, 244
Brown, "Three-Finger," 177
Browning, Pete, 8, 34, 64–65, 69–70, 73, 100–101, 137, 140–42, 152, 171, 207, 211, 223, 232, 242, 246
Buckner, Bill, 18, 257
Buford, Don, 182–83
Burgess, Smokey, 169, 180
Burkett, Jesse, 8, 35–36, 52, 137, 141, 161, 211, 222, 232
Burks, Ellis, 206
Burns, George, 10, 42, 53
Burns, Oyster, 73
Burroughs, Jeff, 219
Busch Stadium, 105, 129, 203–4, 209
Bush, Donie, 17, 182, 218
Butler, Brett, 219, 223, 232, 257

California Angels, 75, 196
Camden Yards, 195
Camilli, Dolph, 217, 223
Campanella, Roy, 239
Campaneris, Bert, 182
Candlestick Park, 105, 212
Carew, Rod, 8, 35, 37–39, 48, 6, 70–71, 84, 100–101, 137, 141, 143, 145, 147–48, 150, 152, 154, 165–66, 174–75, 182, 196, 207, 210, 222, 236, 245, 252
Carey, Max, 53, 233
Carter, Gary, 239

286

INDEX

ABOUT THE AUTHOR

Michael Schell is an Associate Professor of Biostatistics at the University of North Carolina at Chapel Hill, where he primarily collaborates on clinical trials and other cancer research at the Lineberger Comprehensive Cancer Center.

He has authored over 60 articles on statistical methods and cancer research. Schell is a member of the Society for American Baseball Research and an avid Reds fan.